Ancient Empires before Alexander
Part III

Professor Robert L. Dise Jr.

THE TEACHING COMPANY ®

PUBLISHED BY:

THE TEACHING COMPANY
4840 Westfields Boulevard, Suite 500
Chantilly, Virginia 20151-2299
1-800-TEACH-12
Fax—703-378-3819
www.teach12.com

ISBN 1-59803-558-4

Robert L. Dise Jr., Ph.D.

Associate Professor of History, University of Northern Iowa

Robert L. Dise Jr. has taught at the University of Northern Iowa since 1992; prior to joining its faculty, he taught at Clinch Valley College (now the University of Virginia's College at Wise). He received his B.A. in History from the University of Virginia (at Charlottesville), concentrating on the history of the ancient world, and his M.A. and Ph.D. from the University of Michigan, specializing in the history of Rome.

Professor Dise has delivered numerous papers at ancient history, classical studies, and archeological institute conferences and has published articles on the origins and evolution of Roman provincial administration, with a particular focus on the administrative role of the Roman army. In his book, *Cultural Change and Imperial Administration*, he examines the relationship between the progress of Romanization and the elaboration of Roman administration in the provinces of the middle Danube frontier.

Professor Dise regards teaching as the single most important activity that a college faculty member undertakes. At the University of Northern Iowa, he regularly offers courses on the history of the ancient Near East, the history of Greece, the history of Rome, and Classical civilization. He also teaches large sections of the Western civilization survey, the humanities, and occasional seminars on subjects such as the provinces of the Roman Empire. His courses fill quickly, and his past students often come back for more.

Table of Contents
Ancient Empires before Alexander
Part III

Ancient Empires before Alexander

Scope:

For 23 centuries, the figure of Alexander the Great has fired the imaginations of all who hear his story: The heroic young king led his army thousands of miles across the Near East and never lost a battle, conquering the largest empire the world had ever known, only to die a month short of his 33rd birthday. But Alexander's brilliance was so dazzling that it has obscured the fact that he was only the latest in a series of conquerors who had pursued the dream of empire across the stage of Near Eastern history, a grand procession that had already been underway for 2,000 years when Alexander first set foot on the shores of Asia in 334 B.C., a procession composed of names renowned in their own time but now mostly forgotten: Sargon, Ur-Nammu, Hattusilis, Thutmose III, Tiglath-pileser, Cyrus ... conquerors whose empires lay buried deep beneath the lands across which Alexander marched. Some of those empires were nearly as grand and mighty as Alexander's; others were more modest. Some of those empires, like Alexander's, lasted only a few decades; others endured for half a millennium. Most of those empires, unlike Alexander's, are now forgotten.

This is a course about those forgotten empires. Its purpose is to resurrect them from the dust and to restore them to their proper place in the panorama of ancient Near Eastern history. We explore 13 of them, beginning with the empire of Sargon of Akkad in the 24th century—the very first empire in all of human history—and ending more than two millennia later with the empire of Carthage, which outlived Alexander's empire but fell at last before the rising power of Rome. The course is arranged chronologically, and because it is a course about empires rather than about cultures, it focuses on the political and the military and concerns itself with religious, economic, or social issues only as they bear on imperial affairs. In treating each empire, it asks three questions fundamental to understanding any empire in any era: First, how and why did this empire come into being? Was it the creation of one man's genius and leadership, or did it arise out of broader forces? What is the story of its emergence? What opposition did it face, and how did it overcome that opposition? Second, how was this empire governed and defended? What was the relationship between its rulers and their subjects? How was it taxed? How was its army organized, equipped, and commanded? What threats did it face, and how did it confront them? And third, how and why did this empire fall? Was its decline sudden or prolonged? What factors led to its decline and fall? Did it fall due to internal decay, outside attack, or both? And how did the story of its collapse unfold? Answering these questions will require a mix of lecture formats: Some lectures will emphasize the narrative of history, while others will emphasize its analysis. In the end, these forgotten empires will stand revealed for what they were: important chapters in the drama of the history of the ancient world.

The course comprises four broad series of lectures. The first series focuses on the earliest empires in Near Eastern history, all of them concentrated in Mesopotamia. We begin with the mysterious and romantic figure of Sargon the Great, according to legend a foundling child who went on to conquer Mesopotamia and Syria. His empire was followed by the empire of Third-Dynasty Ur—the last flowering of Sumerian civilization and the only empire that Sumer ever forged. After the collapse of Sumer, Babylon first rose to greatness under Hammurabi, a great conqueror as well as a great lawgiver. Hammurabi's empire of First-Dynasty Babylon was short-lived, and in its wake, during the middle of the 2nd millennium, two empires rose to fill the void: the kingdom of the Hurrians in northern Mesopotamia, better known as Mitanni, and the Kassite empire in Babylonia. Tantalizingly little is known of either of these states, even though Mitanni dominated the northern Fertile Crescent for more than two centuries and Kassite Babylonia was the longest-lived of all Mesopotamian empires, enduring for over 400 years.

While empires rose and fell in Mesopotamia, to the north and west other empires were coming into being, which together with the empires of Mesopotamia formed what some scholars have called "the Club of the Great Powers." These will be the focus of the second series of lectures. To the north, the Hittite peoples of central Asia Minor forged the great empire that they called Hatti. To the west, in the coastlands of the eastern Mediterranean, Egypt emerged from its nest in the Nile Valley and conquered an empire that stretched as far north as Syria, where it battled for control with both Mitanni and Hatti. As these empires jockeyed for position in the Near East, on the island of Crete, the Minoans created history's first thalassocracy, or sea empire. Meanwhile, on the mainland north of Crete, the Greeks made their bold entrance onto the stage of history as the Achaeans, under their high king at Mycenae. They quickly developed their own unique political culture and soon spread east across the Aegean to challenge Hatti for supremacy in western Asia Minor.

A terrible cataclysm brought the 2nd millennium to a end, along with the empires that had belonged to the Club of the Great Powers. Mitanni was destroyed by Hatti, but Hatti then vanished in its turn. The Egyptians were driven back inside the confines of the Nile Valley, and the empire of the Kassites collapsed. Out of the ashes rose new powers. It is to these that the third series of lectures is devoted. The hill tribes of Canaan, worshipping a god called Yahweh, united as the kingdom of Israel, briefly filling the power vacuum left by the demise of Egypt's empire before dissolving after the death of its third king, Solomon. More enduringly, a group of peoples formerly subject to Mitanni began the long process of building the empire that would cast its long shadow across the first four centuries of the last millennium: Assyria. From its heartland in northern Mesopotamia, Assyria went on to conquer Babylonia, Syria, southeastern Asia Minor, the Levant, and eventually Egypt, making it the greatest empire the Near East had yet seen, but Assyria collapsed before a last revival of Babylonian power, aided by the Medes of western Iran. The Neo-Babylonian empire spread across the Fertile Crescent, taking up the mantle of Assyria and snuffing out the last remnant of the empire of Israel with the destruction of Judah in 587. But the Neo-Babylonians were to enjoy Assyria's mantle only briefly, for the Medes soon were overthrown by Cyrus, lord of Persis, who went on to overthrow the Neo-Babylonians as well, and all else that stood in his path, and to lay the foundations of the greatest of all Near Eastern empires: Persia.

The final series of lectures focuses on the last great Near Eastern empires, the empires of the mid-1st millennium. We begin with Persia. By the midpoint of the 1st millennium, the empire Cyrus had founded was vastly larger than any that had come before: It spanned the entire Near East, from Egypt and the Balkans to central Asia and the Indus Valley. But its size and its power failed to intimidate the tiny city-states of Greece, and Persia soon found itself locked in a 200-year-long confrontation with Greece that only ended when Alexander gave a royal funeral to Persia's last king and placed the Persian crown on his own head. The Greek conquest of Persia left only one Near Eastern power in existence, located not in the Near East but in the western Mediterranean: Carthage, a colony of Tyre, had built an empire for itself among the Phoenician settlements along the Spanish and African coasts and managed to hold its own against the Greeks in Sicily and Italy, but not against the stirring giant that was Rome. With Rome's defeat of Hannibal in the Second Punic War, the story of the empires of the Near East comes to an end.

The final lecture looks back both at the common threads that link the 13 empires of the course together and at the ways in which they are unique. It also looks forward to the one great legacy that the half-forgotten empires of the ancient Near East bestowed on Alexander and all the conquerors who followed him, from Caesar to Napoleon: the dream of empire.

Lecture Twenty-Five
The Rise of the Persian Empire

Scope:

Our knowledge of Persia, the greatest of all Near Eastern empires, is deeply colored by our sources, the vast majority of which are Greek and therefore focused on Greco-Persian relations. This leaves us ignorant of what happened throughout much of the rest of the Persian empire and paints a picture of the Persians that reflects Greek biases. But the Greek authors also provide a vivid narrative of those episodes in Persian history with which they were familiar. The Persians were part of the Iranian branch of the Indo-Europeans and emerged as the rulers of southwestern Iran after the Assyrians destroyed the Elamites. The founder of Persia was Cyrus the Great, who crushed the Medes in 550 B.C., gained control of western Anatolia and the Greek cities of Ionia in 547 B.C., and finally destroyed the Neo-Babylonian kingdom in 539 B.C. His son, Cambyses, rounded out Cyrus's achievement by conquering Egypt.

Outline

I.   Persia was the greatest of all the empires that ever arose in the ancient Near East. It encompassed more territory than any previous empire had, and more than any subsequent empire would until the rise of the Arab caliphate.

   A. Only Alexander's empire rivaled its extent, but that empire barely outlasted Alexander's death. The Persian empire endured for two centuries.

   B. Presiding over such a multiethnic, multicultural, multilingual realm for as long as they did, the Persians pioneered a singularly successful model for ruling diversity without tyrannizing it.

   C. Our understanding of the history and character of the Persian empire is deeply colored by the nature of our sources for Persian history. Those sources are far less plentiful and are very different in nature from our sources for other Near Eastern empires.

1. First of all, we have very little cuneiform material from the Persian period.
2. Besides the small cuneiform collections, there are also several caches of papyri from Egypt that date to the Persian period.
3. The epigraphic evidence is limited, too, both in quantity and scope.
4. The Hebrew scriptures are another source. Judea was a subprovince of the Persian empire, so the Jewish texts deal with the Persians insofar as the they involved themselves in Jewish affairs.

D. Greek authors provide our most abundant material on Persia.
1. They give us rich, detailed, and often colorful narratives of Persian history, as well as vivid sketches of figures in Persian history.
2. But the Greek authors' interests are specialized. They typically focus on Greco-Persian issues and on those parts of the Persian empire where Greeks came in contact with Persia, such as Anatolia and the eastern Mediterranean.
3. Most importantly, Greek writers display a strong bias in writing about the Persians. They paint the Persians in morally unflattering terms to contrast them with the Greek self-image as manly, virtuous, and self-sufficient.

E. In stark contrast to the textual evidence, archeology has contributed much less to our understanding of Persia than it has both to other areas of the Near East and to the Greco-Roman world.

II. The origins of the Persians are to be found in the great eastward migration of Indo-European speakers from their homeland in the vicinity of the Black Sea. The Persians belong to the Iranian branch of this migration.

A. The Iranians were cattle herders who gradually moved from central Asia into the Iranian plateau.

B. The Persians' ancestors settled in southwestern Iran, in Persis, the modern Fars.

C. The stage for the rise of Persia was set by the Assyrian king Ashurbanipal's destruction of Elam in 646 B.C.

III. Another group of migrating Iranians closely related to the Persians settled in the northern and central Zagros Mountains, around Ecbatana (modern Hamadan), where they became the Medes.

   A. The Medes first appear in Assyrian records in the 9th century, and they played an increasingly important role in the history of the Near East over the next three centuries.

   B. The traditional view has been that the Medes created a regional empire that preceded the Persians', but lately this view has been strongly challenged. The challenge for historians is to ferret out the actual history of the Medes.

IV. The creation of the Persian empire was the work of Cyrus II (*Kuruš*), whom history justly remembers as Cyrus the Great. In less than 30 years, he turned Persia from a peripheral Iranian principality into the greatest empire the Near East had yet known.

   A. Inevitably, Cyrus's brilliant achievements led to the creation of legends about his birth and background.

   B. According to Cyrus's own testimony, he was the fourth generation of his family to sit on the throne of either Persia or Anshan.

   C. The first step in Cyrus's creation of the Persian empire came in 550, with his destruction of the Median kingdom.

   D. Cyrus next turned his attention to western Anatolia, where in 547, King Croesus of Lydia was attempting to capitalize on Cyrus's destruction of the Medes by enlarging his kingdom.

   1. When the Persians and Lydians met in battle, perhaps near the site of Hattusas, Croesus fought Cyrus to a draw.

   2. But the Persians were mountain folk and were used to winter weather, so Cyrus remained in the field and marched on Croesus's capital at Sardis.

   3. Cyrus laid siege to Sardis in the winter of 546. The city fell after two weeks, and with it the kingdom of Lydia came to an end.

   E. Victorious over Lydia, Cyrus went on to subjugate the Greek city-states of Ionia, marking the first fateful encounter between Persia and the Greeks. This time, the Persians won.

F. Cyrus finally turned his attention to Babylonia. The Neo-Babylonians still controlled an empire that stretched from the Persian Gulf to Palestine.

   1. There are hints of fighting between the Neo-Babylonians and Persia prior to the final Persian attack, but Cyrus's invasion also reflected the geopolitical dynamics of the region.

   2. Babylonia also had been allied with Lydia, and Cyrus's conquest of Lydia may have been the pretext for the outbreak of hostilities.

   3. When Cyrus moved, he moved decisively. At the Battle of Opis in 539, he destroyed the Neo-Babylonian kingdom with one swift blow, slaughtering its army. The communities of Mesopotamia rushed to submit to him.

   4. Cyrus cast himself as the divinely sanctioned restorer of Babylonia.

   5. Cyrus's obliteration of the Neo-Babylonian army and government gave him control over territories that extended from the frontiers of Egypt to the Zagros foothills.

   6. He moved quickly to install people whom he trusted in control of Babylonia but avoided taking the royal title himself. Insofar as possible, he left local affairs in native hands.

G. After the fall of Babylon, Cyrus turned his attention to eastern Iran and central Asia.

H. Then in 530, Cyrus was killed while fighting the nomadic Massagetae, who lived in central Asia beyond the Jaxartes River.

I. Before his death, Cyrus had created a new capital for his empire, at Pasargadae.

V. Cyrus's son Cambyses succeeded him on the throne.

A. Cambyses continued the expansion of the empire by conquering Egypt.

B. Herodotus gives us a biased portrait of Cambyses, depicting him as a paranoid tyrant. The truth appears to have been different.

Suggested Reading:

Allen, *The Persian Empire*.

Brosius, *The Persians*.

Wiesehöfer, *Ancient Persia*.

Questions to Consider:

1. If we didn't have the Greeks' accounts of the Persian empire available to us, what would we know about Persia? What lessons do the Greek authors' treatment of the Persians give us regarding the way in which our picture of ancient (and modern) peoples is colored by the sources we use?

2. Was the Persian empire the creation of Cyrus's genius or of some deeper interplay of factors, either within Persia or within the Near East?

Lecture Twenty-Five—Transcript
The Rise of the Persian Empire

Of all the empires that ever arose in the ancient Near East, Persia's was the greatest. It encompassed more territory than any previous empire ever had—and more than any subsequent empire ever would, until the rise of the Arab caliphate. Only Alexander's empire rivaled its extent, but his empire barely outlasted his death. The Persian Empire survived for two centuries. At its greatest, that empire sprawled across more than 3,000 miles of territory—from north Africa and the Balkans to central Asia and the valley of the Indus River. It included a dizzying array of peoples, faiths, cultures, and languages at every level of sophistication and primitiveness. Presiding over such a multi-ethnic, multicultural, multilingual realm for as long as they did, the Persians pioneered a singularly successful model for ruling diversity without tyrannizing it. Theirs was a system that emphasized local autonomy within imperial unity that regarded differences among beliefs, and customs, and languages as a part of the human condition—not some primal defect to be remedied.

So, ruling with a light hand, the Persian Empire was less troubled by revolts than most previous Near Eastern realms. Only the Greeks, Babylonians, and Egyptians consistently resisted Persian rule, motivated by their intense self-awareness and their determination to express that self-awareness through political independence and not mere autonomy. The empire's other peoples were better adjusted and more content. Our understanding of the history and character of the Persian Empire is deeply colored by the nature of our sources. Those sources are far less plentiful and very different in nature than the ones for other Near Eastern empires.

First of all, we have very little cuneiform material. There are a couple of caches of administrative texts from the Persian capital of Persepolis, written in Aramaic—which was the universal language of Persian imperial administration—all told, about 2,500 of them. They deal with various aspects of agricultural and labor organization, landholding, demography, diet, and travel. This is interesting material, but it doesn't tell us much about imperial affairs. The texts are also limited in their chronological scope: They only cover the period from about 510 down to 458 B.C. There's also a cache of cuneiform texts from Nimrud, containing the archives of a Babylonian merchant family that leased royal lands to soldiers and high-court personnel. But these are basically private business records, and their horizon is limited to a particular locale. Why the cuneiform texts peter out after the mid-5th century B.C. isn't immediately clear. It may be that the Persians moved away from clay tablets to papyrus for their record-keeping. If so, they started a general shift in the same direction, because both clay tablets and the cuneiform script disappear entirely from use by the middle of the 1st century A.D.

Besides these small cuneiform collections, there are also several caches of papyri from Egypt that date to the Persian Period. Being perishable, papyrus survives in Egypt's arid climate—but not elsewhere. One of these caches is a trove of records and letters left by a colony of Jewish soldiers serving the Persians at Elephantine. Another is a cache of administrative texts from Saqqara, but it was recovered from the antiquities market in damaged condition—and both its condition and its provenance compromise its usefulness to scholars. Neither of these collections casts much light on anything but its own small corner of the Persian world. The epigraphic evidence is limited, too—both in quantity and scope.

Persian kings occasionally put up monumental inscriptions, usually in Old Persian, the Persians' native language—which is a member of the Indo-European language family—along with Greek, Latin, and English. The best known is Darius I's monumental autobiographical inscription carved on a rock face at Behistun, which narrates the circumstances that led to his accession. But most royal inscriptions give us much less historical information than the Behistun text, and that makes them less useful than we would like them to be for reconstructing Persia's history. The Hebrew Scriptures are another source. Judea was the sub-province of Yehud in the Persian Empire—so the Jewish texts deal with the Persians insofar as they involve themselves in Jewish affairs. Of the texts in the Hebrew Scriptures, Isaiah, Ezra, and Nehemiah all cast a favorable light on the Persians; only in Esther do we find a more negative Persian picture. But it's the Greek authors who provide our most abundant material on Persia. They give us rich, detailed, and often-colorful narratives of Persian history and vivid sketches of figures in Persian history. This means that thanks to the Greeks, in Persia's case alone among the empires of the ancient Near East are we able to describe political, military, and cultural events in detail. It also means that our account of the Persian Empire is much longer than our accounts of other Near Eastern empires. But the Greek authors' interests are specialized. For the most part, they focus on Greco-Persian issues and on those parts of the Persian Empire where the Greeks came in contact with Persia—such as Anatolia and the eastern Mediterranean. This means that we know a fair bit about what went on in those areas, but we know almost nothing about what went on elsewhere. This source problem even has its own name, and it's called "hellenocentrism."

Most importantly, Greek writers display a strong bias in their writing about the Persians. They paint the Persians in morally unflattering terms, in order to contrast them with their own image of themselves as manly, virtuous, and self-sufficient. Here's the warning that the noted Near Eastern historian Amélie Kuhrt gives us in her book, *The Ancient Near East*:

> All the Greek writers were fascinated by the wealth and power of the Persian rulers, so they often recount stories of court intrigue and the moral decadence that comes from living in unlimited luxury. In such anecdotes, the Persian king appears as an essentially weak figure, a prey to the machinations of powerful women and sinister eunuchs. This is an inversion of Greek social and political norms, with which we, as Europeans have usually identified: the image of the cowardly, effeminate Persian monarch has exercised a strong influence through the centuries, making the Persian empire into a powerful "other" in European Orientalism, contrasted with "western" bravery and masculinity. We must remember this in studying the Persian empire: the powerful and widespread impression of its political system is fundamentally flawed.

In his *History of the Ancient Near East*, Marc Van de Mieroop seconds Kuhrt's warning, cautioning us also to beware of the classical writers' depiction of the Persian Empire as doomed and disintegrating as a consequence of its intrigues and the decadent addiction to excessive wealth. Archeology has contributed much less to our understanding of Persia than it has both to other areas of the Near East and the Greco-Roman world. Many important Persian-era sites are today densely inhabited cities—and that, of course, gets in the way of excavation; although, of course, that hasn't stopped excavation in other densely inhabited places like Jerusalem. But perhaps more importantly, Persian excavation projects don't excite the interest—and, therefore, the funding—that other projects do. Very few Persian sites have any direct connection to biblical incidents or personalities. Westerners who fund excavations don't feel the sort of cultural connection to Persia that they do with Greece and Rome. This means that what we know about Persia and what we can say is fundamentally limited by the peculiar perspectives and biases of sources that tell a compelling tale—but a tale of which we must always be skeptical. We see Persia through Greek eyes—not through Persian ones, and in fairness to the great people who were the ancient Persians, we must never forget that.

The origins of the Persians lie in the vast migration of Indo-European peoples spreading east from their homeland in the vicinity of the Black Sea. The Persians were part of the Iranian branch of this migration. The early Iranians were cattle-herders who gradually moved from central Asia into the Iranian plateau. The Persians' ancestors settled in southwestern Iran—in Persis, the modern Fars. But we hear nothing definite about either the Persians or their principality before the 7th century B.C. The stage for the rise of Persia was set by the Assyrian King Ashurbanipal's destruction of Elam in 646. When Assyria crushed Elam, a local Persian dynasty was able to establish both Persis's independence and its own authority. At the same time, the Iranian pastoralists in southwestern Iran were slowly settling down and becoming farmers and townsmen. Persis is also known as Anshan, a name that is derived from the area's main city. Anshan lay deserted between about 1000 and about 700 B.C., but afterwards there was a revival of urban life there and elsewhere in Persis. The earliest appearance of Anshan is in the titles of Persian kings, beginning with Cyrus—who, with his predecessors (Cambyses I, Cyrus I, and Teispes), is called "King of Anshan."

While the Persians were settling in southwestern Iran, another group of migrating Iranians closely related to them settled in the northern and central Zagros, around Ecbatana (modern Hamadan)—where they became known as the Medes. The Medes first appear in Assyrian records in the 9th century B.C. and came to play an increasingly important role in the history of the Near East over the next three centuries. They developed a complex relationship with the Assyrians. They served in the Assyrian army as mercenaries. But more often, they fought with the Assyrians—raiding Assyrian lands and suffering retaliatory attacks in return. The Medes' most dramatic achievement was their central role in the destruction of the Assyrian Empire.

The traditional view has been that the Medes created a regional empire of their own that preceded the Persians', but lately this view has been strongly challenged. The foundation of the traditional view lies in Herodotus's account of the history of the Median royal house. But critical scholars are now inclined to see this as a potpourri of legends woven into a sort of Median national folk epic by Herodotus. The Assyrian evidence doesn't support the existence of a Median empire, even though the historicity of a couple of Median kings is demonstrated by Babylonian records. Archaeological evidence for a Median state is also very sketchy. There are palace-type structures at a handful of sites, but nothing from the supposed Median capital at Ecbatana—and all of the sites decline drastically by the 6th century B.C. So, it may be that Assyrian trade through the Medes' territory brought the mountain dwellers prosperity before the fall of Assyria, which then resulted in a precipitous decline. The challenge for historians is to ferret out the actual history of the Medes.

Herodotus tells us the story of four kings of the Medes. Deioces was the first king of the Medes. Before him, Herodotus says, they were "village dwellers"—or, in Greek terms, uncivilized. Deioces was just and incorruptible, and according to Herodotus's account became king because he was called on so often to resolve his countrymen's disputes that he said they would have to make him their king and build him a great city for a capital. That city was Ecbatana. He ruled for 43 years.

The second king of the Medes was Phraortes. He was said to have made the Persians his subjects and then conquered Asia, which clearly he did not do. He reigned for 22 years and was killed in battle against the Assyrians. Phraortes was succeeded by his son, Cyaxares. Cyaxares reorganized the Median army, probably in response to the defeat that killed his father—separating the spearmen, archers, and cavalry into distinct units, whereas previously they had all fought together. Cyaxares used this restructured army to help in the destruction of the hated Assyrians and reigned for 40 years.

The last king of the Medes was Cyaxares's son, Astyages. Astyages reigned for 35 years and was overthrown by Cyrus the Persian when Cyrus destroyed the Median kingdom. The only Median kings who are well documented in non-Greek sources are Cyaxares and

Astyages. The Babylonian Chronicle names Cyaxares as the Median ruler who allied with Nabonidus to destroy Assyria; it names Astyages as the king defeated and dethroned by Cyrus.

Although Herodotus's account of the Median kingdom is more legend than history, it's clear that the Medes had become a unified kingdom by the late 7th century. For one thing, only the considerable resources made available by a unified kingdom could have enabled Cyaxares to play the role he did in the destruction of Assyria. Furthermore, Cyrus needed only a single battle to destroy the Median kingdom in 550—had they not been a unified kingdom, his task would've been far more complicated. But whether the Medes ever created an empire that stretched from Iran all the way to the Halys River in Anatolia is very doubtful.

The creation of the Persian Empire was the work of *Kuruš* (or Cyrus II), whom history justly remembers as Cyrus the Great. In less than 30 years, between his accession in 559 and his death in 530, he turned Persia from a peripheral Iranian principality into the greatest empire the Near East had ever known. Inevitably, Cyrus's brilliant achievements led to the creation of legends about his birth and background. These are typical of the stories that developed around ancient culture-heroes like Sargon the Great, Moses, and Romulus and Remus. One legend had it that he was born of poor, humble parents and worked his way up through the ranks of the Median court until he overthrew the king.

Herodotus gives his own—typically charming and colorful—account of Cyrus's birth and early childhood. According to him, Cyrus's mother was Mandane, Astyages's daughter, whom he had married to Cambyses, the King of Anshan. Astyages had a dream that the child whom she bore would become king. So, he ordered his servant Harpagus to kill the infant, who passed off the loathsome duty to the royal shepherd, Mithridates, whose wife begged him to substitute her own stillborn child for the royal infant—and so they raised the infant Cyrus as their own. At the age of 10, during a game with other boys, he was chosen as king and beat an aristocratic boy who refused his orders. When the boy's father complained to Astyages and Cyrus was brought before the king, he defended his actions, and Astyages intuitively recognized Cyrus as having royal blood and figured out who he must be. When Mithridates revealed the truth under torture, Astyages cruelly punished Harpagus by butchering Harpagus's son and then serving the lad's cooked remains to the unwitting Harpagus as a royal meal. Astyages allowed Cyrus to return to Cambyses and Mandane, though, because in the opinion of his soothsayers, the *magi*, Cyrus's having been called king by the boys fulfilled the terms of Astyages's dream. Which just goes to show how wrong a guy can be, because to avenge himself on Astyages—once Cyrus was on the throne of Persis (or Anshan)—Harpagus revealed Astyages's original purpose to Cyrus and encouraged Cyrus to revolt.

According to Cyrus's own testimony, he was the fourth generation of his family to sit on the throne of Persis (or Anshan). In the genealogies, the founder of the dynasty was his great-grandfather, Teispes, who reigned around 650 B.C. Teispes's successor was Cyrus I, who was followed on the throne by his son, Cambyses I, who was Cyrus the Great's father. Assyrian records prove the existence of Cyrus I because they record him sending tribute to Ashurbanipal around 640. In a variant form of the genealogy given by Darius I on his Behistun inscription, Teispes's son was Ariamnes. Most scholars think Teispes had two sons: Ariamnes and Cyrus I, and that Anshan and Persis were separate principalities ruled by Cyrus and Ariamnes respectively—but no evidence directly supports the existence of these separate principalities at that time. In any case, Darius claimed descent from Ariamnes and was at pains to associate his own family, the Achaemenids, with the line of Cyrus.

The first step in Cyrus's creation of the Persian Empire came in 550, with his destruction of the kingdom of the Medes. Persia's relationship to the Median kingdom prior to Cyrus is unclear. There's no evidence that directly supports Herodotus's contention that Persia was a vassal state of the Medes. Cyrus defeated Astyages when Astyages's army mutinied on the eve of battle and handed Astyages over to Cyrus, who then kept the fallen Mede in polite but secure captivity at the Persian court. Defeating Astyages vastly increased Cyrus's material and manpower resources and also made him heir to whatever regional hegemony the Median kingdom might have exercised.

Cyrus next turned his attention to western Anatolia—where, in 547, Croesus, King of Lydia, attempted to capitalize on Cyrus's destruction of the Medes by enlarging his own kingdom. When the Persians and Lydians met in battle—perhaps near the site of Hattusas—Croesus fought Cyrus to a draw. Satisfied that he had fended off the Persians at least for the moment, Croesus disbanded his army for the winter and sent requests for aid to Egypt, Babylonia, and Sparta. But the Persians were mountain folk and used to winter weather, so Cyrus remained in the field and marched on Croesus's capital at Sardis. He also sent messengers to the Greek cities on the western shore of Anatolia, the region known as Ionia, to encourage them to join him by rebelling—but they refused. Cyrus laid siege to Sardis in the winter of 546. The city fell after two weeks—and with it, the kingdom of Lydia came to an end.

The traditions about Croesus's fate are contradictory. The Nabonidus Chronicle from Babylonia implies that he was killed. According to Herodotus, though, Croesus became a trusted adviser at the Persian court after his life was miraculously saved—either spared from being killed by a Persian soldier when a previously mute boy suddenly cried out to the soldier to spare Croesus, or when a miraculous torrent of rain doused a pyre on which Croesus was about to immolate himself. But Cyrus's treatment of defeated rivals was singularly generous—so the notion that Croesus, like Astyages, was spared and given an honorable retirement has both emotional appeal and historical merit. Victorious over Lydia, Cyrus went on to subjugate the Greek city-states of Ionia, marking the first fateful encounter between Persia and the Greeks. This time, the Persians won. He placed western Anatolia under direct Persian rule, but almost immediately had to put down a rebellion. He had appointed a local official, Pactyas, to act as treasurer in western Anatolia under the command of the Persian General Tabalos, who was left in Sardis with a garrison force. Pactyas ran off with the funds and raised a revolt with some backing from the Ionian Greeks. Cyrus responded swiftly and harshly by sending his general, Mazares, to pursue the rebel—who was turned over to the Persians by the Aegean city-state of Chios. The Persians made an example of some of the Greek cities that had aided the rebellion and then completed the conquest of the city-states of western and southern Anatolia. Mazares sacked Priene, sold its inhabitants into slavery, and ravaged the plain of the Meander River. Harpagus took over the Persian command after Mazares's death and subjugated the Greek cities of Caria, Caunia, and Lycia. Some submitted peacefully; others had to be besieged. Half of the population of Phocaea simply took ship and fled to their colony of Alalia on Corsica, where they joined the fight against Carthage for control of the island. Once Anatolia was secure, Cyrus finally turned his attention to Babylonia. The Neo-Babylonians still controlled an empire that stretched from the Persian Gulf to Palestine.

There are hints of fighting between the Neo-Babylonians and Persia prior to the final Persian attack, but Cyrus's invasion also reflected the geopolitical dynamics of the region. Hostility between the powers that dominated Mesopotamia and those that dominated western Iran, the Armenian highlands, and Anatolia was a tradition that stretched back nearly 2,000 years. But Babylonia had also been allied with Lydia, and Cyrus's conquest of Lydia may have been the pretext for the outbreak of hostilities. Whatever it was, when he moved, Cyrus moved decisively. At the battle of Opis in 539, he destroyed the Neo-Babylonian kingdom with one swift blow, slaughtering its army. The communities of Mesopotamia rushed to submit to him. The Neo-Babylonian king, Nabonidus, fled to Babylon—where he was taken prisoner as the populace formally welcomed Cyrus into the capital as their new king. Cyrus then cast himself as the divinely sanctioned restorer of Babylonia. He commissioned a program of civic and sacred building construction, proclaiming the restoration of destroyed sanctuaries and the return of their peoples. It was as a part of this program of restoration that he sent the exiles back to Jerusalem from the Babylonian Captivity and commissioned the reconstruction of the Temple—for which Isaiah 45:1 hails him as the Messiah. This was all part of the customary public rhetoric of Babylonian conquerors after a triumph, which guaranteed continuity to the defeated and offered the local elites political cover for collaborating with the victor.

Cyrus's obliteration of the Neo-Babylonian army and government gave him control over territories that extended from the frontiers of Egypt to the Zagros foothills. He moved quickly to install people whom he trusted in control of Babylonia—but avoided taking the royal title himself. Insofar as possible, he left local affairs in native hands. At first, he installed his son, Cambyses, as king in Babylonia. For reasons that aren't clear, after a year he replaced Cambyses with a general named Gobryas as governor. But below the highest echelons, Cyrus retained local Babylonian officials in their posts, a policy that appears to have worked well. There are no hints of the local unrest that had plagued the Assyrians in Babylonia, much less of the sort of open revolt found in Lydia. What measures Cyrus took for the former provinces of the Neo-Babylonian Empire are less clear. The return of the exiles to Jerusalem may hint at a general effort by Persia to restore and strengthen provincial centers in the old Babylonian provinces. Like Astyages and Croesus, Nabonidus was a beneficiary of Cyrus's singular generosity towards former enemies. He became an exile, living on an estate in Carmania in southern Iran for the rest of his life.

After the fall of Babylon, Cyrus created a new capital for his empire, at Pasargadae. The city was located about 50 miles northeast of the city of Anshan. It's named for the tribe Cyrus belonged to—but the style of its buildings was eclectic and imperial. They incorporated Assyrian, Iranian, and even Greek techniques and motifs. So in Pasargadae, Cyrus created a fitting symbol for the breadth and diversity of his vision of the empire—an empire ruled by Persians but home to all the peoples of the ancient Near East. Having secured Babylonia and the west, Cyrus turned his attention to eastern Iran and central Asia. Lying far beyond Greek horizons and of little interest to them, this is the least well-documented part of Cyrus's activity. Greek writers credit Cyrus with the conquest of Bactria and Sogdiana as far as the Jaxartes River. A string of Persian forts built along the Jaxartes include Cyreschata, whose foundation was later linked to Cyrus. Though it's not clear how much of the region he actually conquered, it looks as though he brought most of Afghanistan and south central Asia under some sort of Persian control. Then, in 530, while fighting the nomadic Massagetae who lived in central Asia beyond the Jaxartes, Cyrus the Great was killed in battle.

Cyrus's son, Cambyses, succeeded him on the throne. Cambyses continued the expansion of the empire by conquering Egypt. King Amasis of Egypt had actively supported Cyrus's opponents and taken steps to strengthen Egypt's position vis-à-vis Persia. He allied with Polycrates of Samos as a balance against Persia's control of Ionia. He also conquered Cyprus to check Persian control of the Levant. Cambyses carefully laid the groundwork for the Persian invasion of Egypt by doing three things: building a fleet to counter Egypt's naval supremacy; taking Egypt's outposts; and securing the invasion routes across the Sinai. His navy consisted of the cutting-edge *trireme*, which were top-of-the-line warships propelled in combat by three vertical banks of oars. The ships were crewed by Persia's maritime subjects, but the commanders were all Persians. He also took Cyprus from Egypt to prevent its use as a base against Persian bases in the Levant, and he established diplomatic links with the Arab tribes that controlled the routes through the desert.

He launched his attack on Egypt in 526. Victory was swift. The Persians defeated the Egyptian army in a battle on the easternmost branch of the Nile Delta, and the Egyptians fell back to the fortress of Memphis. They murdered the Persian herald sent to summon them to surrender, and the Persians besieged and took Memphis after 10 days. The new Egyptian king, Psammetichus III, was taken prisoner. The peoples of Libya, Barca, and Cyrenaica quickly approached the Persians with offers of submission. Cambyses then consolidated Egypt's southern frontier by making an arrangement with the Napatan kings who ruled beyond the first cataract. Cambyses may also have secured the routes across the eastern Sahara by conquering the Egyptian outpost at the Kharga Oasis.

Herodotus gives us a biased portrait of Cambyses, depicting him as a paranoid tyrant. The truth appears to have been different. His picture is grounded in hostile Egyptian propaganda from the mid-5th century B.C. Egyptian sources contemporary with the conquest see Cambyses much differently. What happened to color our sources? By Herodotus's time, Egyptian attitudes toward Persian rule had soured thanks to the burden of Persian taxation and the ruthless suppression of two Egyptian revolts in 486–485 and in 460 to 453. There was also the loss of status and property suffered by those who backed the losing side in these two rebellions. In point of fact, Cambyses's policy towards Egypt mirrored Cyrus's policy in Babylonia. He forged links with the local elites and installed them in honored—but not politically powerful—positions, using their familiarity with local conditions to make acceptance of Persian rule palatable. He honored and respected local religious cults with their powerful and influential priesthoods. While Cambyses was consolidating his control of Egypt, there was a severe political crisis back home—in the course of which he came to an untimely end. According to the account left by the next king, Darius the Achaemenid, Cambyses secretly murdered his brother, Bardiya (or "Smerdis," as Herodotus calls him). An impostor—Gaumata the Magian—then arose, posing as Smerdis, and the entire empire rallied to his side against Cambyses—who died of an accidental wound in Syria while returning to defend his throne. Darius, after praying to the one god Ahuramazda, led a group of great Persian barons against Gaumata and killed him—after which Ahuramazda bestowed the kingship on Darius. It may be likelier that what actually happened was that Bardiya took advantage of discontent with his brother's prolonged absence in Egypt to usurp the throne—and that he was then murdered by an aristocratic conspiracy led by Darius.

Cambyses's death brought an end to Cyrus's dynasty, and Darius's accession ushered in both a new family, the Achaemenids, and a new era in Persia's imperial history—when the empire achieved its final form and met its mortal enemy: the Greeks.

Lecture Twenty-Six
The Outbreak of the Greek Wars

Scope:

Darius I put the finishing touches on the empire founded by Cyrus, conquering the Indus Valley, establishing a Persian bridgehead in the Balkans, and giving the administrative structure of the empire its definitive form. But a botched effort to expand Persian authority into the islands of the central Aegean led to a massive rebellion among Persia's Anatolian Greek subjects, who received token support from their relatives in Athens. After he crushed the Ionian revolt, Darius determined to neutralize the threat posed by the city-states of mainland Greece. His first expedition foundered in a storm. The second, aimed at Athens, was defeated at Marathon. Thus began the epic Persian confrontation with Greece, which continued, in one form or another, until Alexander's destruction of the Persian empire.

Outline

I. Among Persian monarchs, Darius I is second in importance only to Cyrus the Great. With him, the Achaemenid dynasty came to the throne it was to occupy until the end of the empire. With him, the Persian empire received its definitive shape and administrative structure. And with him, Persia's long and fatal confrontation with the Greeks began.

    A. Darius became king under highly questionable circumstances. This may be one reason why his accession was greeted by widespread revolts.

        1. Many of the rebellions were the usual efforts by subject Near Eastern peoples to exploit the moment of potential weakness represented by a royal transition.

        2. But there were also revolts in the Persian homeland, which suggests that there were larger doubts about Darius's claim to the throne and that fracture lines existed within the young Persian empire.

        3. Whatever the truth behind Darius's accession and the hostility that greeted it, he reacted swiftly and decisively against the challenge to his authority and crushed the revolts.

B. Darius was the last Persian king to expand the empire, bringing it to its greatest extent. When he was done, it stretched from Libya and the Balkans in the west to Bactria (modern Afghanistan) and the borders of India in the east.

II. The advance into the Aegean islands proved fateful when, in 499 B.C., it sparked a rebellion among the Greek city-states of Ionia. This six-year-long Ionian revolt was the first spasm in a military and diplomatic confrontation with Greece that was to last off and on for the remainder of the Persian empire's history and would ultimately result in its destruction.

    A. The Ionian revolt sprang from a number of causes.

        1. The underlying cause was the Ionians' resentment of Persian rule. This grew out of the Greeks' distaste for Persian infringement of their beloved autonomy.

        2. The immediate cause of the revolt, according to Herodotus, was the failure of the Persian attack on the island polis of Naxos, in the central Aegean.

    B. The revolt began very successfully for the rebel cities, but its prospects dimmed when it failed to attract much support outside Ionia.

        1. The rebels began by overthrowing their Persian-backed tyrants.

        2. Then, in a surprise attack, rebel troops succeeded in capturing Sardis, the capital of the Persian satrapy in western Anatolia.

        3. The rebels sought aid from the city-states of the Greek mainland, but for the most part they were rebuffed.

        4. The Persians gathered their forces and launched a counteroffensive within a year.

        5. The climactic battle took place at sea, at Lade. The Persians won an overwhelming victory.

        6. The Persians initially punished the rebels with cold-blooded brutality. But after 493, the Persians adopted a more conciliatory approach.

        7. The final stage in the consolidation of Persian authority came after the Naxos revolt. In the north Aegean, Mardonius led a land-sea expedition along the coast to reaffirm Persian authority.

III. The participation of the mainland city-states Athens and Eretria in the Ionian revolt had shown the Persians that their northwestern frontier could never be secure so long as the city-states of mainland Greece remained unsubdued. The Greco-Persian Wars began as a Persian effort to neutralize the Greek threat to their western provinces and a Greek effort to neutralize the Persian threat to their autonomy.

    A. The wars pitted two antagonists against one another whose military and material resources were vastly different in scale, with the Persians enjoying an overwhelming advantage.

        1. The Persians possessed immense numerical superiority. They could draw on the manpower assets of an empire that extended from the Aegean and Egypt to India.

        2. The Persians also possessed immense economic resources.

        3. Finally, the Persians possessed unity of command. That unity came from the fact that these vast resources were commanded and deployed by only one man: the Great King of Persia.

    B. By contrast, any sensible person would have placed the Greeks at a decided disadvantage.

        1. There was no unity among the Greeks at all. There was no kingdom or empire of Greece. The Greek world consisted of hundreds of completely independent little city-states, called poleis.

        2. Furthermore, Greece was poor. It had limited agricultural production and few mineral resources.

        3. The poleis of Greece also had small populations and therefore had limited pools of military manpower.

        4. But the poleis of Greece did possess important, though not readily apparent, strengths. Most notable of these was their commitment to the rule of law and the notion of citizenship.

        5. The Greeks also possessed military strengths that were not readily apparent but that allowed them to move with speed and agility.

IV. In 491, Darius began his bid to neutralize the Greek threat.

    A. The Persians possessed considerable intelligence about the Greek world, obtained through Greek exiles and their own reconnaissance.

B. Additionally, Darius undertook a diplomatic offensive to exploit the Greeks' chronic disunity by winning the submission of as many poleis as possible.

C. In 490, Darius launched an expedition against Greece to punish the poleis that had defied him.

D. The Athenians', Spartans', and Eretrians' efforts to work out joint defense plans fell through and left them vulnerable to defeat.

E. The Greeks' intelligence gathering was poor to nonexistent, so the Persians were able to surprise them by island hopping across the central Aegean, rather than following the expected route along the Thracian coast.

F. After destroying Eretria, the Persians crossed over the straits between Euboea and Attica and landed at the nearby plain of Marathon, planning to march from there to Athens, about 25 miles away.

    1. Marathon was an obvious landing spot for the Persians.

    2. The Athenians made no effort to oppose the Persians' landing but swiftly marched their heavy infantry to the edge of the plain, blocking the roads to Athens.

    3. For about a week, the two forces faced each other across a couple of miles of open ground, stalemated by their different tactical goals and by disputes within the Athenian command.

    4. The Athenians timed their attack carefully and altered the deployment of their phalanx to compensate for their inferior numbers.

    5. The fighting was bitter and prolonged. The Athenians finally defeated the Persians, but the Persians managed to evacuate their troops even as fighting raged on the landing beaches.

G. Round one in the Greek Wars had gone to the Greeks. Round two would soon begin.

Suggested Reading:

Allen, *The Persian Empire.*

Burn, *Persia and the Greeks.*

Green, *The Greco-Persian Wars.*

Questions to Consider:

1. Do you find the account of Darius's expedition against the Scythians credible? What were the logistical challenges that faced the Persian army on this expedition, if the account is accurate?

2. What were the relative advantages and disadvantages, political and military, that the Persians and the Greeks brought to their confrontation with one another? Did the Greeks enjoy a decisive advantage in this struggle? How might the Persians have neutralized the Greeks' strengths?

Lecture Twenty-Six—Transcript
The Outbreak of the Greek Wars

Among Persian monarchs, Darius I is second in importance only to Cyrus the Great. With him, the Achaemenid dynasty came to the throne it was to occupy until the end of the empire. With him, the Persian Empire received its definitive shape and administrative structure—and with him, Persia's long and fatal confrontation with the Greeks began. Darius became king under highly questionable circumstances. This may be one reason why his accession was greeted by widespread revolts. As we've seen, Cyrus's son and successor, Cambyses, had died in the course of a rebellion in 522. The prelude to the rebellion was the murder of Cambyses's brother, Bardiya—perhaps at Cambyses's own hands. The rebellion itself was led by a shadowy figure, Gaumata the Magian, who supposedly rallied the common people to him by pretending to be Bardiya. After praying to Ahuramazda, Darius claims to have led a conspiracy of great Persian barons against Gaumata, putting down his rebellion and killing him—after which Ahuramazda gave Darius the throne.

Many of the rebellions were the usual efforts by subject Near Eastern peoples to exploit the moment of potential weakness represented by a royal transition. There were uprisings in Babylonia, Bactria, and Armenia, as well as parts of central Asia. But there were also revolts in the Persian homeland, which suggests that there were larger controversies about Darius's claim to the throne, and that fracture lines existed within the young Persian Empire. Was Darius involved in the conspiracies against Cambyses or Bardiya? What about the legitimacy of Darius's claim to power? In his autobiographical Behistun inscription, Darius is at great pains to assert that he and Cyrus the Great descended from a distant common ancestor, a purported individual named Achaemenes, but this is almost certainly a fiction, especially since both Darius's father and grandfather were alive when he seized the throne—and if this common descent were true, they ought to have had a better claim on the crown than he did.

Furthermore, the back-story of Gaumata the Magian suggests that he was a Mede—and, therefore, that his attempt to gain power threatened Persian ethnic hegemony. Or it may be that Gaumata, as a *magus* (or priest) represented an older strain of Persian religion, and that his rebellion was a revolt of the common people against an attempt by the royal house to impose their Zoroastrian faith on their still-pagan Iranian subjects. Whatever the truth behind Darius's accession and the hostility that greeted it, he reacted swiftly and decisively against the challenge to his authority and crushed the revolts. He marched in person against Babylon, defeating the rebel army and seizing the city in late 522. He then sent off forces under other generals to deal with the other rebellions.

Early in 521, loyal governors defeated the rebel leader in Persia, who had claimed yet again to be the true Bardiya. By the spring of 521, Darius himself had put down the rebellions in Media and Parthia. The last embers were snuffed out by June. In a decisive break with the clemency that had characterized Cyrus's rule, Darius then executed the leaders of the Iranian rebellion, killing them both publicly and cruelly. The worst of the traitors, those who had led the rebellion in Persia itself, were impaled. Darius is noteworthy for being the last Persian king to expand the empire. He brought it to its greatest extent—and when he was done, its boundaries stretched from Libya and the Balkans in the west to Bactria and the borders of India in the east.

Unfortunately, our information about his conquests is very spotty. The most glaring example is his subjugation of the Indus River Valley. We have no details about how he did it. This dramatically underscores the limitations of having to depend on Greek sources for our knowledge of Persia's history, because the main reason Greek writers didn't discuss the conquest of India would appear to be that they didn't find this expedition particularly interesting. After all, it didn't involve any Greeks. So we're not even sure about such basic information as the date of the conquest. We have to infer it from the dates of inscriptions that either do or don't mention India as part of the empire. Based on those, we think it probably took place about 518 B.C.

Following the conquest of the Indus Valley, Darius returned to the west and, around 513, launched an expedition into the Balkans and the Ukraine. Herodotus is our source for this campaign, but his account is strongly shaped by his determination to cast it in a mold that foreshadows the later Persian attack on Greece itself. According to Herodotus, Darius's goal was to neutralize the threat posed by the nomadic Scythians, who had been raiding Persia's northern provinces, but apparently Darius also intended to acquire a permanent foothold in southeastern Europe. He built a pontoon bridge two-thirds of a mile long across the Bosporus (a feat not duplicated until A.D. 1973), setting up white stone columns at either end that detailed his order of battle. The suspicion that Darius intended to establish a permanent bridgehead in Europe is strengthened by the fact that he chose a line of march that took him through the interior of Thrace instead of along the coast, where he could've been more easily supplied, and by the fact that he kept erecting inscriptions along his route—which was a way of indicating that he was annexing the area through which he marched.

The campaign apparently saw the Persian army march through Thrace and across the Danube; then from the Danube all the way east through the Ukraine to the Volga—and then back, a total distance of some 2,000 miles. But during the whole expedition, Darius was unable to force the elusive Scythians into a decisive confrontation, and so the campaign was indecisive and proved barren of results. Although Darius's expedition failed in what Herodotus says was its primary objective—the neutralization of the Scythian threat, it did result in that permanent Persian presence in the Balkans. When he withdrew to Anatolia, Darius organized Thrace as the satrapy (or province) of Skudra. It comprised the territory from the Danube to the Aegean, and from the Black Sea to the Strymon River—with the kingdom of Macedonia, west of the Strymon, as a vassal buffer state under its king, Amyntas. Meanwhile, as the Scythian expedition was underway and the satrapy of Skudra was being set up, the Persian governors (or satraps) in Anatolia were slowly expanding Persian control into the Greek islands of the eastern Aegean. By the end of the 6th century, they'd established Persian authority over all the large islands off the Anatolian coast. Samos was taken by the Persians early in Darius's reign, around 520. Chios and Lesbos fell to the Persians about 10 years later. But this advance into the Aegean Islands proved to be fateful when, in 499, it sparked a rebellion among the Greek city-states of Ionia. This six-year-long Ionian Revolt was the first spasm in a military and diplomatic confrontation with Greece that was to last off and on for the remainder of the Persian Empire's history—and would ultimately result in its destruction.

The Ionian Revolt sprang from a number of causes. The underlying one was the Ionians' resentment of Persian rule. This grew out of the Greeks' distaste for Persian infringement of their beloved autonomy. For one thing, Darius had imposed an annual tribute in place of Cyrus's occasional levies. He had also hit the cities with demands for military service, particularly the provision of ships and manpower to support the Scythian expedition. The Greeks especially resented the tyrants whom the Persians had imposed as their agents to rule over the Ionian cities.

The immediate cause of the revolt, according to Herodotus, was the failure of the Persian attack on the island polis of Naxos in the central Aegean. Around 500 B.C., a group of political refugees from Naxos appealed to Aristagoras, the former Persian-backed tyrant of Miletus, for aid. He arranged Persian support, going all the way up to Darius for approval. An expedition of Ionian ships and Persian troops sailed to Naxos, but dissension within the expedition's leadership led to Naxos being warned of its approach, and its citizens were ready when the Persians arrived. The four-month-long siege failed, and the expedition returned to Anatolia empty-handed. Aristagoras, fearing Darius's displeasure, then passed word to Ionia to throw off Persian rule—promising the Ionian cities democracy in place of tyranny if they did so.

The revolt began very successfully for the rebel cities, but its prospects dimmed when it failed to attract much support outside of Ionia. Rebels began by overthrowing their Persian-backed tyrants. Aristagoras's successor as tyrant at Miletus was murdered. Then, in a surprise attack, rebel troops succeeded in capturing Sardis—the capital of the Persian satrapy in western Anatolia. The satrap, Artaphernes, withdrew to the citadel, where he held out with the Persian garrison. The city caught fire—reportedly by accident—and was destroyed. The rebels sought aid from the city-states of the Greek mainland, but for the most part they were rebuffed.

The Spartan king, Cleomenes, ejected the Ionian envoy when he made the mistake of being honest and telling the Spartans that it would take the astonishing total of three months for their troops to march from Sardis along the royal road to the Persian capital at Susa. The Ionians were much more successful at Athens, which agreed to contribute 20 ships to the rebel cause. The small community of Eretria on the nearby island of Euboea dispatched another five. The rebels also got the support of the Persian-dominated Greek cities of Cyprus, Caria, and the Hellespont—which joined the rebellion following the destruction of Sardis. But these defections threatened Persia's communications with the satrapy in Thrace and the sea lanes connecting the Levant with the west, and that prompted a vigorous Persian response. The Persians gathered their forces—and within a year, launched a counteroffensive. Cyprus was retaken in 497 in a simultaneous land-sea battle that saw the rebels victorious at sea—but the Persians victorious on land. Three Persian columns then marched against the rebels in western Anatolia, but for three years the result was a stalemate.

Finally, the Persians decided that an incremental approach was ineffective—and in 494, they combined their forces and laid siege to Miletus, the center of the rebellion. The climactic battle took place at sea, at Lade. The rebels brought 353 ships to the battle; the Persians brought 600—largely Phoenician. Athens and Eretria had already withdrawn their small squadrons from supporting the rebellion, so there were no mainland Greek forces present. The rebels were torn by dissension among the various city-state contingents, and this dissension betrayed them: The 60-vessel Samian squadron deserted and sailed home just as the battle was being joined, costing the allies 20 percent of their already outnumbered fleet's strength. The result was that the Persians won an overwhelming victory.

The rebel defeat at Lade led to the collapse of the revolt. Miletus soon fell to the besieging Persian army. The Persians initially punished the defeated rebels with cold-blooded brutality. Miletus was sacked and burned, and its male population either butchered or deported to Persia—while the women and children were sold into slavery. Each island city was netted with a human chain that walked across the island to round up all the inhabitants. Many cities were destroyed and their temples razed. As at Miletus, the men were killed or deported, and the women and children were sold into slavery. But after 493, the Persians adopted a more conciliatory approach. Artaphernes had the Ionian cities take vows to settle their mutual differences through arbitration instead of violence. He resurveyed the territories of each city to establish a fairer basis for assessing their taxes to the Persian crown. When Darius's son-in-law, Mardonius, arrived in 492, he replaced the Persian-backed tyrants with democracies—which ironically marked the largest single advance for democracy in the Greek world to that date.

The final stage in the consolidation of Persian authority after the revolt took place in the north Aegean, where Mardonius led a land-sea expedition along the coast to reaffirm Persian authority in the wake of the rebellion. Herodotus frames this as an expedition against Athens to punish her for aiding the revolt, but this seems unlikely since the Persians made no effort to isolate Athens diplomatically—as they did later. As he had done in Anatolia, Mardonius removed the tyrants in Persia's subject cities in the north Aegean and installed democracies—but then the gods intervened. As the fleet sailed along the coast, it was wrecked by a violent northern gale off Mount Athos in the Chalcidice. Supposedly 300 ships were lost and 20,000 men drowned. The participation in the mainland city-states Athens and Eretria in the Ionian Revolt had shown the Persians that their northwestern frontier could never be secure so long as the city-states of mainland Greece remained unsubdued. The Greco-Persian wars began as a Persian effort to neutralize the Greek threat to their western provinces—and a Greek effort to neutralize the Persian threat to their autonomy. The wars raged from 499 to 449 B.C. They pitted two antagonists against one another, whose military and material resources were vastly different in scale—with the Persians enjoying an overwhelming advantage. The Persians possessed immense numerical superiority. They could draw on the manpower assets of an empire that extended from the Aegean and Egypt all the way to India.

Herodotus credits the Persians with an army in excess of 2.5 million men and a fleet of over 1,200 *triremes*. Obviously, only a fraction of these assets could be mobilized and supplied for an offensive on a single front—but still, the scale of Persian resources was greater than anything a Near Eastern empire had ever possessed before. The Persians also possessed immense economic resources. They had nearly inexhaustible stores of precious metals. They controlled access to the agricultural surpluses of Egypt and southern Russia, which were necessary to feed the larger city-states of Greece.

Finally, the Persians possessed unity of command. This important point is little noted by the sources. That unity came from the fact that these vast resources were commanded and deployed by only one man: the Great King of Persia. This is the apparent advantage of any authoritarian system of government: At its center, all control lies in the hands of a single decider.

By contrast, any sensible person would have placed the Greeks at a decided disadvantage. There was no unity among the Greeks at all. There was no kingdom or empire of Greece. The Greek world consisted of hundreds of completely independent little city-states (or *poleis*) located both in the area of the Aegean and in colonies scattered around the Black Sea and in southern Italy and Sicily. Adding to the disunity, many *poleis* had faction-prone forms of government, like oligarchies and democracies. The polis had emerged in the wake of the Greek Dark Ages, during the 9th and 8th centuries B.C. *Poleis* jealously guarded their independence from one another—making it very difficult to form them into solid alliances, and very easy to employ a strategy of divide and conquer against them. They frequently fought among themselves, often treating their defeated neighbors as brutally as any Near Eastern state had done—doing things like slaughtering the military-age males and enslaving the women and children.

Furthermore, Greece was poor. It's a mountainous country with very limited amounts of arable land. Mineral resources were available locally—but nothing on a Persian scale. Athens had deposits of silver, but most of Greece's gold came from the Balkans. Lack of mineral and agricultural resources was a major reason why the Greeks had colonized the Mediterranean so extensively. The *poleis* of Greece also had small populations—and, therefore, limited pools of military manpower. Athens was probably the most populous, with perhaps a quarter-million people—many of whom were slaves and, therefore, ineligible for military service. Most *poleis* would have had much smaller populations—more in the range of several tens of thousands.

But the *poleis* of Greece did possess important—though not readily apparent—strengths. For one thing, the polis was grounded in *nomos*, the rule of law, which meant that no man—no matter who he might be—was master, and all men were subject to the same rules. Any leader who set himself above the law was reckoned to be a *tyrannos*—a tyrant. It was also grounded in the notion of citizenship—the idea that every man born from the blood of the community has a share in power and responsibility. This notion that by our very nature as human beings the proper way for us to live is as citizens in communities under the rule of law—not as subjects under some tyrant's whim—is an idea originated by the Greeks and bequeathed by them as their greatest contribution to the rest of mankind and history. It meant that Greeks were willing to live, fight, and die for their *poleis*, precisely because they were their *poleis*.

The Greeks also possessed military strengths that weren't readily apparent. They devised a particularly effective form of the *trireme*— longer, lower, and more maneuverable than the *triremes* used by the Phoenicians. Some of them had also devised tactics and training that enabled their *triremes* to suddenly alter course, shearing off their opponents' oars and leaving them helpless victims for either ramming or boarding.

Finally, during the 7th century B.C., the Greeks had perfected a highly effective form of infantry combat: the hoplite phalanx. Hoplites were spearmen, both heavily armed and heavily armored. They fought in a disciplined close-order formation called a phalanx, usually eight ranks deep and a hundred or more men wide. Moving forward at a walking pace presenting a bristling hedge of spear points, the phalanx would close with an enemy formation, thrusting at them until a gap could be opened in the enemy's line—at which point the hoplites would draw their short swords and wade into the crumbling formation opposing them, stabbing and chopping until the enemy broke and fled. The only vulnerability of the phalanx was to archery and to attacks on its exposed flanks and rear. The major battlefield weakness the Greeks suffered from was their weakness in cavalry—an arm that was necessary both for scouting, for screening, and for protecting the vulnerable flank and rear of the phalanx.

In 491, Darius began his bid to neutralize the Greek threat. The Persians possessed considerable intelligence about the Greek world. Numerous prominent exiles lived at the Persian court, refugees from the factional in-fighting that plagued Greek cities. Hippias, the former tyrant of Athens, came after he was deposed in 510. Demaratus, the exiled king of Sparta, arrived in Persia in the late 490s. Darius also sent out reconnaissance parties to gather information about the Greek world firsthand. He even dispatched his personal physician—who was Greek—with a team of Persian officers to reconnoiter the coasts and ports, not just of mainland Greece, but also of Greek Italy and Sicily. Additionally, Darius undertook a diplomatic offensive to exploit the Greeks' chronic disunity by winning the submission of as many *poleis* as possible.

In 491, he sent envoys to the *poleis* of mainland Greece to demand earth and water, the traditional tokens of submission. Intimidated by Persia's size and power, many *poleis* complied—but Athens and Sparta defiantly refused and even abused the Persian envoys. The Spartans tossed the envoys down a well and told them to get their own earth and water. The Athenians threw them into a pit "like criminals," as Herodotus says. These were gross violations of the ancient principle of diplomatic immunity—and, therefore, equally gross acts of sacrilege.

In 490, Darius launched an expedition against Greece to punish the *poleis* that had defied him. The fleet comprised several hundred *triremes* and hundreds more transports and landing ships, drawn from the cities of Phoenicia. Herodotus gives a figure of 600 for the *triremes*, but this is probably a conventional figure meaning "a really big Persian fleet"; a likelier strength is probably half that. Like modern landing craft, the landing ships were equipped with specially built ramps in the bows for disgorging troops and horses directly onto the shore. The landing force had a strength of rather more than 25,000 troops. It probably included about 1,000 cavalry; the rest were infantry. The troops were drawn from the garrisons of the satrapies; the elite element was the Persian mounted troops. The expedition was commanded by Datis, a Mede who had succeeded the wounded Mardonius in command and Darius's nephew and personal representative, Artaphernes.

The Athenians', Spartans', and Eretrians' efforts to work out joint defense plans fell through and left them vulnerable to defeat in detail. The most crippling problem was factional dissension within the *poleis* themselves. An Athenian effort to reinforce Eretria was deterred by news of severe in-fighting in Eretria over whether to resist or surrender. Athens itself was riven by in-fighting between those factions favoring resistance and those favoring submission— but Spartan troops were delayed by the need to celebrate a religious festival. The Greeks' intelligence gathering was poor to non-existent, so the Persians were able to surprise them by island-hopping across the central Aegean, rather than following the expected route along the Thracian coast. This was undoubtedly why the Greeks failed to attack the Persian force while it was at sea and most vulnerable.

The Persians' first target was Naxos in punishment for its resistance in 499. The Persians landed unopposed, destroyed the town and its temples, and deported all the people they could find. Next, the Persians attacked the city of Carystus on the southern tip of Euboea, which gave in after a brief siege. They were let off with handing over hostages and sending troops to accompany the Persian expedition. Eretria was the Persians' next target. After a week-long siege, the city fell through treachery. The Persians burned the temples in revenge for Sardis and deported the inhabitants of the town.

After destroying Eretria, the Persians crossed over the straits between Euboea and Attica and landed at the nearby plain of Marathon—planning to march from there to Athens, about 25 miles away. Marathon was an obvious landing spot for the Persians. It was close to their new base at Eretria. Their ally—the ex-tyrant Hippias—knew the area. It had level ground good for cavalry and plenty of water and pasturage. The Athenians made no effort to oppose the Persians' landing—but swiftly marched their heavy infantry to the edge of the plain, blocking the roads to Athens. The full strength of the Athenian army would've been about 9,000 hoplites. The only aid that Athens received was a force of 1,000 hoplites from the small neighboring polis of Plataea.

For about a week, the two forces faced each other across a couple of miles of open ground, stalemated by their different tactical goals and by disputes within the Athenian command. The Athenians fortified their position, protecting themselves with an abattis of felled timber to prevent the Persian cavalry from flanking them. The Persians wanted to lure the Athenians out into the open, where their cavalry would be decisive—while the Athenians wanted to close quickly on the Persian infantry, where their heavily armed and armored infantry would have the advantage—but avoid the Persian cavalry. Each night the Athenians advanced their protected line a little farther out onto the plain, towards the Persian position. After several nights, they were within about a mile of the Persians. Command of the Athenian forces was shared between the 10 commanders of the tribal regiments of the Athenian phalanx. Half of them favored a cautious, defensive approach—the other half, a more aggressive one. The latter group was led by Miltiades, who had been a leader in the Ionian Revolt and had then fled back to Athens. The decision in favor of attacking the Persians came when the 10 generals agreed to give a vote to the polemarch (or commander-in-chief) Callimachus, who threw in with Miltiades's faction. The Athenians timed their attack carefully and altered the deployment of their phalanx to compensate for their inferior numbers. Ionian deserters had informed Miltiades during the night that the Persian cavalry had been withdrawn to the rear to be watered and pastured. In the darkness, Miltiades extended his line to a width of about a mile, the same as the Persian line, thinning it out in the center to less than the customary eight ranks, but deepening it on both flanks. He launched his attack at dawn. It was a swift charge rather than the usual slow advance, in order to minimize Persian reaction time and the hoplites' exposure to Persian archery. The Greeks crashed into the Persian position, and the hand-to-hand fighting began. It was fierce, and the issue was in doubt until the weight of the deep phalanx on either wing wore down the Persians' flanks, and the Persian troops there were driven back. But meanwhile, the ethnic Iranian troops in the center defeated the thinner phalanx facing them, broke it, and pursued the fugitives across the plain.

Meanwhile, the Persian cavalry had arrived on the battlefield—but was unable to intervene because the infantry combat was so close and confused. Aware that their flanks had been broken, the Persians in the center had to retreat hastily—hotly pursued by the Athenians. They fought to defend the exits that led to the beach, but the Greeks broke through and drove many Persians into the marsh that lay near the beach—where the Persians drowned since they couldn't swim. The fighting carried onto the beach, where—despite the combat raging around them—the Persian landing ships managed to evacuate first the cavalry and then the infantry. It was in this part of the battle that the polemarch, Callimachus, died—along with one of the Athenian regimental commanders, but the Athenians were able to board and seize seven of the landing ships. Herodotus records that 192 Athenians were killed at Marathon. The Persian dead supposedly totaled 6,400, which ought to have meant that they suffered total losses, killed and wounded, of 10,000 or more—a ruinous rate of 40 percent, enough to send almost any army packing. But their losses must actually have been much lower since the Persian squadron didn't return home—but instead promptly sailed around Attica to try to land the army again and take Athens before the Athenian troops could march back. Anticipating such a move, Miltiades supposedly double-quicked the Athenian phalanx home in a night march and arrived just in time to deter a Persian landing. This makes for dramatic narrative in Herodotus, but the quick Persian voyage and the Athenian army's march are both fiction.

Exhausted and disordered from the fight and the confused evacuation, the Persians would've needed more than an afternoon to sail the nearly 60 miles around the coast of Attica and arrive at Athens. The Athenian army—exhausted after a night deployment, a dawn attack, and combat lasting hours—would've been in no condition to reassemble and jog, in armor, 26 miles over mountain roads to arrive back at Athens by nightfall. The trip probably took both at least two days—but in the end, the Persians withdrew and sailed back to Anatolia. Round One in the Greek wars had gone to the Greeks. Round Two would soon begin.

Lecture Twenty-Seven
Xerxes and the Invasion of Greece

Scope:

Frustrated but undeterred by defeat at Marathon, Darius determined to renew his effort to subdue Greece but was distracted by revolts in Babylonia and Egypt. His successor, Xerxes, picked up the effort where Darius left off, and in 480 B.C. he led the most massive military expedition in all of antiquity against the 31 city-states that had refused his call for submission to Persian authority. Marching along the coast of the northern Aegean, Xerxes met the Greeks at Thermopylae, where the Greeks sought to delay the Persian land advance until their fleet could defeat the Persians at sea. In a hard-fought battle, the Spartan-led Greek force was overwhelmed, and Xerxes marched to Athens, which he destroyed. The Athenians had retreated to the nearby island of Salamis, however, and in an epic naval battle in the straits between Salamis and the mainland, they crushingly defeated Xerxes' navy. Xerxes returned to Asia but left behind a large land force to continue the fight the next year.

Outline

I. Frustrated but undeterred by the repulse of his expeditionary force at Marathon, Darius I laid plans to attack Greece again, but he was unable to mount a second assault before his death.

   A. An Athenian naval counteroffensive that tried to capitalize on the victory at Marathon sputtered out.

   B. Meanwhile, in the summer of 486 B.C., a rebellion against Persian rule had broken out in Egypt.

II. Darius's successor, Xerxes, was a conscientious ruler, but he was unable to match his father's achievements. Under his rule, the growth of the empire stagnated, and while he was able to hold it together, his efforts to put an end to the Greek menace led to a series of catastrophic defeats that left the empire weakened and vulnerable.

   A. We are crippled in studying Xerxes' reign because of the unevenness of our source material. Virtually everything we know comes from Greek authors.

B. It appears that Xerxes' accession met with no opposition in Persia itself but was greeted by the customary rebellions in the provinces.

    1. Xerxes moved swiftly to snuff out the revolt that had broken out in Egypt before his father's death.

    2. The most dangerous rebellion to greet Xerxes' accession was in Babylon, next door to the Persian heartland. Xerxes dealt with the Babylonian rebels as harshly as he had dealt with the rebels in Egypt.

III. Once he had crushed the rebellions in Egypt and Babylonia, Xerxes could give his full attention to the unresolved problem of Greece. To settle matters once and for all, he decided to hurl the full might of the Persian empire against the Greeks, in a massive invasion that he would lead in person.

    A. He began his campaign shrewdly, with a diplomatic offensive aimed at isolating Athens and Sparta, the ringleaders of resistance to Persian authority.

    B. The land and naval forces that Xerxes assembled for the invasion drew on all the resources of the Persian empire, as well as Persia's allies.

    C. The Hellenic League's resources were much smaller than those of the Persians, and their preparations were clouded by unfavorable omens.

        1. The Greeks' most sacred oracles gave dire warnings of defeat, though they were couched in typically cryptic terms.

        2. As if that were not bad enough, the Greeks' preparations were marked by procrastination.

        3. When assembled, the allied army totaled about 110,000 men, mostly from the Peloponnese.

        4. The allies conferred supreme command on both land and sea on the Spartans; Themistocles was appointed to command Athens's fleet.

    D. The Persians' and Greeks' strategies were very different.

        1. Xerxes' strategy was simple: to focus on the land war, where he could employ his overwhelming superiority in numbers.

2. The Greeks' strategy was to defeat the Persians at sea, blocking their land advance in a location that would neutralize the Persian army's numerical advantage while the Greek navy tackled the Persian fleet.

E. In April of 480, Xerxes' army crossed the Hellespont. Its numbers made it unwieldy, and its advance was slow, dogged by the problems of supplying and moving so many men.

F. After they abandoned Thessaly, the allies fell back to the pass of Thermopylae in central Greece.
    1. Thermopylae was a strategic chokepoint. By holding it, the allies could block the Persians' advance on land; meanwhile, the allied fleet engaged and defeated the Persians at sea, at Cape Artemisium off the northern tip of the island of Euboea.
    2. In late August, Xerxes moved south from Macedonia. It took him more than two weeks to move his huge army south through Thessaly. He arrived before Thermopylae in the second week of September.

G. The Battle of Thermopylae has for good reason become history's paradigm of the last stand against long odds. The battle raged for three days but was actually an adjunct to the naval fighting at Artemisium.
    1. Xerxes began the combat by sending in first-class Iranian troops, the Medes, telling them to take the Greeks alive and bring them to him, but the Greeks held them off.
    2. Next, hoping for a quick resolution, Xerxes committed the best troops in the Persian army, the elite Ten Thousand Immortals, but to no avail.
    3. Meanwhile at Cape Artemisium, the naval fighting was indecisive, although the allied fleet generally had the better of it tactically.
    4. The second day's battle was again inconclusive, both on land and at sea.

5. On the third day, a local resident revealed the existence of the path around Thermopylae to Xerxes, who sent the Ten Thousand Immortals to flank the pass. The allied blocking detachment withdrew at their approach, and Sparta's King Leonidas, informed that he was being flanked, dismissed the bulk of the allied troops, remaining behind with a rear guard to cover their escape. Leonidas was killed shortly thereafter.

6. Thermopylae and Artemisium were costly for both sides, but particularly for the Persians. The Persians lost 20,000 top-quality infantry and about half of their fleet to combat and to storms.

H. After clearing the pass at Thermopylae, Xerxes advanced south, needing to finish off the Greeks before autumn settled in. The Persians had a massive numerical advantage, but as at Thermopylae, geography barred them from employing it fully.

I. The Battle of Salamis took place at the end of September, probably on the 29th.

1. Xerxes' plan was to sweep down the channel between Salamis and the mainland like a tsunami, overwhelming the smaller, lower Greek vessels with his superior numbers of towering Phoenician and Egyptian triremes.

2. The details of the battle are obscure, since Herodotus's account focuses more on singling out individuals for praise than on narrating the action. Aeschylus's play *Persians* helps, since he fought at Salamis, but difficulties still remain.

3. The Persian front line numbered around 100 ships, tightly packed alongside one another. Together with the difficult configuration of the straits, this quickly caused problems for the Persian fleet.

4. As the dense Persian formation began to loosen, the allied fleet moved forward to engage.

5. The battle was joined, and it was fierce. The Persians' superior numbers proved to be their greatest handicap in the face of the Greeks' tactical skill.

6.   Although the allies won a clear victory over the Persian fleet, it was not a decisive victory. The Persian fleet's losses were not crippling, and it still possessed an overwhelming numerical superiority, but Xerxes chose not to renew the fight.

J.   Xerxes decided to withdraw before winter arrived. He returned to Asia with the fleet and much of the army, but he left behind a large force in Thessaly commanded by Mardonius. Persia may have lost a battle, but it had not yet lost the war.

Suggested Reading:

Allen, *The Persian Empire*.

Burn, *Persia and the Greeks*.

Green, *The Greco-Persian Wars*.

Questions to Consider:

1.   What were the strengths and weaknesses in Xerxes' strategy in the invasion of 480?

2.   Salamis is often presented as one of the decisive battles of world history, sealing the defeat of Persia's effort to conquer Greece. Do you agree or disagree with that estimation? Did the Persians see it as dooming their invasion?

3.   What should Xerxes have done to neutralize Greek interference in Persia's empire?

Lecture Twenty-Seven—Transcript
Xerxes and the Invasion of Greece

Frustrated but undeterred by the repulse of his expeditionary force at Marathon, Darius I laid plans to attack Greece again, but he was unable to mount a second assault before his death. The Athenians didn't have any better luck. They tried to follow up on their victory with a naval counteroffensive, but it quickly sputtered out. The goal of this effort seems to have been to block the route the Persians had used to cross the Aegean by getting control over the islands along the way. The Athenians mustered their entire fleet of 70 *triremes* and placed it under Miltiades's sole command. He retook some of the island *poleis* in the Cyclades, but the citizens of Paros resisted. Miltiades besieged the town and nearly captured it—but finally had to withdraw when it looked as though the Persians might be coming with a relief force. Miltiades was wounded during the siege. The wounds eventually killed him—and when he died, so did the counteroffensive. Meanwhile, in the summer of 486, a rebellion against Persian rule had broken out in Egypt. The cause of the revolt is unclear. Some scholars have attributed it to the defeat at Marathon, which shattered the myth of Persian invincibility. But it may have just been due to Darius's advancing age and the anticipation of a change of ruler. In any case, the revolt simmered throughout the remainder of the year and was still going on late in 486, when Darius died.

His successor, Xerxes, was a conscientious ruler, but he wasn't able to match his father's achievements. Under his rule, the empire's growth stagnated—and while he was able to hold it together, his efforts to put an end to the Greek menace produced a series of catastrophic defeats that left the empire weakened and vulnerable. The unevenness of the source material hampers our efforts to study Xerxes's reign. Everything we know comes from Greek authors—and most of that comes from Herodotus. Only bits and pieces are available, scattered around other sources. There's a little Jewish texts, and a little more from Babylonian ones, and scraps here and there in Egyptian sources—so our narrative of Xerxes's reign ends up pretty skewed. It makes it look like his reign was dominated by the Greek wars. There is no question that those wars were events of the first magnitude—but since we have literally no information about what took place during the 22 years of Xerxes's reign on the Indian frontier or the central Asian frontier, we shouldn't simply assume that the entire story of his tenure on the throne was the story of the war with the Greeks.

It appears that Xerxes's accession met with no opposition in Persia itself but was greeted by the usual rebellions in the provinces. In Persian eyes, he had legitimacy because, although he wasn't Darius's oldest son, he was Darius's oldest son by his paramount wife—the Great Queen, Atossa. Xerxes did have an older brother, Artobazanes, but he was born of a second-rank queen, an unnamed daughter of Gobryas. Xerxes moved swiftly to snuff out the revolt that had broken out in Egypt before his father's death. He appointed his younger brother, Achaemenes, as satrap of Egypt. Probably acting on Xerxes's orders, Achaemenes instituted a harsh policy toward the rebels. Temple lands were confiscated, and Xerxes refused to pander to the Egyptians' sympathies by portraying himself as their pharaoh—the way that Cambyses and Darius had done. He made it clear that Egypt was now under foreign rule. The most dangerous rebellion to greet Xerxes's accession was in Babylon, next door to the Persian heartland. Xerxes dealt with the Babylonian rebels as harshly as he had dealt with the rebels in Egypt. Babylon was always a restive possession for any outside conqueror, as we've seen—it had given the Assyrians endless problems, which they were never able to solve.

The details of the revolt against Persia are very sketchy, since it wasn't of much interest to Greek authors. It appears to have begun in 484 and lasted for several years. Who led the revolt isn't clear: The names of two separate rebel kings are known from cuneiform texts. But it is clear that, as elsewhere, Xerxes acted decisively to suppress the rebels. He dispatched the Persian General Megabyzus with a large force to put down the revolt. Once it was defeated, he systematically destroyed the symbols of Babylonian national identity. The walls of the city of Babylon were leveled. The great ziggurat in Babylon (the famous Tower of Babel) was demolished. The priests of the local gods were executed. The great statue of Bel-Marduk, to which Cyrus and Cambyses had paid homage, was taken away and melted down.

It may be that there was a religious dimension to this uprising. Xerxes writes:

> Among the countries [that were in rebellion] there was a place where previously false gods had been worshipped. Afterwards, by the favor of Ahuramazda, I destroyed their sanctuary of

the demons and I proclaimed, "The demons shall not be worshipped." Where previously the demons were worshipped, there I worshipped Ahuramazda reverently. [Kuhrt II, 680]

Whether the rebellion in Babylon led to a new policy of religious intolerance towards local peoples or whether this reflects changing religious attitudes among the Zoroastrian ruling classes of Persia is unclear. What is clear is that Babylonia was shattered by this rebellion. Its prosperity and economic activity declined sharply. The lands of merchants and citizens were confiscated and parceled out to Persian notables. It took Babylonia a long, long time to recover.

Once he'd crushed the rebellions in Egypt and Babylonia, Xerxes could give his full attention to the unresolved problem of Greece. To settle matters once and for all, he decided to hurl the full might of the Persian Empire against the Greeks in a massive invasion that he would lead in person. He began his campaign shrewdly, with a diplomatic offensive aimed at isolating Athens and Sparta, the ringleaders of the resistance. Persian heralds were sent off to all the *poleis* to demand their submission, pointedly excluding Athens and Sparta. Most *poleis* in the path of the Persian invasion either "medized" (that is, submitted to Persia) or remained neutral. In the end, of the hundreds of *poleis* in mainland Greece, only 31 defied Xerxes's demand. They banded together in a loose alliance called the "Hellenic League," to resist Persia, pledging to set aside their quarrels until the Persian threat was ended. The League was led by Sparta in overall military and naval command. Pleas for assistance to the Greek *poleis* of Sicily were refused, though—since those *poleis* feared an attack by Carthage, acting in alliance with Persia. The land and naval forces that Xerxes assembled for the invasion drew on all the resources of the Persian Empire as well as Persia's allies.

Herodotus says that it was an army and a fleet "far greater than any other in recorded history." He claims that Xerxes's army dwarfed the one that Darius led against the Scythians and was incomparably larger than the armies that fought in the Trojan War. Indeed, he says that it was larger than all of these other armies put together. He admits that since nobody left a record, he can't give a precise figure for the strength of Xerxes's army, but he speculates that the total force Xerxes brought with him—soldiers, sailors, marines, and camp followers—numbered nearly 5.3 million people. But to the skeptical mind of a modern historian, these figures are quite literally fantastic.

The troops alone, marching in a column of fours on Greece's narrow roads, would have stretched more than 500 miles. In modern American terms, taking the interstates, the rear guard of the army would've been leaving downtown Washington, D.C., just as the advance guard was entering downtown Detroit, Michigan. Add in the camp followers, and the length of the column would grow to more than 1,000 miles—which would take the column from Washington, D.C., to Des Moines, Iowa. But Herodotus says that they took three routes through Greece, so the columns would have been only about 350 miles long—each. That's the distance from D.C. to Akron, Ohio. No problem, right?

Herodotus's figures for the naval forces are less incredible than his figures for the army, but only by comparison. He details a fleet of more than 1,200 *triremes* and 3,000 50-oared *penteconters*. The truth is probably closer to 1,000 warships of all the various types. And how many troops? Most scholars think only about 200,000—only. That still makes it the largest land force ever assembled for a single campaign before modern times. The warships' crews and the crews of the thousands of supply ships may have added as many as 400,000 additional men to the total—so, a mere 600,000 men. Only Persia could have done this—and only Persia at the height of its power, under Xerxes.

Xerxes ordered massive engineering projects to ease the passage of his huge force. He had a canal dug through the base of the Athos peninsula of the Chalcidice to avoid the treacherous weather that had scuttled Mardonius's expedition in 492. The canal was dug by hand, using Persian troops and locally conscripted labor. Supervised by Phoenician engineers, the canal was one-and-a-third miles long and 65 feet wide to permit the passage of oared *triremes*. It took two years to build. He also had the coastal road through the Thracian satrapy improved—paving it where necessary and building bridges over the rivers, as well as guard-posts and courier-stations. He had a Greek engineer design two immense combination suspension and pontoon bridges spanning the Hellespont, so that his army could march across rather than having to be ferried. Each bridge was a mile long—one with 314 ships, the other with 360—lashed loosely together, beam to beam, held in place against the four-knot current by anchors with cables more than 330 feet long. The roadways were built of planks and brushwood on cables made of fibers twisted taut above the decks of the ships and attached to massive land piers on either side of the strait.

In 481, Xerxes mustered his army at Sardis and his fleet on the coast of western Anatolia and was ready to attack. The Hellenic League's resources were much smaller than those of the Persians, and their preparations were clouded by unfavorable omens. The Greeks' most sacred oracles gave dire warnings of defeat, though they were couched in the usual cryptic terms. Delphi told the Spartans that either one of Sparta's two kings must die—or Sparta itself must be destroyed. Athens was first warned by the oracle to abandon Attica and flee to the ends of the earth—then told to trust to her so-called "wooden walls." As if that weren't bad enough, the Greeks' preparations were marked by procrastination. Xerxes had already mustered his army at Sardis before Sparta even called a planning conference of the 31 member states of the resistance. Once it finally assembled, the allied army totaled about 110,000 men—mostly from the Peloponnese. About 40,000 were hoplites; the other 70,000 were light-armed troops. There was almost no cavalry. The allies' fleet mustered about 400 *triremes*, half of them Athenian. While the allied fleet was much smaller than the Persian one, it had the advantage of consisting of more uniform types of ships—schooled in similar tactics, with no language barriers to hinder communication. On the other hand, much of it was new: On the initiative of the far-sighted leader Themistocles, Athens had only recently finally expanded her fleet to more than 200 *triremes* using the proceeds from a rich silver vein discovered in Athenian territory in 483. The allies conferred supreme command on land and sea on the Spartans; Themistocles was appointed operational command of Athens' fleet.

The Persians' and Greeks' strategies were very different. Xerxes's strategy was simple: to focus on the land war, where he could employ his overwhelming superiority in numbers. The Greeks' strategy was to defeat the Persians at sea—blocking their land advance in a location that would neutralize the Persian army's numerical advantage while the Greek navy tackled the Persian fleet. The allies realized that if the Persians lost command of the sea, they would eventually have to withdraw their large army because they couldn't supply it off Greece's limited resources. In April of 480, Xerxes's army crossed the Hellespont. Its numbers made it unwieldy, and its advance was slow, dogged by the problems of supplying and moving so many men. In June, the allies pulled back from their initial positions in northern Thessaly after they realized those positions could be outflanked. This ceded Thessaly to the Persians. By July, the Persian army had reached

Macedonia; there, Xerxes rested his forces while he brought forward supplies and prepared the routes to the south. The roads were improved and widened. Supply depots were established along the march routes, and ships brought fresh supplies over from Anatolia. Large numbers of troops were dropped off to guard the supply lines and to assist in moving supplies forward.

After they had abandoned Thessaly, the allies fell back to the pass of Thermopylae in central Greece. Thermopylae was a strategic chokepoint. By holding it, the allies could block the Persians' advance on land while the allied fleet engaged and defeated the Persians at sea at Cape Artemisium, off the northern tip of the island of Euboea. At Thermopylae, named for the nearby hot springs, the coastal road was tightly hemmed in by mountains on one side and the rocky seacoast on the other. The pass narrowed at either end and was protected by a defensive wall. The narrowness of the pass would prevent the Persians from either taking advantage of their numbers or their cavalry—and enable the allies to employ economy of force in defending the position. The allied force comprised about 10,000 men—6,500 of whom were heavy infantry commanded by the Spartan king, Leonidas, and built around a core of 300 elite Spartan hoplites. There were also several thousand helots (or state serfs) accompanying the Spartan contingent as light troops, but there was no cavalry. The pass had one weakness, though—a narrow path wound around it through the mountains. Leonidas posted a detachment of 1,000 men to block that path.

In late August, Xerxes moved south from Macedonia. It took him more than two weeks to move his huge army south through Thessaly. He arrived before Thermopylae in the second week of September. Given the length of its march columns, it took several days for the entire Persian force to arrive and encamp. Meanwhile, the Persian fleet was delayed by coastal storms that sank a large number of ships and damaged many more. Probably exaggerating, Herodotus claims that 400 warships were destroyed by this fierce Nor'easter. Xerxes's cavalry scouted the Greek position and reported seeing men doing gymnastics and combing their long hair. Xerxes found this behavior ridiculous. But the exiled Spartan king, Demaratus, who was in his entourage, warned him that these ridiculous men were the bravest soldiers in all of Greece. For four days Xerxes held back, certain that the Greeks would withdraw now that they could see that they were outnumbered 20-to-1. Of course, they didn't withdraw because their mission was to block Xerxes's advance long enough for the Greek fleet to crush the Persian one. Finally, in frustration and needing to defeat the Greeks and draw down his strength in Greece before the onset of autumn and then winter, on the fifth day Xerxes had no choice but to attack. The Battle of Thermopylae has for good reason become history's paradigm of the "last stand against long odds." The battle raged for three days. Xerxes began the combat by sending in first-class Iranian troops, the Medes—telling them to take the Greeks alive and bring them to him, but the Greeks fought them off. It wasn't because of any deficiency on the part of the Medes as soldiers. They attacked with bravery and determination. Given that they fought throughout the day and took terrible losses but refused to abandon the attack until ordered by the king to withdraw, Herodotus's statement that the Medes made it clear to everyone that Xerxes had many men in his army but few soldiers is little more than an anti-Persian smear. Next, hoping for a quick resolution, Xerxes committed the best troops in the Persian army, the elite 10,000 Immortals—but to no avail. The confined spaces at Thermopylae prevented the Immortals from exploiting their numerical superiority. Meanwhile, the Greeks' longer spears and heavier armor and shields gave them significant advantages over the lightly armed Persians, and the Greeks suffered few casualties. The Spartans were in the forefront of the fighting, and their discipline and training were evident as they employed clever feints that would have been fatally risky with lesser troops—such as feigning retreat to lure the Persians into hasty pursuits that disarranged their formations, enabling the Spartans to suddenly wheel around and strike.

Meanwhile, at Cape Artemisium, the naval fighting was indecisive—although the allied fleet generally had the better of it tactically. The Greeks had 270 *triremes* at Artemisium, about half of them Athenian, facing a numerically superior Persian fleet—from which 200 ships had been detached to cut off the allied escape route to the south. Faced by superior numbers, the Greek ships formed up in a circle with their prows outward, rowing out to ram the encircling Persian vessels. The battle continued all day without any conclusion, and both sides retired to the shore for night. An overnight storm then wrecked the 200-ship Persian encircling detachment, while a 53-ship reinforcing squadron arrived from Athens for the allies.

The second day's battle was again inconclusive, both on land and at sea. The allied fleet was still outnumbered by the Persians, though less severely than before—but despite sinking a number of Cilician vessels, it was unable to win a clear-cut victory. Back at Thermopylae, the fighting continued as it had the day before. Xerxes had hoped the Greeks would be so exhausted or reduced by casualties that he could force the pass—but Leonidas rotated his units in and out of the front line, keeping them fresh, and their casualties remained low. On the third day, a local resident, Ephialtes of Malis, revealed the existence of the path around Thermopylae to Xerxes, who sent the 10,000 Immortals to flank the pass. The allied blocking detachment withdrew at their approach, and Leonidas—informed that he was being flanked—dismissed the bulk of the allied troops, remaining behind with a rearguard to cover their escape. The rearguard comprised what was left of the 300 Spartans, as well as the 400-man contingent from Thebes, whose loyalty was not trusted—and the 700 hoplites from the Boeotian polis of Thespiae, who insisted on standing by the Spartans. Wanting to fix the Greeks in position, the Persians attacked into the pass, where the remaining allies met them in close combat. The Persians exploited their numbers to keep constant pressure on the allies—who were unable to retire for rest and whose spears were soon splintered, making the combat hand-to-hand with short swords. Leonidas was killed, and only by hard fighting were the Spartans able to retrieve his body.

At this point, the Immortals arrived—and the allies retired to a hillock. The remaining Thebans surrendered, but the Spartans and Thespians fought to the death—surrounded and under a hail of arrows. Meanwhile, at Artemisium, the Persian ships attacked in a crescent formation to envelop the Greek squadrons, but the Greeks counterattacked. The ensuing battle cost both sides heavily, the Egyptians and the Athenians distinguishing themselves in the fighting. By evening, half the Athenian vessels were no longer battle-worthy. News of the fall of Thermopylae arrived in the evening, and the decision was then made to retire south. Thermopylae and Artemisium were costly for both sides, but particularly for the Persians. The Persians lost 20,000 top quality infantry and about half of their fleet, both to combat and to storms. The allies lost about 4,000 men—half of them helots—and a couple of dozen ships, having been able to salvage most of their damaged vessels. Many noble Persians died at Thermopylae in battle with the Spartans, including two of Xerxes's brothers and one of Darius's brothers.

After clearing the pass at Thermopylae, Xerxes advanced south, needing to finish off the Greeks before autumn settled in. As they marched through Boeotia, the Persians were welcomed by the *poleis* that had medized, but they ravaged the territories of other *poleis*—especially Plataea and Thespiae. The allies abandoned the Athenian mainland because the frontier with Boeotia could be too easily flanked and built a wall across the Isthmus of Corinth to defend the Peloponnese. They stationed their naval forces at the island of Salamis, close by Athens, to which most of the Athenian population had been evacuated to keep them out of the Persians' clutches. In late September, Xerxes occupied Athens and burned the temples on the Acropolis in revenge for the destruction of Sardis in the Ionian Revolt. Herodotus recounts that the allies were panic-stricken at the sight of the burning city and wanted to decamp south, leaving the evacuated Athenian civilians on Salamis to their fate. But Themistocles explained the tactical advantages of the position at Salamis to them and threatened that the Athenians might simply abandon the allies to their fate by removing themselves and their fleet and then go re-found their polis in the western Mediterranean—since a polis is its citizens, not its buildings. That brought the allies to their senses.

Xerxes opted to defeat the allies' fleet before advancing south to force the Isthmus. Both sides had replenished the losses they had suffered at Artemisium, giving the Persians a massive numerical advantage—but as at Thermopylae, geography barred them from employing it fully. Xerxes had drafted additional ships from the *poleis* of the Aegean Islands and brought about 1,000 warships into the anchorage between the mainland and Salamis. The Athenians had built up a reserve of ships for just such an occasion, and the allied fleet numbered about 380 *triremes*—half of them from Athens. The confined waters of the channel between the mainland and Salamis, studded with small islands, restricted the Persians' ability to deploy their numbers effectively against the numerically inferior Greeks.

Furthermore, the allies knew the currents in the straits between Salamis and the Athenian mainland intimately and took advantage of that knowledge and the confined waters of the straits to make the Persian fleet's superior numbers and larger vessels work against it. The Battle of Salamis took place at the end of September, probably on the 29th. Xerxes's plan was to sweep down the channel between Salamis and the mainland like a tsunami—overwhelming the smaller, lower Greek vessels with his superior numbers of towering Phoenician and Egyptian *triremes*. He intended his ships to present a solid front, which would prevent the Greek ships from taking advantage of their greater maneuverability and stouter construction to employ ramming tactics, and would enable the contingents of archers on the Persian ships to fire down on the Greeks' decks. The allies' plan was to disrupt the Persians' formations in order to expose their broadsides for ramming, and to enable the hoplite marines to swarm on board the disabled Persian vessels.

The details of the battle are obscure, since Herodotus's account focuses more on singling out individuals for praise than on narrating the action. Aeschylus's play *The Persians* helps, since he fought at Salamis, but difficulties still remain. Even the initial deployments of the fleets are unclear. The Persian fleet may have been drawn up along the mainland side of the straits, or it may have been spread across the width of the straits—blocking the channel. The allied fleet may have been waiting along the Salamis shore, or it may have deployed up the channel—prefatory to sailing down. It does seem clear that Xerxes sent a large detachment of ships around Salamis to block any allied flight that might take place in that direction. The Persian front line numbered about 100 ships, tightly packed alongside one another. Together with the difficult configuration of the straits, this quickly caused problems for the Persian fleet. The Phoenicians were on the right, towards the mainland shore; the Ionian Greeks were on the left, with the other national contingents in between. Behind the front ships, the supporting ships of their national contingents sailed in files as much as 10 ships long, which turned the Persian advance into a dense mass of oared vessels streaming up the channel between the mainland and Salamis. The maneuvering was complicated by the long promontory of Kynosoura that projects east off of Salamis—constricting the channel, and by the presence of several 0ands around which the ships had to maneuver. The promontory congested and slowed the Ionian squadron on the left as it tried to sail around it, disrupting the Persian formation.

As a consequence of the confusion on the left, the Phoenicians in the more open waters on the right swept farther ahead. As the dense Persian formation began to loosen, the allied fleet moved forward to engage. The allies sailed in several columns, led by the squadron from the island polis of Aegina; the Athenians took up the rear. The columns swung forward into line of battle, with the Athenians along the mainland shore facing the Phoenicians. The battle was joined, and it was fierce. The Persians' superior numbers proved to be their greatest handicap in the face of the Greeks' tactical skill. The ships of the Persian center and left were so congested they began fouling one another's oars and colliding with each other. The Athenians meanwhile backed water—retreating before the Phoenicians, drawing them ahead of the rest of the Persian line. Then a swell rolled down the channel and threw the tall Phoenician *triremes* off their balance, exposing their broadsides and giving the Athenians their opportunity. Instantly, they ceased backing water and went over to the attack, ramming the Phoenician ships and shearing off their oars. The Athenian hoplite marines swarmed onto the disabled ships' decks and slaughtered their crews. The Phoenicians fought hard—but were sunk, beached, or forced to flee. The Athenians then turned to aid the allied center and right and clinched the victory.

Although the allies won a clear victory over the Persian fleet, it was not a decisive victory. The Persian fleet's losses weren't crippling, and it still possessed an overwhelming numerical superiority—but Xerxes chose not to renew the fight. The Persians had probably lost about 200 ships—but thanks to the extreme congestion in the channel, many of their vessels hadn't even gotten into action before they received the order to withdraw. The allies had probably lost 40 to 50 ships, but many others were too badly damaged to return to action soon. It may be that the decisive blow dealt at Salamis was less to the Persian fleet than to Persian morale. Xerxes decided to withdraw before winter arrived. He returned to Asia with the fleet and much of the army, but he left behind a large force in Thessaly commanded by Mardonius. Persia may have lost a battle, but Persia had not yet lost the war.

Lecture Twenty-Eight
From Plataea to the Peace of Callias

Scope:

The Persians saw the defeat of their fleet at Salamis as a reverse, but not a decisive one. When Xerxes returned to Asia, he left behind a large force to renew the campaign to subjugate Greece. The Persian commander, Mardonius, launched a diplomatic offensive to try to break up the anti-Persian coalition, but to no avail. In the late summer of 479 B.C., the Persians and Greeks met in battle at Plataea. Although the battle was close until the end, the Greeks ultimately scored a crushing victory. In the wake of Plataea, an alliance of Greek city-states, led by Athens, launched a vigorous counteroffensive aimed at driving the Persians from Europe and liberating the Greek cities of Anatolia. The Persians were forced to abandon their satrapy in the Balkans and to surrender control over the coast of Ionia. But after they annihilated an Athenian expedition in Egypt, the Greek counteroffensive stalled, and Athens and Persia concluded an uneasy truce.

Outline

I. Undeterred by the reverse at Salamis, in 479 B.C., Persia prepared to renew its effort to subdue all of Greece. Xerxes' son-in-law, Mardonius, who had long experience of Greece and its affairs, was in overall command of Persian land and sea forces.

   A. Once again showing that the Persians appreciated the linkage between diplomacy and military operations, prior to the 479 campaigning season Mardonius launched another diplomatic offensive in the hope of exploiting the divisions that characterized Greek politics.

   1. In a stunning testimonial to Persian flexibility, Mardonius particularly focused on wooing Persia's arch-nemesis, Athens, whose defection would have cost the Greek allies the best and strongest units of their fleet, as well as the second-largest contingent in their army.

   2. The Athenians were no slouches at subtle diplomacy either. They made sure that news of Mardonius's peace overture was leaked to Sparta.

B. In the early spring of 479, the Persians mustered their fleet at Samos, off the Ionian coast of Anatolia.

C. Meanwhile, the allied fleet gathered at Aegina, under Spartan command.

D. Unlike the Persian fleet, the Persian army in Greece had not been defeated by the Greeks, since Thermopylae was a Persian victory. The army was strong and of high quality, on the whole a better army than the one Xerxes had led in the previous year's campaign.

E. The allied Greek army was under the command of Leonidas's nephew, Pausanias, who was the regent for Leonidas's young son. It was the largest army ever assembled by the Greeks, but its lack of cavalry constituted a serious weakness.

F. Mardonius began military operations once it was clear that his efforts to separate the Athenians from the Greek alliance had failed.

II. The Battle of Plataea, coming almost exactly a year after Salamis, was one of the most decisive battles in history. Scholars debate many of its details, but all agree that it was hard fought and that its outcome was anything but certain. The Greeks very nearly lost.

A. The basic problem confronting both Mardonius and Pausanias was how to lure their opponents onto ground favorable for their army's preferred tactics.

B. The two armies faced each other for a couple of weeks, but prolonged inaction held dangers for both sides.

    1. For the allies, the danger lay in internal dissension, which was a Greek national trait.

    2. For Mardonius, the problems were logistical. He was no longer able to forward supplies to his army by sea and had to haul his supplies 100 miles over land from Thessaly.

C. Forced to act, Mardonius finally broke the stalemate by unleashing his cavalry against the allies' supply lines. This interdiction campaign turned the logistical tables on the Greeks and forced them to move.

D. Pausanias's effort to move his army quickly turned into a fiasco. Mardonius had brilliantly created this opportunity, and once it came, he seized it aggressively.

    1. Hoping to avoid exposing his troops to Persian attack, Pausanias ordered the allied army to withdraw at night, in the face of the enemy, which is the riskiest of all maneuvers in wartime. The predictable result came to pass: The Greek army became scattered and quickly lost its cohesion.

    2. Discovering that the allies had withdrawn, Mardonius assumed that they were in headlong flight and ordered an immediate pursuit. Here's where he blundered, by assuming that the Greeks were in flight rather than disorderly retreat. His overconfidence resulted in a disorderly pursuit that squandered his chance at a decisive victory.

    3. Seeing the disorder in the Persian ranks, Pausanias ordered his Spartans and the Tegeans to charge. The Persians lost the advantage of their archery, and the battle was now fought on the Greeks' terms.

    4. The Persians successfully held off the Spartans attacking the camp until the Athenians showed up. The Athenians, who were good at such things, breached the palisade around the camp and then, together with the Spartans, poured in for the kill.

E. Far more so than Salamis, Plataea was a battle of epic importance. It marked the definitive end of Persia's efforts to conquer Greece; those efforts were never to be resumed.

III. The disasters at Salamis in 480 and Plataea in 479 marked a watershed in Persian imperialism. Persia ceased to expand and henceforth adopted a defensive posture, concerned more with defending its empire than enlarging it.

A. We have little information about what steps the Persians took following Plataea to defend their positions in the northern Aegean. The victorious Greeks formed an alliance, known as the Delian League, to defend Greece against any future Persian attacks and to liberate those Greek poleis under Persian rule.

B. The allies launched a counteroffensive against Persia in 478, under Spartan command, but although it was a great success, political intrigues soon brought it to a halt.

C. Under Cimon, a brilliant commander who was the son of Miltiades, the victor of Marathon, the league next launched an offensive against Persia's possessions throughout the Aegean. It quickly became a thinly veiled exercise in Athenian imperialism, not a campaign of liberation.

D. By the early 460s, Persia had reconstituted its fleet, but Cimon learned of it and led the league in a preemptive attack that dealt a shattering blow to Persia's power in the eastern Mediterranean, reminiscent of Mycale.

E. Following Persia's defeat at the Eurymedon, the league offensive against Persia gained momentum, and Persia's strategic position deteriorated rapidly.

F. Athens also actively aided rebels within the Persian empire, most notably in Egypt. But the Persians offered stiff resistance to Athens's offensive in the eastern Mediterranean, and Athens's adventure in Egypt ended in disaster.

G. After the destruction of the Athenian expeditionary force in Egypt, Persia went on the attack and soon recovered most of Cyprus.

H. Hostilities between Athens and Persia finally ended around 449, probably with an agreement now known as the Peace of Callias.

Suggested Reading:

Allen, *The Persian Empire.*

Burn, *Persia and the Greeks.*

Green, *The Greco-Persian Wars.*

Questions to Consider:

1. Did Greek command of the sea after Salamis play any role in the Plataea campaign? Was Salamis, in fact, the decisive battle in the Persian invasion of Greece, or was Plataea?

2. What could the Persians have done to defend themselves better against the Athenian counteroffensive after Plataea?

3. Was the Persian failure on the battlefield against the Greeks inevitable, or was it a matter of faulty tactics that gave the Greeks an advantage?

Lecture Twenty-Eight—Transcript
From Plataea to the Peace of Callias

Undeterred by the reverse at Salamis, in 479 B.C. Persia renewed its effort to subdue all of Greece. Xerxes's son-in-law, Mardonius, who had long experience of Greece and its affairs, was in overall command of the Persian land and sea forces. Once again showing that the Persians appreciated the link between diplomacy and military operations, before the 479 campaigning season opened, Mardonius launched another diplomatic offensive in the hopes of exploiting the divisions that characterized Greek politics. In a stunning testimonial to Persian pragmatism, Mardonius particularly focused on wooing the empire's arch-nemesis, Athens, whose defection would have cost the Greek allies the best and strongest units of their fleet—as well as the second-largest contingent in their army. He realized that Athens had good reasons to consider medizing. Attica was still a no-man's land between the allied and Persian forces—the allies' army being concentrated at the Isthmus of Corinth, and the Persians' being based in central Greece.

The Athenian population was still camped out on Salamis, unable to return to their devastated homes. Through Alexander, King of Macedon, who had made a second career out of being a conduit between the allies and Persia, Mardonius offered the Athenians attractive terms. They included complete retroactive amnesty for Athens's 20 years of hostility to Persia; complete autonomy—that is, control over her own internal affairs; full restoration of her territory and the possibility of expanding it at the expense of the anti-Persian city-states if Athens so desired; and financial assistance in rebuilding the Athenian temples that the Persians had destroyed the year before. The Athenians were no slouches at backdoor diplomacy either, so they made sure that news of Mardonius's peace feelers got leaked to Sparta.

Realizing what was at stake and after much negotiation, the Spartans finally relented and agreed to defend Attica by sending Spartan troops north to confront the Persians. So in the early spring of 479, the Persians mustered their fleet at Samos, off the Ionian coast of Anatolia. According to Herodotus, the fleet numbered only some 300 *triremes*, most of them from the *poleis* of Ionia. There were probably Phoenician squadrons present, too, but the Egyptians seem to have opted out and stayed home. Morale was a problem among the

Persian crews and their commanders because the memory of Salamis was both fresh and dark.

Meanwhile, the allied fleet gathered at Aegina under Spartan command. It's said to have totaled 110 ships. This number is the same as the Aeginetan and Peloponnesian contribution to the fleet at Salamis, so it probably was comprised of ships from those two sources. Athens refrained from sending ships—at least at first—as a way of keeping pressure on the allies not to renege on their commitment to defend Attica. Unlike the Persian fleet, the Persian army in Greece had not been defeated by the Greeks—since Thermopylae, after all, was a Persian victory. It was strong and of high quality, man-for-man a better army than the one Xerxes had led during the previous year's campaign. Although Herodotus claims that Mardonius's army included some 300,000 men, it probably numbered a little more than a third of that. It's thought that he had about 60,000 Persian troops, who were quartered in Thessaly, as well as about 20,000 levies from the medizing Greek *poleis* in Boeotia. Another 40,000 men formed a strategic reserve in northern Greece. This means that Xerxes had withdrawn about half of the previous year's expeditionary force to Anatolia, leaving behind an army that was much easier to supply than the army of 480—and was also much more mobile because it was less encumbered with baggage and camp followers.

Mardonius's army was particularly strong in cavalry, and it included the best troops in the Persian Empire. The hard core of the cavalry was the regiments of the imperial guard, who were heavily armed and heavily armored. There were also numerous battalions of light-armed cavalry from Iran, supplemented by units of auxiliary horse from Greece and India. The infantry included the 10,000 Immortals as well as various Persian and Median units and hoplites contributed by the medizers. Because it comprised mostly Iranian and Greek troops, the motley character of the previous year's army was gone. There was much more uniformity in weapons and equipment, making it much easier to organize and deploy on the battlefield—and there were far fewer language problems, which greatly simplified command and control.

The allied Greek army was under the command of Leonidas's nephew, Pausanias, who was the regent for Leonidas's young son. It was comparable in size to the allied army of the previous year, the largest army ever assembled by the Greeks. It mustered nearly

110,000 infantry. Sparta contributed 10,000 hoplites, half of them the elite Spartiates, as well as 35,000 helots serving as light infantry. Athens provided 8,000 hoplites, and Corinth another 5,000. All told, the army had a total of 38,700 hoplites, drawn from no fewer than two-dozen *poleis*. But as strong as it was in high-quality heavy infantry, the allied army still had virtually no cavalry, which presented them with a tactical dilemma nearly identical to the one the Athenians had faced at Marathon—that is, the Greeks had to avoid open ground because the Persians' cavalry could swarm around the flanks of the phalanxes and either strike them in the rear or force them to form a defensive square formation, which would render the phalanx immobile and make it an ideal target for Persian archery. But open ground was also the ground most suitable for hoplite warfare, because the phalanx was too unwieldy to maneuver on broken ground. So, the Greeks' lack of cavalry neutralized their heavy infantry's main tactical strength. Their lack of cavalry also meant that the allied army's supply lines were vulnerable to harassment and interdiction by the Persian horse.

Mardonius began operations once it was clear that his efforts to separate the Athenians from the Greek alliance had failed. Gathering his troops from their winter quarters, he marched south into Attica— which the Persians ravaged once more, destroying whatever they'd missed the previous year. Then, when he received word that Spartan troops had advanced north through the Isthmus, Mardonius pulled his troops back into Boeotia. He didn't do this because the Persians were afraid of the Spartans—they weren't after their victory at Thermopylae. It was simply that he wanted to entice the Spartans away from the rugged ground of Attica and onto the more cavalry-friendly terrain of Boeotia. Once in Boeotia, Mardonius settled his army in along the Asopus River, facing Plataea—a position from which he could cover the passes leading to and from Attica. Once Mardonius had pulled back, Pausanias led the Spartans to Athens, where he was joined by the 8,000 Athenian hoplites. Together they advanced into Boeotia. With the two armies now confronting one another, the stage was set.

The Battle of Plataea, coming almost exactly a year after Salamis, was one of the decisive battles of history. Scholars debate many of its details, but all agree that it was hard-fought and that its outcome was anything but certain. The Greeks very nearly lost. The basic problem confronting both Mardonius and Pausanias was how to lure their opponents onto ground favorable for their army's favorite tactics. The Persians were based in a large stockaded camp on the plain beyond the Asopus, in country favorable for cavalry maneuvers. The Greeks were settled in near Erythrae, in the foothills of Mount Cithaeron, where cavalry couldn't fight en masse.

After killing Mardonius's cavalry commander in a skirmish, Pausanias confidently moved the Greek army forward from Erythrae to a ridge above the Asopus—facing the Persians on the plain below, but in a position that was still tactically inaccessible to Persian cavalry. Unfortunately, the position had one major deficiency: It lacked secure communications to the rear. The two armies confronted each other for a couple of weeks, but prolonged inaction held dangers for both sides. For the allies, the danger lay in internal dissension, which was a Greek national trait. In the Athenian army, for example, a clique of officers who favored oligarchy over democracy and medizing over loyalty to the alliance began plotting against the senior commanders. Aristides, the Athenian commander, discovered the plot—and the conspirators fled. For Mardonius, the problems were logistical. Now that the Athenian squadron had finally joined the allied fleet, the Greeks controlled the local waters on the eastern coast of Greece. This meant that Mardonius was no longer able to forward supplies to his army by sea and had to haul them overland 100 miles from Thessaly—which was both time-consuming and very expensive, especially for an army of 120,000 men. Since it was impossible to sustain 120,000 men by local foraging, Mardonius needed either to defeat the Greeks quickly or retreat closer to his base of supply in the north. Forced to act, Mardonius finally broke the stalemate by unleashing his cavalry against the allies' supply lines. This interdiction campaign turned the logistical tables on the Greeks and forced them to move.

In their first raid, the Persian horsemen destroyed an allied supply convoy of more than 500 oxen, which were expensive and difficult to replace. The Persians compounded the Greeks' problems when their mounted archers drove off the Spartans guarding the spring that provided the allied army with water—then fouled the spring. Then, the Persian cavalry prevented the Greeks from clearing the spring and also prevented them from getting water from the Asopus. With his army rapidly becoming parched, Pausanias was forced to retreat, and that laid the allied troops open to attack. Because Pausanias's effort to move his army degenerated into a fiasco, Mardonius had brilliantly created this opportunity—and once it came, he seized it aggressively. Hoping to avoid exposing his troops to Persian attack, Pausanias ordered the allied army to withdraw at night in the face of the enemy, which is the riskiest of all maneuvers in wartime. The predictable result came to pass: The Greek army became scattered and quickly lost its cohesion. The Athenians, Megarians, and Corinthians arrived below the walls of Plataea itself—but had become far separated from the Spartans and the hoplite contingent from Tegea, which was marching with them.

To make matters worse, a pig-headed Spartan battalion commander had protested that retreat in the face of the enemy, even because of looming dehydration, was tantamount to cowardice and refused to move. The rest of the Spartans lagged behind so as not to lose contact with his isolated troops. As day broke, they headed off towards Plataea, and the dissident commander finally sulked along in their wake. About halfway to Plataea they halted, and he rejoined them. Discovering that the allies had withdrawn, Mardonius assumed that they were in headlong flight and ordered an immediate pursuit. Here's where he blundered, by assuming that the Greeks were in panicked flight rather than disorderly retreat. His over-confidence resulted in an equally disorderly pursuit that squandered his chance at a decisive victory. The Persian infantry hurried toward the Spartan position and set up a rampart of their wicker shields, from behind which they loosed volleys of arrows on the Spartan and Tegean lines. Pausanias summoned the Athenians to come to his aid, but Persia's medizing Greek allies had moved forward and barred the way. The Spartan and Tegean hoplites stoically endured the rain of arrows until Pausanias saw that behind the wicker rampart the Persian infantry, in its eagerness to be in on the kill, had lost order and formation and become a crowded mob. Seeing the disorder in the Persian ranks, Pausanias suddenly ordered the Spartans and Tegeans to charge. The Persians lost the advantage of their archery, and the battle was now fought on the Greeks' terms. The allied hoplites crashed into the wicker rampart and smashed it flat. At close range, their discipline, training, and heavier armor gave the Spartans a lethal advantage. But even though outgunned, the Persian infantry fought with undaunted courage and determination, earning their enemies' admiration—and they held their own against the best that Greece had to offer until Mardonius was killed, dying like the great Persian he was in the thick of the combat, swinging a sword from the back of his white charger. Then, finally, the Persian infantry fell back to their stockaded camp—their retreat covered by the cavalry.

Meanwhile, the Athenians had had their hands full with the medizing Greeks. The medizers fought as hard as the Persian infantry had and didn't finally give way until the Athenians had annihilated an elite band of 300 Theban hoplites. Then they retreated to Thebes, and the Athenians rushed across the foothills to aid the Spartans. At the camp, the Persians had rallied and were successfully holding off the Spartans until the Athenians showed up. The Athenians, who were good at such things, made a breach in the camp's palisade—and then, together with the Spartans, poured in for the kill. Total allied dead in the battle came to 1,360. The Persian dead numbered somewhere between 10,000 and 12,000. Together with the wounded, Persian losses amounted to about a third of the troops on the field.

According to Greek tradition, on the same day as Plataea, the Greek fleet won an equally spectacular victory at Mycale, on the coast of Anatolia. The Persian fleet had been reduced to little more than 100 ships after the Phoenician contingent was sent home because it was so demoralized. What remained was largely Ionian Greek ships, whose loyalty was as dubious as the Phoenicians' morale. When the allied fleet approached Samos, the Persians withdrew to the mainland coast, where they beached their vessels and built a stockade around them. The allies then beached their fleet too, armed themselves as infantry, and approached the Persian stockade overland. The Persians unleashed a torrent of arrows, and the allies hurled themselves at the stockade—which the Athenians breached, as they had at Plataea. A slaughter resulted, made worse because the Ionians chose this moment to turn on their Persian masters.

In the end, the Persian fleet was destroyed, and the Aegean was now a Greek lake. The allies promptly sailed to the Hellespont to destroy the Persian bridge, but found that it had been dismantled and the cables were stored at Sestos. Most of the fleet sailed home, but the Athenian squadron laid siege to Sestos and brought the cables back as proof that no Persian army would ever cross into Europe again. Far more so than Salamis, Plataea was a battle of historic importance. It marked the definitive end of Persia's efforts to conquer Greece; those efforts were never to be resumed. It also placed the strategic initiative in the hands of the Greek *poleis*—now flush with victory, bitter with resentment, and thirsting for revenge.

The disasters at Salamis and Plataea were turning points in Persian imperialism. Persia ceased to expand and, henceforth, adopted a defensive posture—concerned more with defending its empire rather than enlarging it. We know very little about Persian history in the decades after Plataea because virtually all of our information comes from Greek sources, which—as we've seen—are primarily interested in Greek affairs. After the defeats of 480 and 479, Xerxes apparently returned to the heartland of the empire, where we hear almost nothing more about him. Our lack of information may reflect the sources' hellenocentrism, or it may indicate that he was so stunned by the magnitude of the defeats that he concerned himself only with pursuits other than imperial politics, such as completing his father's building projects in Persepolis.

We don't know much about what steps the Persians took to defend their position in the northern Aegean following Plataea. The victorious Greeks formed a new alliance—known as the "Delian League"—to protect Greece against further Persian aggression, and to liberate the Greek cities still under Persian rule. Taking an oath to be bound together until iron would float in the sea, the member *poleis* of the League contributed either military resources or cash to the joint effort—which was to be headquartered on the sacred Aegean island of Delos and led by Athens. The main allied striking force, their fleet, comprised about 300 *triremes*—half of them Athenian. The allies launched a counteroffensive against Persia in 478 under Spartan command, but although it was a great success, political intrigues soon brought it to a halt. The Spartan King Leotychidas, the victor of Mycale, failed to oust pro-Persian factions from control in Thessaly and was exiled for life by a Spartan court on charges of corruption. Pausanias led an expedition to Cyprus that succeeded in gaining control of most of the island—then sailed to the Bosporus and seized Byzantium from the Persians. These were significant strategic victories. The establishment of allied positions on Cyprus barred the Phoenician fleet from sailing west to the Aegean. The capture of Byzantium severed communications between the Persian satrapy in Thrace and the rest of the empire. But like Leotychidas, internal Greek politics soon took Pausanias down. A number of allied captains accused Pausanias of acting arrogantly. They asked the Athenians to assume command of the allied fleet. Pausanias was recalled, put on trial, and acquitted of abusing his powers as commander, but there was suspicion that he had conspired secretly with Persia—so he was relieved of his command. He was replaced by Cimon, a brilliant commander who was the son of Miltiades, the victor of Marathon. Under Cimon, the League next launched an offensive against Persia's possessions throughout the Aegean. It quickly became a thinly veiled exercise in Athenian imperialism, rather than a campaign of liberation.

The Persian fort at Eïon—at the mouth of the Strymon River, just east of the Chalcidice—fell in 476. The non-Greeks there were enslaved, and an Athenian colony was established at the site. The Athenians attempted to found another colony inland, up the Strymon, at the Nine Ways—but it was destroyed by the natives. In 475, the League fleet took the infamous pirate stronghold of Scyros in the western Aegean. Once more, the non-Greeks living there were enslaved, and an Athenian colony was installed in their place. But it's doubtful whether Scyros had any Persian ties, and it seems to have played no role in Xerxes's invasion. So although the pirates on Scyros were a danger to Greek commerce, its conquest and the installation of an Athenian colony weren't legitimate activities of the League. In the late 470s, the League targeted Carystus, on the southern tip of Euboea. Carystus had been sacked by the Persian expeditionary force on its way to Marathon in 490, so it had medized in 480—which made it a target for League vengeance. Carystus surrendered and then was compelled to join the League against its will.

Soon after the fall of Carystus and its forcible incorporation into the League, the large island polis of Naxos, a League member, attempted to withdraw for unknown reasons. It was brutally punished. Its walls were destroyed. It was stripped of its fleet, forced to pay an indemnity and to pay tribute to the League from now on. The justification for the severity of Naxos's punishment was that withdrawal from the League was forbidden—because the League was a permanent alliance and iron had not yet floated in the sea. Because our Greek sources are primarily concerned with how the League became an Athenian Empire, they tend to ignore League efforts that were directed at Persian territories— evidently, there were a number of them. They were probably concentrated on the coastal cities, and by the early 460s seem to have consolidated control over the Aegean sufficiently that the League could undertake expeditions outside the area.

By the early 460s, Persia had reconstituted her fleet, but Cimon learned of it and led the League in a preemptive attack that dealt a shattering blow to Persia's power in the eastern Mediterranean, reminiscent of Mycale. The Persian fleet numbered about 350 ships and was based in Pamphylia, on the south coast of Anatolia, accompanied by a large land force. Another squadron of 80 Phoenician ships was expected to arrive soon from Cyprus. The Persians' intentions are unknown, but may have included a plan to advance into the Aegean to recoup some of the empire's losses there. Cimon assembled a League fleet of about 300 vessels, 200 of them Athenian, and sailed to Pamphylia—where he seized Phaselis, opposite the Persian base at the mouth of the Eurymedon River. He probably had about 5,000 hoplites available, not counting marines.

Seeking to avoid battle before they were ready, the Persians pulled their ships back into the basin of the Eurymedon, but Cimon aggressively pursued them. The battle was joined and soon decided. The Persians ventured out to meet the League fleet, but fled towards shore at the first contact—showing their demoralization. Some Persian ships were sunk, others captured, and still more ruined running up on the beach at high speed. The Persians lost 200 ships at the Eurymedon and in a follow-up action with the Phoenician reinforcing squadron. When the Persian troops advanced to the beach to protect the fugitive sailors, Cimon forced a landing—and his hoplites and marines engaged the Persians. The fighting was severe and costly to the Athenians, but the Persians were driven off, and their camp was captured. For the Athenians, the Eurymedon confirmed the superiority of their fleet and army over the Persians'.

Following Persia's defeat at the Eurymedon, the League offensive against Persia gained momentum, and Persia's strategic position deteriorated rapidly. Cimon led a League force to the Hellespont, where he captured Persia's last remaining outposts. With that, the Persian presence in Europe came to an end after 60 years. But then, in 461, Cimon fell from power as a result of political intrigues in Athens. He led Athenian troops to Sparta's aid when a rebellion broke out among the helots following a devastating earthquake in 462. In his absence, his opponents—Ephialtes and Pericles—won control of the government. When Cimon arrived in Sparta, the Spartans told the Athenian troops to go back home. After this humiliation, Ephialtes and Pericles engineered Cimon's ostracism—forcing him to leave Athens for 10 years. When Ephialtes was assassinated soon afterwards, Pericles began his 30-year career as Athens's leader. After Cimon's fall, the League offensive against

Persia expanded under Pericles's leadership into the eastern Mediterranean. Athens's annual casualty lists now routinely include men lost fighting on the coasts of Syria and Palestine, which means Pericles was raiding the Levant. Pericles also sent a fleet of 200 ships to attack Cyprus, though whether this was merely a raid or an attempt at conquest isn't clear.

Athens actively aided rebels within the Persian Empire as well. Under Inaros, a descendant of the Egyptian king toppled by Cambyses 60 years earlier, a major revolt had broken out in the Nile Delta. Inaros defeated the Persian garrison and appealed to Athens for aid. Pericles diverted the League fleet from Cyprus to aid the rebels. It won a dramatic victory— 50 Persian ships were sunk, and the Persian commander, Achaemenes, was killed. But the Persians offered stiff resistance to Athens's offensive in the eastern Mediterranean. Defeated but unbroken, the Persian garrison of Egypt doggedly held out against Inaros and the League forces. The Egyptian war dragged on for a half-dozen more years, draining both Athens's and the League's resources, because the League kept a large military and naval force permanently stationed in Egypt.

In 459, Xerxes's successor, Artaxerxes, tried to counter Athens's intervention in Egypt by inciting opposition to Athens within Greece—but to no avail. Megabyzus was sent to Greece, offering Persian subsidies for an invasion of Attica—which would force the Athenians to withdraw from Egypt. Sparta spurned the Persian offer, however. The memories of Xerxes's invasion were still too fresh and the danger from Athens still not grave enough to allow her to accept Persian gold. Frustrated in his efforts to turn Greek against Greek, in 455, Artaxerxes sent a large army and navy to Egypt that finally put an end to the revolt and annihilated the Athenian expeditionary force. The Persians defeated the combined forces of Athens and the rebels and penned the Athenians up on an island in the Nile Delta. Precariously supplied by sea, the League forces held out for 18 months, but in 454, Persian engineers diverted the waters surrounding the island—enabling Persian troops to assault the League stronghold. The result was a crushing victory for the Persians. We have no reliable figures on Greek losses, but supposedly 6,000 of the Athenian and League defenders were taken prisoner, and most of the others were slaughtered. Only a handful escaped overland, crossing the Libyan Desert on foot to the Greek colonies in Cyrenaica.

The Greeks' naval losses are no more certain than their other casualties, but may have run as high as 250 warships. The disaster was then compounded when an Athenian relief force of 50 ships arrived carrying troops, unaware of the disaster, and was ambushed by a Persian army and a Phoenician naval squadron. Most of the relief force was destroyed. Finally—revenge for Salamis and Plataea. After the destruction of the Athenian expeditionary force in Egypt, Persia went on the attack and soon recovered most of Cyprus. But Cimon returned from exile, and in 451 launched a vigorous counteroffensive to recover the island. He led 140 ships to Cyprus, where he besieged the Persian base at Citium. But then he died during the siege—and without his passionate hatred of Persia to drive it, the counteroffensive stalled. The League expeditionary force withdrew from both Cyprus and Egypt.

Hostilities between Athens and Persia finally came to an end around 449, probably with an agreement now known as the "Peace of Callias"—named for the wealthy Athenian who supposedly negotiated it. Since Thucydides makes no mention of any Peace, scholars have doubted its existence—but the evidence, nevertheless, points to some sort of agreed cessation of hostilities. There is no indication of further clashes between Athens and Persia after the death of Cimon. The later writer Diodorus Siculus indicates that there was an exchange of embassies between Athens and Persia, prompted by exhaustion and defeats. Given the uncertainty about the existence of the Peace of Callias, it shouldn't surprise us that its terms are the subject of debate. The traditional picture is that given by Diodorus: The Greek cities of Ionia were to be left autonomous— that is, left to run their own internal affairs (though they may still have owed tribute to Persia). Persian troops were not to come within three days' march (or about 35 miles) of the Aegean Sea. No Persian warships were to sail west of Phaselis, near the southwestern tip of Anatolia (that is, they weren't to enter the Aegean)—nor were they to sail west of the Blue Rocks in the Black Sea (located just inside the Black Sea from the Bosporus). In return, Athens agreed not to attack Persian territory. So, after 50 years, Persia's 5th-century wars with the Greeks came to an end—but no peace is permanent.

Both sides would tend to their own affairs, but those affairs were now entangled and could never be disentangled—short of cutting the Gordian Knot.

Lecture Twenty-Nine
The Persian Empire from 450 to 334

Scope:

Once Athens turned its energies away from attacking Persia and toward building its own empire in Greece, Persia was able to consolidate its position in Anatolia and the eastern Mediterranean but was unable to regain the strength it had wielded before its disastrous invasion of Greece. The Persians realized that in order to safeguard their western provinces from Greek attacks, it was necessary to find more effective tools to use against the Greeks than military force. Those tools were diplomacy and the Persians' immense wealth, which they used adeptly, beginning with the closing years of the Peloponnesian War, when they subsidized Sparta. Afterward they shifted their resources between the Greek cities, keeping the Greeks at each other's throats and making the Great King the arbiter of Greek affairs. Then, in the middle of the 4th century B.C., Persia became distracted by internal problems, and a new and unexpected power united Greece under its banner, against Persia: Macedon.

Outline

I. Following its defeat in the war with Greece, Persia was in retreat until the middle of the 5th century B.C., but afterward, shrewd and capable rulers were able to restore the situation.

   A. Xerxes was assassinated in 465, the victim of a plot among his courtiers. The conspirators also murdered the crown prince, Darius, and placed one of Xerxes' other sons, Ardashir, also known as Artaxerxes, on the throne.

   B. Once he was more or less secure on the throne, Artaxerxes found himself facing significant threats to the empire's position in the eastern Mediterranean, most of them involving Persia's arch-enemy, Athens. But Artaxerxes was a capable ruler, and he eventually succeeded in stabilizing the situation.

   C. Despite the truce, tensions remained high between Athens and Persia into the 430s, with sporadic confrontations and clashes. Most of this had the nature of low-level friction around the peripheries of their empires and never flared into anything serious.

II. Persian power in the west revived at the end of the 5th century, as they skillfully exploited the most destructive example of the Greeks' penchant for internecine conflict: the lengthy and debilitating Peloponnesian War between Athens and Sparta.

    A. Darius II came to the throne following another orgy of dynastic bloodletting.

        1. Artaxerxes was succeeded in 424 by his son Xerxes II, who reigned only 45 days before he was assassinated after a night of heavy drinking by a palace cabal led by his half-brother, Sogdianos, who then took the throne.

        2. When Sogdianos demanded that Ochus, who was also his half-brother, come to Susa, Ochus raised an army and declared himself king, with the backing of senior military officers and the satrap of Egypt. He deposed and cruelly executed Sogdianos by gorging him with food and drink and then dropping him into an ash bin when he fell asleep. Sogdianos had been on the throne a little more than six months.

        3. Darius II then eliminated all of the other conspirators who had murdered Xerxes, either by dropping them into ash bins too or just having them stoned.

    B. Darius II and the satraps of western Anatolia took advantage of the Peloponnesian War to recoup Persia's position in the Aegean and to gain leverage in Greek politics.

    C. In 407, Darius sent his younger son, Cyrus the Younger, to serve as viceroy in Anatolia, with the mission of supporting Sparta and pressing Persia's advantages. Cyrus forged a close alliance with the Spartan commander Lysander and provided lavish funds for Spartan use. This proved decisive for the Spartan victory.

III. Darius II was followed on the throne by his designated heir, Artaxerxes II. Although he came to the throne peacefully, the early years of his reign were clouded by the rebellion of his younger brother, Cyrus; a war with Persia's erstwhile ally, Sparta; and the successful secession of Egypt from the empire. Despite these problems, Persia was able to establish itself as the arbiter of Greece.

A. Cyrus resented his brother's accession to the throne and is said to have plotted to assassinate Artaxerxes during his coronation. If so, he didn't follow through. However, in 403, back in Anatolia, he immediately began planning his rebellion. The resulting fight cost Cyrus his life.

B. Even before Cyrus had begun his bid for the throne, Egypt had rebelled, in response to the turmoil on the Persian throne. The rebellion began in the Nile Delta in 405 and resulted in Egypt winning independence from Persia and maintaining that independence for the next 60 years.

C. A war with Sparta in Anatolia arose out of Spartan bad faith. It broke out in 399 when Sparta reneged on the terms of its agreement with Persia during the Peloponnesian War. Persia would eventually emerge victorious.

D. After the war with Sparta, Persia was able through the use of subsidies to manipulate the situation in Greece so as to keep the major poleis in conflict with one another, leaving its possessions in Anatolia secure.

E. When Athens showed signs of wanting to rebuild its empire, Persia switched sides and allied with Sparta. In 386, Persia brokered an end to the Corinthian War, the so-called King's Peace.

F. Following the King's Peace, Artaxerxes turned his attention to restoring Persia's position elsewhere in the eastern Mediterranean.

G. Meanwhile, Greece remained locked in intercity conflict, which exhausted the poleis and prevented any threats to Persia but also made them turn to Persia as the arbiter of their feuds.

H. On the other side of the Aegean, the mid- to late 360s were marred by a series of satrapal rebellions in Persian Anatolia, which nearly led to the disintegration of the empire west of Mesopotamia.

    1. Virtually all the satraps of Anatolia were involved in the rebellions in one way or another.

    2. The satraps drew aid from hostile foreign sources, allying themselves with Athens, Sparta, or Egypt.

    3. Artaxerxes skillfully used treachery and the personal ambitions of key rebel leaders to suppress the rebellion.

    4. Royal authority had finally been restored in Anatolia by the time of Artaxerxes II's death in 359.

IV. The Persian empire revived during the reign of Artaxerxes II's son, Artaxerxes III Ochus, but the effort of restoring royal authority distracted him from the Greek threat.

    A. Artaxerxes III came to the throne in a now-customary orgy of dynastic bloodshed. The youngest of Artaxerxes II's sons by the Great Queen Stateira, Ochus cold-bloodedly carved his way through his brothers to take the throne.

    B. Soon after he came to the throne, Artaxerxes III had to contend with a renewed satrapal rebellion in Anatolia.

    C. Artaxerxes III's most important accomplishment was the reconquest of Egypt, which was accompanied by the reassertion of royal authority in the Levant.

        1. He made his first effort against Egypt in 353, but it failed.

        2. The failure of the campaign in 353 sparked rebellions in Phoenicia and Cyprus, which were aided by Egypt. Artaxerxes swiftly suppressed the rebellions, but without undue brutality.

        3. The fate of Egypt was decided by Persian victory in an amphibious battle at Pelusium in 343. After Pelusium, the other fortresses in Egypt quickly surrendered, and the Nile once more belonged to Persia.

    D. Artaxerxes III died in 338, along with most of his family, in a palace massacre engineered by the eunuch Bagoas. Bagoas later installed a distant royal relative, Darius III, to the throne.

    E. Darius III was a capable ruler and a sound strategist, but he soon faced a challenge that few if any rulers, in any age, would have been able to master: Alexander the Great.

Suggested Reading:

Allen, *The Persian Empire*.

Cook, *The Persian Empire*.

Olmstead, *History of the Persian Empire*.

Questions to Consider:

1. Did the Persian ability to dominate Greece by the use of diplomacy and subsidies indicate that this was a superior strategy for dealing with the Greek threat, compared to the one of conquest attempted by Darius and Xerxes? What were the advantages of the strategy of diplomacy and subsidies? What were its weaknesses?

2. What distracted Persia's attention from the Greek threat during the middle of the 4th century? Was there some weakness in the Persian system of government that impaired Persia's ability to deal with such distractions as well as with the necessity of heading off threats from Greece?

Lecture Twenty-Nine—Transcript
The Persian Empire from 450 to 334

Following her defeat in the war with Greece, Persia was in retreat until the middle of the 5th century B.C.—but afterwards, shrewd and capable rulers were able to restore the situation. Xerxes was assassinated in 465, the victim of a plot among his courtiers. The conspirators also murdered the crown prince, Darius, and placed one of Xerxes's other sons, Ardashir (or Artaxerxes) on the throne. The main players in the conspiracy were Artabanus, one of Xerxes's favorites, and the General Megabyzus. In league with one of the royal eunuchs, they murdered Xerxes in his bedchamber. We have no clear idea what motivated Megabyzus—but treachery was habit-forming for Artabanus, and he soon plotted against Artaxerxes as well. Some habits can be fatal. The plot was revealed, and Artaxerxes promptly had Artabanus executed. Once he was more or less secure on the throne, Artaxerxes found himself facing threats to the empire's position in the eastern Mediterranean—most of them involving Persia's archenemy, Athens. As we have seen under the bitterly anti-Persian leadership of Cimon and Pericles, Athens was pressing ahead with the counteroffensive she had launched after the defeat of Xerxes's invasion.

The Athenians' major aim seems to have been to gain control of Cyprus for use as a base in interdicting Persian trade and raiding the ports of the eastern Mediterranean. We have documentary evidence of Athens's piratical raids against the Levant, in the form of inscriptions that list the various Athenian citizens killed during military operations there in the 450s. To add to Artaxerxes's troubles, soon after his accession a major rebellion broke out in Egypt, which attracted substantial Athenian support. The rebellion was led by one Inaros, who was related to the last dynasty to rule independent Egypt before the Persian conquest 60 years earlier. Inaros requested aid from Athens, which Athens happily provided—seeing an opportunity to do major damage to Persia's power and wealth, and to secure access to Egypt's inexhaustible supplies of grain. The Athenians sent hundreds of ships and thousands of troops to aid the rebels and set up a base inside the labyrinthine channels of the Nile Delta. But Artaxerxes was a capable ruler, and he eventually succeeded in stabilizing the situation. To bolster the defenses of the Levant against Athenian raids, Artaxerxes studded the coastlines of

Syria, Lebanon, and Judea with forts. His dispatch of Ezra to Judea in 458 B.C. and Nehemiah in 445 may have been connected with this effort to shore up Persian control in the area.

Artaxerxes also launched a multi-pronged diplomatic and military counteroffensive against the rebels in Egypt and their Athenian supporters—and in the end, won a stunning victory. He sent envoys to Sparta offering aid if she would put military pressure on Athens within Greece, but the Spartans turned him down. In 455, he dispatched an expeditionary force to Egypt to suppress the revolt. The next year, the Persians succeeded in trapping and annihilating the Athenian expeditionary force—and then decapitated the rebellion by taking Inaros prisoner. The revolt finally sputtered out in 449, and Egypt grudgingly returned to Persian control. Despite Persia's dramatic victory in Egypt, Athenian attacks on Cyprus continued for several more years.

Finally, in 449, Persia and Athens are thought to have concluded some sort of truce, often called "the Peace of Callias," which gave Athens control over the Aegean and guaranteed the autonomy of the Greek *poleis* of western Anatolia—but required Athens to guarantee that she wouldn't interfere in Persian affairs elsewhere. Despite the truce, tensions remained high between Athens and Persia into the 430s—with sporadic confrontations and clashes, though the theater of operations shifted from the eastern Mediterranean to the eastern Aegean and western Anatolia. Most of this had the nature of low-level friction around the peripheries of their empires and never flared into anything serious.

Athens turned the Delian League into an Athenian thalassocracy that included the coastal *poleis* of western Anatolia as well as the island communities of the Aegean. Control over these communities was essential to her because she depended on grain shipments from the Black Sea to feed her large population. Then, in 440, Athens and Pissouthnes, the Persian satrap in western Anatolia, found themselves in confrontation over the island polis of Samos—which was a charter member of the Delian League but rebelled against Athens's overbearing behavior and received Persian support. As a consequence of the so-called "Samian War," the island finally ended up being incorporated into Athens's empire as a subject state in 439. But while Athens was defending her authority in the islands of the Aegean, Persia was making gains on the Anatolian mainland. By the end of 440, she had regained control over several *poleis* along the Propontis in northwestern Anatolia. She was able to retake much of interior Caria, in southwestern Anatolia, forcing Athens to combine the Carian and Ionian tribute districts of her empire. But Athens compensated by seizing several coastal *poleis* in northern Anatolia from the Persians—most notably Amisus and Sinope, where Athens placed colonies in 438, and taking back one or two of the lost communities on the Propontis.

Persian power in the west revived more fully at the end of the 5th century B.C., as the Persians skillfully exploited the most destructive example of the Greeks' penchant for fratricidal conflict: the lengthy and debilitating Peloponnesian War between Athens and Sparta. This revival took place during the reign of Darius II Ochus, who came to the throne following another orgy of dynastic bloodletting. Artaxerxes was succeeded in 424 by his son, Xerxes II, who reigned only 45 days before he was assassinated after a night of heavy drinking by a palace cabal led by his half-brother, Sogdianos—who then took the throne. When Sogdianos demanded that Ochus—who was also his half-brother—come to Susa, Ochus raised an army and declared himself king, with the backing of senior military officers and the satrap of Egypt. He deposed and cruelly executed Sogdianos by gorging him with food and drink and then dropping him into an ash-bin when he fell asleep. Sogdianos had been on the throne a little more than six months. Darius II then eliminated all of the other conspirators who had murdered Xerxes—either by dropping them into ash-bins, too, or just having them stoned. Darius II and the satraps of western Anatolia took advantage of the Peloponnesian War to recoup Persia's position in the Aegean, and to gain leverage in Greek politics. There's evidence that Sparta and her allies approached Persia for aid early on in the Peloponnesian War, when Artaxerxes was still king, but that they didn't have any luck. Athens captured some of the ambassadors before they got to their destination, and the others met a chilly reception from the Persians—who found their proposals vague and inconsistent.

What turned Darius against Athens was Athens's support for the Anatolian satrap—their former rival, Pissouthnes—when he rebelled against the crown in 420. Darius sent out the capable Tissaphernes as satrap to crush the rebellion, which he did by about 415. Darius's opportunity to restore Persian authority in western Anatolia came when Athens suffered a catastrophic defeat in the Sicilian Expedition in 413. The subject *poleis* of Athens's empire saw their chance to throw off the democracy's imperial yoke, and rebellions quickly erupted throughout the Aegean and along the western coast of Anatolia. The Spartans assembled a fleet to support the rebels—and Tissaphernes and the satrap of northern Anatolia, Pharnabazus, both extended their support. In 411, Sparta concluded a treaty with the Persians that granted Persia complete control over all the Greek *poleis* of Anatolia. In return, Persia provided Sparta with the funds needed to keep her fleet in being and to retain her footholds in Ionia and the Hellespont—where she had a chokehold on Athens's grain supply from the Greek *poleis* on the northern Black Sea coast. In 407, Darius sent his younger son, Cyrus the Younger, to serve as viceroy in Anatolia—with the mission of supporting Sparta and pressing Persia's advantages. Cyrus forged a close alliance with the Spartan commander, Lysander, and provided lavish funds for Spartan use. This proved decisive. The fighting at sea raged for three more years, with the advantage going back and forth between the Spartans and the Athenians—but Persian support gave Sparta an edge as Athens's resources slowly dwindled until they were finally exhausted.

In 405, using Persian funds, Lysander equipped a fleet of 200 ships and attacked Athens's remaining outposts in the Hellespont. Athens drained her coffers to equip one last fleet of 180 vessels and sent it north to confront him. At Aegospotami, after several days of standoff, Lysander surprised the Athenian ships and took them while they were beached. He then captured the crews, who had been foraging, and executed 3,000 of them. Lysander then sailed south and blockaded Athens, which was too broke to field another fleet. Starvation set in, and finally the city was forced to surrender. Citing Athens's services against Persia 75 years before, Sparta spared her defeated enemy the massacre and enslavement that other Greek cities called for—but Athens's walls were demolished, her empire dissolved, and her fleet reduced to 10 ships. But while Sparta had won the fighting in the Peloponnesian War, the real victor was Persia. By adroit diplomacy and shrewd use of her immense wealth, Persia had enabled Sparta to defeat Athens and had achieved her long-cherished goals. First, she had destroyed the power of the polis that had masterminded the eradication of Persian power in the Balkans, the Aegean, and western Anatolia—and that had for a time even threatened Persian control of the eastern Mediterranean. Second, she had also established herself as the arbiter of Greek affairs—the authority to which the quarrelsome Greek *poleis* would turn for support against one another. She had, in other words, done what Darius I and Xerxes had set out to do: neutralize the Greek threat to Persia—and she had done it by discovering that her most potent weapon against the Greeks wasn't the vast military might of her empire, but rather its vast wealth.

Darius II was followed on the throne by his designated heir, Artaxerxes II. Though he came to the throne peacefully, the early years of his reign were clouded by the rebellion of his younger brother, Cyrus; a war with Persia's erstwhile ally, Sparta; and the successful secession of Egypt from the empire. But despite these problems, Persia was able to establish herself and maintain herself as the arbiter of Greece. Cyrus resented his brother's accession to the throne and is said to have plotted to assassinate Artaxerxes during his coronation. If so, he didn't follow through—but in 403, back in Anatolia, he immediately began planning his rebellion. By 401, he was ready. To supplement the Persian troops he had available in Anatolia, Cyrus mustered a force of 12,000 Peloponnesian War veterans to fight in his cause—a cause that had the support of Sparta, thanks to his friendship with Lysander. Fearing that the Greek mercenaries would balk at marching into the heart of Asia and taking on the full might of the Persian Empire, Cyrus misled them about his plans. As they started east, he first told them that he was going to use them to suppress Pisidian bandits—then, as they progressed further east, Cilician pirates. The Spartan fleet mustered off Cilicia to aid Cyrus in penetrating into Syria, so Cyrus's deceptions had a superficial credibility.

The mercenaries' suspicions were finally aroused by the absence of fighting as they marched farther and farther east, and Cyrus had to buy their continued loyalty by increasing their pay—but being mercenaries and being paid, they kept marching. Cyrus penetrated into upper Mesopotamia without encountering significant resistance—and then marched down the Euphrates to Cunaxa, just north of Babylon. There, he met his brother and the loyalist army in battle. The result was a victory—but a victory with a tragic end. The Greek mercenaries defeated the Persian infantry facing them, but Cyrus saw Artaxerxes and charged headlong towards him into the fighting. He succeeded in wounding Artaxerxes in personal combat, but was then killed by the king's retainers. Orphaned by Cyrus's death in the moment of their triumph and bereft of commanders when Artaxerxes treacherously had their leaders murdered under a flag of truce, the Greek mercenaries chose new leaders, including the later historian Xenophon—and fought their way home across the western Persian Empire. This was the legendary March of the Ten Thousand. By the spring of 400, they had reached the Black Sea. The lesson they brought back with them was that a force of Greek infantry could march all the way into the heart of the Persian Empire and back. It was noted and remembered. Even before Cyrus had begun his bid for the throne, Egypt had rebelled in response to the turmoil in the heart of the Persian Empire. The rebellion began in the Nile Delta in 405—and resulted in Egypt winning her independence from Persia and maintaining that independence for the next 60 years.

The rebellion was led by Amyrtaeus, the descendant of a leading figure in the Great Revolt in the middle of the 5th century. He was reckoned as the sole ruler of Dynasty 28 and reigned until 399. Artaxerxes immediately gathered an army to retake Egypt, but it was diverted to defend Mesopotamia against Cyrus's rebellion—and then the re-conquest was abandoned, as Persian resources had to be diverted again to Anatolia to deal with a war with Sparta. That war arose out of Spartan bad faith. It began in 399 when Sparta reneged on the terms of her agreement with Persia from the Peloponnesian War. She had retained the *poleis* of western Anatolia as part of her own empire, rather than turning them over to Persia—as she had promised to do. Furthermore, Sparta had given open aid to Cyrus's rebellion. A Spartan officer, Clearchus, had commanded Cyrus's mercenary force and had been executed by Artaxerxes after being taken captive. Sparta had also provided Cyrus with naval support and a contingent of Spartan troops to accompany him on his march to Cunaxa. Tissaphernes was promoted by Artaxerxes to Cyrus's old position as viceroy of Anatolia and began to seize the *poleis* along the coast. Sparta sent an army and a fleet to Anatolia to confront him. The Spartan army included 5,000 Peloponnesian troops as well as 6,000 veterans of Cyrus's revolt, freshly returned from Persia. The Spartans lacked unified command, though, so the army and the fleet operated without coordination, and the army lacked siege equipment, so it couldn't take any Persian fortifications—which meant that it spent its time marching back and forth through the countryside, looting the natives and leaving them angry.

Learning that Persia was building a large fleet in Phoenicia to send to the Aegean, Sparta sent reinforcements to Anatolia under the command of Lysander and the Spartan King Agesilaus—but they were still unable to win a decisive victory. Lysander was sent to the Hellespont, where he managed to capture some Persian-held towns. Agesilaus used combined-arm tactics to defeat a force of Persian cavalry. He then raided extensively in western Anatolia but couldn't win a decisive victory, though he did take a lot of loot. The new Persian fleet, commanded by an Athenian admiral named Conon, finally arrived in 395 and seized the island of Rhodes—cutting Sparta's supply lines to Egypt. The same year, the Persians backed the formation of an anti-Spartan alliance between Thebes and Athens—later joined by Argos, Corinth, and other *poleis*. This led to the recall of Agesilaus and his army from Anatolia, relieving the pressure on Persia and effectively ending the war. Lysander was sent to confront the allies, but he and a small body of his troops were defeated below the walls of Thebes—and he was killed.

After her war with Sparta, by using subsidies, Persia was able to manipulate the situation in Greece so as to keep the major *poleis* in conflict with one another—leaving her own possessions in Anatolia secure. The Corinthian War—from 395 to 386—pitted Athens, Thebes, Argos, and Corinth against Sparta. It turned into a stalemate, with Sparta dominant on land—but the allies dominant at sea after a fleet supplied to them by Persia crushed the Spartan fleet at Cnidus. Following Cnidus, Persia expelled the Spartan governors and garrisons from the *poleis* of the eastern Aegean—but on the advice of the Athenian admiral, Conon, she refrained from imposing her own direct authority on them. Persia also provided funds and labor to Athens to rebuild her fortifications, which she had been forced to dismantle at the end of the Peloponnesian War. Finally, Persia provided money to Corinth to build a fleet with which to challenge Spartan control of the western trade routes through the Gulf of Corinth. But when Athens showed signs of wanting to rebuild her empire, Persia switched sides and allied with Sparta. In 386, she brokered an end to the Corinthian War, the so-called "King's Peace."

Sparta sent out feelers in 392, when she struck a deal with the Persian viceroy Tiribazus for a formal peace—offering to formally turn over control of the Greek *poleis* of Anatolia, but Artaxerxes renounced the deal. Frustrated, Sparta resumed her offensive against Persia in western Anatolia. She regained several coastal bases but wasn't able to do much more. Finally, after several years of inconclusive naval skirmishing with Athens, in 387 Sparta approached Persia for an alliance. Persia accepted because Athens had betrayed her by intriguing with Persian rebels and trying to revive her empire. Athens had begun to "liberate" Spartan-controlled *poleis*, only to force them to pay tribute and compel them to accept Athenian hegemony. Athens had also sent naval and military aid to Evagoras, the ruler of the town of Salamis on Cyprus, who had seized control of the island and allied himself with Egypt.

In late 387, Tiribazus summoned envoys from the warring *poleis* to hear Artaxerxes's terms for peace between them. With Persia controlling their purse-strings, they had little choice but to accept. The terms included the following provisions: All states in Asia, including Cyprus, were to be subject to Persia; all states in Greece, no matter how small, were to be autonomous—except the islands of Lemnos, Imbros, and Scyros, which were to belong to Athens. Any state that refused those terms would be subject to attack. Sparta was to be Persia's agent in enforcing the King's Peace. Following the King's Peace, Artaxerxes turned his attention to restoring Persia's position elsewhere in the eastern Mediterranean. Tiribazus was successful in regaining control of Cyprus. He suppressed Evagoras, pushing him back into his old haunts around Salamis—where he continued on as a Persian vassal until he was murdered in 374. But Artaxerxes's three efforts to re-conquer Egypt ended in failure.

The first expedition was such a complete failure that the Egyptians were able to expand their power north into parts of Palestine. The second one, in 373, supposedly included 200,000 troops and a fleet of 300 *triremes*—commanded by Pharnabazus, a commander who had cut his teeth fighting against the Spartans in Anatolia. But the Egyptians flooded and dammed the region around their position in the eastern Delta—making it almost unapproachable—and blocked the mouths of the river with pontoons protected by forts to prevent the Persian fleet from entering the Delta. Although the Persians succeeded, with Greek advice, in gaining a beachhead—they were unable to advance out of it and eventually had to retire. Finally, Artaxerxes's son and heir, Ochus, marched on Egypt in 359—but was halted by the Egyptians' still-formidable defenses and then recalled to Persia when Artaxerxes fell ill and died.

Meanwhile, Greece remained locked in inter-city conflict, which exhausted the *poleis* and prevented any threats to Persia—but also made them turn to Persia as the arbiter of their feuds. Artaxerxes soon found himself turned into the mediator of every petty dispute among the *poleis* of Greece. A steady stream of embassies came to Susa to lay boundary disputes and factional squabbles at the king's feet. But Greece proved incapable of stability, and internecine warfare continued. The Greeks threw off Sparta's authority but were unable to find unity as Thebes, Athens, and Sparta formed shifting and hostile alliances. Persia tried to impose a second "King's Peace" on the Greeks in 371—but failed when Thebes rejected the principle of "autonomy" because it would dissolve her control over the Boeotian League. Thebes then emerged as the leading power in Greece when she crushed Sparta's army in open battle at Leuctra later in 371, ending Spartan power forever.

In 368, Persia called a peace conference at Delos, but it broke down into squabbling, and a subsequent conference at Thebes fared no better. On the other side of the Aegean, the mid-to-late 360s were marred by a series of satrapal rebellions in Persian Anatolia, which nearly led to the disintegration of the empire west of Mesopotamia. The origins of the rebellions lay in court intrigues. The high aristocracy of Persia was as riddled with personal jealousies as any similar group in history, and these jealousies expressed themselves in rumors of plots and corruption—which, true or untrue, could cost a man his life and make it worth his while to rebel rather than appeal to honesty. Virtually all the satraps of Anatolia were involved in the rebellions one way or another. Datames, satrap of Cilicia, rebelled and held off a royal army sent against him in 367—forcing Artaxerxes to give him de facto recognition to his autonomy. Ariobarzanes, satrap of Dascylion, rebelled shortly after Datames. Autophradates, satrap of Lydia, soon joined Ariobarzanes's revolt. Mausolus, satrap of Caria, gave only formal loyalty to Persia. Orontes, satrap of Armenia and Mysia, served as the rebels' figurehead leader. The satraps drew aid from hostile foreign sources, too—allying themselves with Athens, or Sparta, or Egypt. Artaxerxes skillfully used treachery and the personal ambitions of key rebel leaders to eventually suppress the rebellion. Orontes was bought off with promises of security in his old satrapal positions. Dynastic turmoil in Egypt eroded Egyptian backing for the rebels. Autophradates and Mausolus, seeing that the rebellion was wavering, asked for and received mercy and confirmation of their positions as satraps. Ariobarzanes and Datames were assassinated. Royal authority had finally been restored in Anatolia by the time of Artaxerxes II's death in 359.

The Persian Empire revived during the reign of Artaxerxes II's son, Artaxerxes III Ochus—but the effort of restoring royal authority distracted him from the Greek threat. Artaxerxes III came to the throne in a now-customary orgy of dynastic bloodshed. The youngest of Artaxerxes II's sons by the Great Queen Stateira, Ochus, cold-bloodedly carved his way through his brothers to take the throne. According to Greek sources with a strong anti-Persian moral bias, Artaxerxes II had 360 concubines and 115 sons, but only 3 were sons of his Great Queen Stateira. The eldest son, Darius, was executed for conspiring against his elderly father. The second son, Ariaraspes, was persuaded that he'd fallen under suspicion and committed suicide. A fourth son, Araspes, not of the Great Queen, was murdered at the instigation of the third son, Ochus—who then became Artaxerxes III.

How much of this is true and how much an anti-Persian Greek smear is unknown. Ochus left behind a reputation as being the cruelest and most tyrannical of all the Persian kings, though his actions in dealing with rebels belie his reputation—which raises the possibility that it, too, is a Greek smear.

Soon after he came to the throne, Artaxerxes had to contend with a renewed satrapal rebellion in Anatolia. Artabazus, hereditary satrap of Dascylion, rebelled in alliance with the now-elderly Orontes, satrap of Mysia and Armenia—who, of course, had been the figurehead leader of the previous satrapal rebellion. The rebellion probably was prompted by Ochus's demand that Artabazus disband his private army of Greek mercenaries. The rebellion quickly fell apart, without the necessity of a major campaign. Artabazus fled and took refuge with Philip, the King of Macedon, when the support he was promised by Thebes failed to materialize. Orontes proved himself a master at survival by mollifying Ochus and remaining in power—in fact, his family remained in control of Armenia for nearly two more centuries. Artaxerxes III's most important accomplishment was the re-conquest of Egypt, which was accompanied by the reassertion of royal authority in the Levant. He made his first effort against Egypt in 353, but it failed. We know of this campaign from a passing mention in a speech of Demosthenes's, the Athenian orator, but details of what happened are lacking.

The failure of the campaign in 353 sparked rebellions in Phoenicia and Cyprus, which were aided by Egypt. The King of Sidon received

4,000 mercenaries from Egypt. Evagoras II was expelled by a usurper in Cyprus who organized a rebellion among nine Cypriote cities. Artaxerxes swiftly suppressed the rebellions—but without undue brutality. He sent a fleet with a force of Athenian mercenaries to Cyprus, where the rebels sued for peace and remained in power as loyal Persian vassals. He did harshly punish Sidon when he captured it in 345, but not without provocation. The Sidonians had murdered Persian officers and diplomats—so Artaxerxes executed the Sidonian king and let the Persian troops plunder the city. Greek stories that he also massacred the population must be a fiction, since the city was functioning normally a dozen years later. The fate of Egypt was decided by an amphibious battle at Pelusium in 343. Both sides employed Greek troops as the core of their armies. Artaxerxes had at least 15,000 of them, including contingents sent from Thebes and Argos. After diverting the water that protected the Egyptians' fortifications, Artaxerxes's troops fought their way into the Egyptian position in a costly and drawn-out battle.

The deciding moment was an attack from the river by 80 Persian *triremes* and 5,000 marines. An Egyptian counterattack failed, and resistance collapsed when the Greek mercenaries fighting for Egypt accepted a safe conduct and sailed home. After Pelusium, the other fortresses in Egypt quickly surrendered—and the Nile once more belonged to Persia. Artaxerxes III died in 338 along with most of his family in a palace massacre engineered by the eunuch Bagoas. We know nothing of what prompted Bagoas to engineer this bloodbath. He had commanded a wing of the Persian army in the Battle of Pelusium and had led the capture of the rest of Egypt. He had become the second-ranking person in Persia—but as a eunuch could never take the throne himself. Bagoas elevated Artaxerxes's sole surviving son, Arses, to the throne as Artaxerxes IV—but killed him almost two years later, once again along with his family. Bagoas then placed a distant relative of the royal family on the throne as Darius III. Renowned for his bravery and probably disturbed by a pattern of previous behavior, he promptly had Bagoas executed. Darius III was a capable ruler and a sound strategist, but he soon faced a challenge that few—if any—rulers in any age would have been able to master: Alexander the Great.

What kind of empire did Darius rule? How was it run, and how was it defended? When Alexander marched east, what would he encounter?

Lecture Thirty
The Government and Army of Persia

Scope:

As was the case with all other Near Eastern empires, Persia was a monarchy, ruled by a king whose power was absolute. The Persian king was the earthly regent of the one god, Ahura Mazda, and was a great warrior as well as the guarantor of justice. The approach taken by the Persians to imperial administration was flexible, adapted to local circumstances. Darius I seems to have been the main architect of the administrative system, which was built around some 20 large provinces known as satrapies, in turn often subdivided into smaller administrative units. Local affairs were left in native hands. Persian systems of revenue administration and communication were highly sophisticated. The Persian army was as diverse as the empire's population but was built around a core of ethnic Iranian units. Its main combat arms were infantry and heavy cavalry; their primary weapon was the bow.

Outline

I. At the heart of the Persian empire stood the king, a figure whose qualities, like those of other Near Eastern monarchs, were carefully defined by a royal ideology.

    A. The Persian king was a divine-right monarch, the earthly regent of the one god, Ahura Mazda.

    B. Persian kingship was associated with the physical and moral qualities familiar from other Near Eastern royal ideologies.

        1. As part of his duties as defender against the forces of chaos, the Persian king was the divinely appointed guarantor of justice and the social order.

        2. Of course, the king possessed great physical prowess and outstanding skills as a warrior.

    C. The power of the king was absolute. His word was the source of all law.

    D. The king's surroundings were structured to emphasize his special power and position.

        1. Court ceremony was elaborate and designed to emphasize his majesty and power.

2. He was secluded from his subjects, and access to him was tightly controlled.

3. His appearance was magnificent: His dress and surroundings were opulent beyond anything permitted to any of his subjects.

E. Legitimacy of descent was crucial to the legitimacy of the king's authority.

II. Darius I was the architect of the classic Persian system of imperial administration.

A. Persian administration was distinguished by its flexibility, varying its practices according to local conditions.

1. The Persians acknowledged and respected the diversity of languages, cultures, and political traditions among their subject peoples.

2. The Persians do not even seem to have tried to impose close control on the normally troublesome nomadic peoples of their empire.

3. The Persians' embrace of diversity also shows in the variety of languages and scripts that they used in their imperial administration.

4. As early as Cyrus, the Persians understood the importance of adapting to the political traditions of conquered peoples in order to accommodate them to imperial rule.

B. The geographical focus of Persian rule remained the Persian homeland in western and southwestern Iran.

C. Since the king was the center of the empire, the focus of imperial administration was the royal court, but we actually know very little about its structure and organization.

D. Herodotus is our main source for the provincial organization of the Persian empire. He tells us that Darius established the 20 large satrapies that formed the basis of subsequent Persian administration.

E. Each satrapy had an administrative center that functioned as its capital.

F. Because of their size, many satrapies were subdivided into smaller administrative units, but we know very little about them.

G. Local affairs were left in local hands, and there was a high degree of local autonomy.

H. The revenue system that the Persians developed for their empire was intelligent and efficient. The Persians are the ones who introduced money to the Near East.

I. To link their sprawling empire together, the Persians built a sophisticated communications network.

J. Darius's administrative and communications reforms greatly increased prosperity throughout the Persian empire.

    1. He improved agriculture by encouraging the introduction of new crops and diversifying the uses of existing ones.

    2. He and his successors also expanded existing irrigation projects and built new ones.

III. The Persian army reflected both the vastness and the diversity of the empire it defended.

A. This was the largest army ever mustered by a Near Eastern empire.

B. Like every other Near Eastern army, the Persian army's organizational structure was based on decimal units.

C. The core of the Persian army was its ethnic Iranian units. The elite corps was the Ten Thousand Immortals.

D. To supplement the Iranian troops, there were contingents from all of the empire's subject peoples and allies.

E. The cavalry formed an immensely important part of the Persian army. Chariots played only a minor role.

F. Local defense in the satrapies was provided by regular troops posted in small garrisons around the countryside.

G. The Persians created a system of military land grants that provided a ready reserve force that could be mobilized swiftly. Estates were granted to Persian nobles, with the nobles obliged to provide troops for royal service when summoned.

H. During the last century of the empire's existence, mercenaries became a significant element in the Persian army.

I. The Persian navy was always recruited from subject peoples. We hear of no native Persian squadrons. We have no information about Persian fleets in the Persian Gulf or the Indian Ocean.

J. In assessing the effectiveness of the Persian army and navy, we should not confuse size with strength. The Persian military suffered from real weaknesses.

1. Its recruitment from a multitude of ethnic groups must have made communications very difficult.

2. Similarly, the bewildering array of ethnic tactical practices had to have complicated the effective deployment of the army.

3. The worst deficiency, though, may have been a failure to adapt, to find a way to best the phalanx without simply copying it. Perhaps the Persian army suffered from a failure of institutional culture, a deeply ingrained conservatism of thought that in the end brought it down.

Suggested Reading:

Briant, *From Cyrus to Alexander*.

Cook, *The Persian Empire*.

Questions to Consider:

1. Did the Persian approach to ruling a culturally diverse empire resemble the approaches of certain previous Near Eastern empires? Which ones? How did it differ from the approaches of others? Which ones? What accounts for those similarities and differences?

2. How absolute was the Persian king's power in practice? Was the Persian empire sufficiently centralized to make his absolute authority effective?

3. Given its organization and equipment, what sort of tactics would have been most suitable for the Persian army? Did it employ those tactics against the Greeks?

4. What might the Persians have done to turn to their advantage the fact that they had a multilingual army equipped with a wide variety of weapons and used to a wide variety of fighting techniques?

Lecture Thirty—Transcript
The Government and Army of Persia

At the heart of the Persian Empire stood the Great King, a figure whose qualities—like those of other Near Eastern monarchs—were carefully defined by a royal ideology. The Persian king was a divine-right monarch—the earthly regent of the One God, Ahuramazda. All power and authority derived from Ahuramazda, and it was believed that he had given Persia and its king dominion over all the lands and people of the earth. This bestowal of imperial dominion on Persia and its king were essential parts of Ahuramazda's wonderful plan for an orderly world, from which all peoples would benefit. The tomb reliefs of Darius I depict him attending the One God at a fire altar, with the diverse peoples of the empire gathered below—assembled in loyalty to the king and obedience to the God's authority. Darius says that the reason why Ahuramazda gave him kingship was because the earth "was in commotion" and it was his job to "put it down."

The theme of the king as the defense against disorder occurs in several of Darius's other inscriptions as well—especially the Behistun text. The motif of rebellion, which causes unrest, is linked to the growth of "the lie" (or "falsehood"). The concept of falsehood is linked to revolt against the divine and royal order. Rebellion against the king is equivalent to the worship of false gods—and thus a denial of Ahuramazda. This theme and the theme of the king as the defense against earthly chaos, of course, echo themes found in the relationship between Assyrian kings and their chief god, Ashur. Persian kingship was associated with the physical and moral qualities familiar from other Near Eastern royal ideologies.

As part of his duties as defender against the forces of chaos, the Persian king was the divinely appointed guarantor of justice and the social order. Ahuramazda had equipped him with moral insight that enabled him to distinguish right from wrong in ways that other men could not. The king metes out justice fairly—and only after due consideration of the merits of the case and the person before him. The god also gave him self-control, for the king never acts impulsively. Of course, the king possessed great physical prowess and outstanding skills as a warrior. He was a supremely able horseman. Like Egyptian and Assyrian kings before him, he wields both bow and spear with superb skill—whether on foot or on horseback. The power of the king was absolute. His word was the source of all law. Even trivial matters were often referred to him for decisions. The king literally was the government of Persia—the seat of government was located wherever he happened to be. So strictly speaking, there was no "capital" per se. The king's surroundings were structured to emphasize his special power and position. Court ceremonial was elaborate and emphasized his majesty and power. He was secluded from his subjects, and access to him was tightly controlled. When he appeared, his appearance was magnificent. His dress and surroundings were opulent beyond anything permitted to any of his subjects.

Legitimacy of descent was crucial to the legitimacy of the king's authority. From Darius I on, all Persian monarchs were members of the Achaemenid clan, and Darius was at pains to create links between the Achaemenids and the line of Cyrus. The reigning king chose his successor—and sometimes, elder sons were passed over in favor of younger ones. Most kings seem to have been monogamous, but several are known to have had more than one wife. Darius I had six. Artaxerxes II had three. Darius III had two—but then Philip of Macedon had seven, and Alexander had three. Kings were buried in a royal tomb complex at Persepolis, but there was no cult of dead kings. The tomb of Cyrus was just a simple mausoleum and still survives today.

Darius I was the architect of the classic Persian system of imperial administration. That administration was distinguished by its pragmatism, adapting its practices according to local conditions. The Persians acknowledged and respected the diversity of languages, cultures, and political traditions among their subject peoples. Their appreciation of this diversity is seen on the massive ceremonial stone platform at Persepolis—with its depiction of 29 different peoples carefully distinguished from one another by clothing and hairstyles, each bringing their unique contribution to the majesty of the empire. The administrative texts that survive from Persepolis clearly demonstrate that people from around the empire were employed in all capacities at Persepolis, even in the imperial administration. The Persians don't even seem to have tried to impose tight control on the normally troublesome nomadic peoples of their empire. The herdsmen of the Zagros, for example, were left outside the provincial system, since their way of life made that sort of administration impractical. Instead, their chieftains were bound to the king by mutual oaths of loyalty, and they agreed to contribute troops to the royal army and keep the passes open for trade. The Persians also didn't try to constrain the Arab tribes of the desert fringe, who controlled the trade routes through the desert. The desert tribes paid no tax to Persia—but instead gave regular gifts of incense to the king as a token of their loyalty.

The Persians' embrace of diversity also shows in the variety of languages and scripts that they used in their imperial administration. Having no written tradition before they created their empire, but ruling peoples with long traditions of bureaucratic administration, the Persians adopted what they encountered for local use. They introduced Elamite and its cuneiform script for administrative uses in Persia proper. In Mesopotamia they continued the use of Babylonian styles of record-keeping. In Egypt they utilized hieroglyphic and demotic scripts and papyrus scrolls. For the empire as a whole they adopted Aramaic as their administrative language, written in an alphabetic script on parchment or papyrus. As early as Cyrus, the Persians understood the importance of adapting to the political traditions of conquered peoples in order to accommodate them to imperial rule. In Babylonia, Cyrus presented himself as a traditional Babylonian king, took part in Babylonian religious rituals, and left the customary royal building inscriptions in Babylonian style. Cambyses hired a local official to teach him how to behave properly as an Egyptian king—and even adopted an Egyptian throne-name, Mesuti-re (meaning "offspring of Re").

The geographical focus of Persian rule remained the Persian homeland in western and southwestern Iran. That's where the four imperial residences were located. Susa, the old Elamite center in modern Khuzestan, was the most important and was the imperial residence during the winter. Ecbatana (modern Hamadan) in the mountains of Media was the summer residence. Persepolis and Pasargadae in the old Iranian heartland of Persis served as occasional residences and as ceremonial centers. But the royal court was mobile, so there was no true capital—except wherever the king happened to be located. Since the king was the center of the empire, the focus of imperial administration was the royal court, but we actually know very little about its structure and organization.

The titles of court officials often bore little or no relation to their functions. The "spear-bearer" and "bow-bearer," for example, seem to have had civil and ceremonial roles rather than military ones. The "Court Marshal" was a ceremonial official rather than an administrative one. There doesn't seem to have been any sort of "Privy Council" to assist the king in policy deliberations. Suggestions that there was a "Council of Seven" great Persian nobles haven't been borne out by the evidence. It appears that any royal councils were ad hoc consultations with whomever happened to be at court when the king wanted an opinion. Herodotus is our main source for the provincial organization of the Persian Empire. He tells us that Darius established the 20 large satrapies that formed the basis of subsequent Persian administration. The outlines of this system had probably already been sketched out by Cyrus. So what Darius probably did was reorganize and tighten Cyrus's work. The governors of the satrapies were called satraps. They were drawn either from the royal family or from the topmost ranks of the Persian aristocracy. Being rich, they weren't paid in money. They were compensated by receiving estates, whose income was theirs to keep— though the land itself remained royal property. These estates were located throughout the empire and typically were administered by royal agents. In principle, satraps served at the pleasure of the king, but they often served for long periods of time and amassed substantial power. Some satrapies, like Dascylion, became semi-hereditary.

Darius I tried to create safeguards against satrapal rebellion. He garrisoned contingents of royal troops in each satrapy, under officers who reported directly to the crown. These were kept separate from those units under the satraps' direct command. He also separated financial authority from administrative authority, so that satraps lacked control over the treasuries of their provinces. He created a corps of royal inspectors general, "the king's eyes and ears," to monitor the satraps' activities for signs of disloyalty. They had authority to conduct surprise inspections of satrapal records to audit accounts, and to question members of both the satraps' staffs and the general public regarding satrapal performance and behavior. Each satrapy had an administrative center that functioned as its capital. The capitals of satrapies were normally located in traditional administrative centers. Babylonia's, for example, was in Babylon; Egypt's was in Memphis. Satrapal residences were palatial structures modeled on the Persian royal court. The aim was to impress the provincials. Often they were palaces that were taken over from pre-Persian kings. The satrapal palaces served as administrative centers, too. It was from them that the regional bureaucracies operated.

Petitions to the satrap were sent there, and copies of his responses were filed in the archive for later reference, as were satrapal resolutions endorsing local governmental decisions regarding city lands and income—and, of course, any communications received from the king.

Because of their size, many satrapies were subdivided into smaller administrative units, but we know very little about them. Apparently, the subdivision was undertaken both for administrative effectiveness and because large satrapies typically contained ethnically and culturally diverse populations. These sub-provinces often appear to have been run by people of local extraction—thus, the sub-province of Yehud (or Judea) within the satrapy of Beyond the River was administered from Jerusalem, by Jews. Another sub-province was Samaria, which was run by a local clan under the supervision of the satrap of Beyond the River seated in Damascus. Similarly, local affairs were left in local hands, and there was a high degree of local autonomy. Natives were left to govern themselves according to their own traditions, and local law remained in force—instead of being replaced by Persian law. The Persians actively sought the cooperation of the local authorities because they knew that they needed them to do 99 percent of the work of running the day-to-day affairs of the empire.

Early Persian rulers protected local religious cults and prided themselves on restoring local religious traditions that had been disrupted. In Egypt and Babylonia, the Persians were careful to uphold local cults in order to ensure control of the wealthy sanctuaries and the loyalty of those sanctuaries' priests. In lesser places, like Jerusalem, they granted privileges to temples because they acknowledged the support that their gods had given to Persia. This got a positive response from the Jews: Isaiah 44:28 through Isaiah 45:13 depicts Cyrus as chosen by Yahweh to release the Jews and to rebuild the Temple at Jerusalem. To most people, then, there would've been little difference when the Persians took control, because their local religious and cultural activities would have continued uninterrupted. But hostility could cost you that tolerant attitude, and the shrines of enemies were often destroyed—such as the Temple of Apollo at Didyma and the temples on the Athenian Acropolis.

The revenue system that the Persians developed for their empire was both intelligent and efficient. Each satrapy was assessed a fixed annual tribute—primarily in silver, but also in supplies like grain and horses. Herodotus details each satrapy's assessment. Babylonia paid the largest amount of silver—1,000 talents. India paid 360 talents in gold dust. The precious metals collected in taxes were either forwarded to Persepolis or kept in reserve for exceptional expenditures. The revenue generated and stockpiled was immense. Classical authors tell us that Alexander captured 180,000 talents in gold alone from Persian treasuries, causing massive inflation when he released it onto the market. The gold-to-silver ratio went from 1-to-13 to 1-to-10, and both of the metals lost half of their value compared to copper. The satrapy assessments were based on careful calculations of the productivity of the land and the wealth of the population.

Revenues were deposited and tallied in royal treasuries. These were repositories of precious objects—gold and silver bullion, as well as coinage. There were at least a half-dozen of these treasuries, each of which was responsible for a region of the empire. The ones we know of were located at Susa, Hamadan, and Persepolis in Iran; Memphis contained the one for Egypt; Babylon for Mesopotamia; and Sardis for Anatolia. The treasuries provided supplies to the king and his officials, as well as to royal couriers and work parties. Detailed summaries of these disbursements were compiled each year and forwarded to the king. The treasuries were under the control of royal treasurers, who had the title *ganzabara*. The treasurers reported directly to the king and not to the satraps. In fact, satraps probably needed royal authorization to withdraw sums and supplies from the treasuries—but we know that there were other storehouses that the satraps and their staffs could draw on.

We have an account from Elephantine in Egypt that highlights the labyrinthine process of getting things done. It deals with a boat used by two Egyptians for government purposes, who filed a request that the boat be repaired. The request went through the bureaucracy all the way to the satrap of Egypt, Arsames, who instructed his subordinates to have the boat put in dry dock and have the Elephantine accountants and the chief carpenter inspect the boat to see whether the repair was necessary—and provide a detailed inventory of what materials would be needed. That report was made out, with a recommendation that the old materials from the boat be put away in the storehouse. Arsames approved the request, and the work was done—probably late.

The Persians are the ones who introduced money to the Near East. Money (or coinage) had been invented by the Lydians of western Anatolia in the late 7th century B.C. Darius introduced a bi-metal coinage in gold and silver. The gold daric weighed about three-tenths of an ounce and was 98 percent pure. The silver *siglos* (or shekel) weighed two-tenths of an ounce and was 90 percent pure; 20 shekels equaled a daric. The coins were decorated with the figure of a bearded and crowned king in a half-running, half-crouching position—carrying a bow and a dagger. But the monetary economy was focused on the cities and never reached far into the countryside or the lower levels of society, where barter seems to have continued to be the main means of economic exchange.

To link their sprawling empire together, the Persians built a sophisticated communications network. The central element in this network was the road net that crisscrossed the empire—from Bactria to Ionia, and India to Egypt. The most famous road was the Royal Road, which ran 1,700 miles from Sardis to Susa. Persian engineers even went so far as to cut grooves into the road surface on treacherous stretches in the mountains, so that wagon wheels could align themselves in the grooves and not slide off. The road net was equipped with way stations for the use of official travelers. Darius seems to have modeled them on Assyria's system. The way stations were at regular one-day travel intervals of about 15 miles and were provided with excellent accommodations, supplies, and fresh horses. Of course, use of the way stations was limited to individuals bearing sealed warrants from the king or some other responsible official. These warrants allowed travelers to obtain food and fodder by presenting their warrants at the way stations along their route. The relevant way station manager furnished the stipulated amount of supplies and then reported it to the central accounting office—where the warrant issuer's accounts were debited.

Access to supplies was carefully regulated—travelers weren't authorized additional supplies if they happened to dawdle on their journeys. The availability of supplies and remounts at these way stations made it possible to communicate rapidly across the empire. A message could travel the length of the Royal Road in a week, passed off from courier to courier in one-day relays. Less urgent traffic, though, might require as long as three months to make the journey. According to Herodotus, couriers were undeterred by bad weather. His description of their indefatigable service was later adopted by the U.S. Postal Service: "Nothing stops these couriers from covering their allotted stage in the quickest possible time— neither snow, rain, heat, nor darkness."

There were also security posts at strategic chokepoints, like mountain passes and river crossings, to monitor travelers and to suppress banditry. The posts were manned by detachments of royal troops. Upkeep of the supply and guard posts probably fell on the satraps. For emergency communications requiring more speed than a mounted courier could provide, the Persians built a system of hilltop fire beacons that were able to transmit simple alerts warning of invasions and rebellions with great speed.

Road-building wasn't the Persians' only accomplishment. Darius even dug a canal to link the Nile with the Red Sea—150 feet wide, it ran from the Pelusian branch of the Nile Delta, to the Bitter Lakes, to the Gulf of Suez: a total distance of 125 miles (compare that to the 107 miles for the modern Suez Canal). Darius's administrative and communications reforms greatly increased prosperity throughout the Persian Empire. He improved agriculture by encouraging the introduction of new crops and diversifying the uses of existing ones. Rice was introduced into Mesopotamia from Egypt. Sesame was introduced into Egypt in return. Pistachios were brought into Syria from Anatolia. Alfalfa was introduced into northern Greece from Media as fodder for horses during Xerxes's invasion. The Persians encouraged the use of flax for fiber in making linen cloth, instead of simply cultivating it for seed and oil. Darius and his successors also expanded existing irrigation projects and built new ones—and to prevent evaporation and conserve water, they built the irrigation channels underground.

The vastness and diversity of the empire was reflected in the army that defended it. The Persian army was the largest army ever mustered by a Near Eastern empire. Herodotus's figures would give it a total strength of more than 2 million. As we've seen, this is a huge exaggeration. But even if it were only 500,000 men, it was still much larger than the Roman army of the Principate and comparable to the total strength of the Roman army of the later empire. Like every other Near Eastern army, the Persian army's organizational structure was based on decimal units. Our information comes from Xenophon's *Cyropaedia* and from actual army supply manifests excavated at sites in Persia and Egypt. Its basic unit was the battalion of 1,000 men (called a *hazarabam*). Each battalion was composed of 10 companies of 100 men each (a *sabatam*). Each company was divided into 10 squads of 10 men each (a *dathabam*). Ten battalions were grouped into a division of 10,000 (a *baivarabam*).

As we can see from the supply manifests from Egypt, though, actual available-for-duty strengths were typically less than these figures—sometimes only half or fewer. But then, that's typical of armies both in antiquity and even in modern times. The heart of the Persian army lay in its ethnic Iranian units. The elite corps was the 10,000 Immortals. The Immortals were so-called because whenever one of them died or retired, his spot was immediately filled by a new recruit. The Immortals were infantry, chosen from the finest troops in the army's Persian and Median regiments. Within the Immortals was an especially elite 1,000-man regiment called the "Kinsmen." These functioned as the king's bodyguard. Persian soldiers' arms and equipment were very much in the tradition of other Near Eastern armies. They wore light armor. Instead of helmets, they had soft felt caps. On their torsos they wore tunics, though sometimes with scale armor attached. Their arms were light, too. Their shields were made of wicker. They carried short spears. Their main side arm was a long dagger. Their most deadly weapon was a powerful compound bow, firing arrows made with cane shafts. According to Herodotus, all the Iranian contingents had basically the same equipment. That equipment suggests that they were intended for mobile warfare tactics—emphasizing stand-off missile weapons, rather than the close-in fighting with pike and sword favored by the Greeks.

To supplement the Iranian troops there were contingents from all the empire's subject peoples and allies. This led to considerable variation in equipment and also in suitability for employment on the battlefield. The Indians wore cotton and were equipped with bows firing iron-tipped cane arrows, like the Iranians. The Arabians wore long flowing robes and carried longbows. The Ethiopians dressed in animal skins and were armed with longbows, firing stone-tipped arrows and spears tipped with animal horn spear points. The Libyans wore leather and carried javelins—while the Anatolians carried short spears, javelins, and daggers; wore wicker helmets; and carried small shields. So far as Herodotus indicates, contingents drawn from the subject peoples were usually commanded by Persian generals—who, in turn, appointed their subordinate unit commanders. Cavalry formed an immensely important part of the Persian army. The ethnic

Iranian cavalry were equipped similarly to the Iranian infantry—with wicker shields, bow, spear, and dagger. There are indications that there was a royal cavalry guard corps of 10,000 men—a sort of mounted parallel to the Immortals. Non-Iranian cavalry contingents were armed more exotically. Most carried weapons similar to their ethnic infantry—but according to Herodotus, the Sagartians were armed only with lassoes.

From the late 5th century B.C. on, we begin to hear of heavy-armored cavalry in the Persian army. In these units, both men and horses were equipped with metal breastplates—like those worn by Greek hoplites. This was the origin of the later units of *cataphractarii* and *clibanarii* in the Sassanid Persian and Roman armies. Chariots played only a minor role in Persian armies. The chariot was an awkward weapon, easily countered on the battlefield by light infantry, which could decimate chariot units—and by cavalry, which was far more maneuverable. Scythe chariots turned out to be poor weapons. Their one success, recorded by Xenophon, was against scattered troops on a foraging expedition—and even then they needed support from heavy cavalry. But Alexander's disciplined infantry easily defeated the Persian scythe chariots at Gaugamela. Local defense in the satrapies was provided by regular troops posted in small garrisons dotted around the countryside.

According to Xenophon, each satrapy had a 1,000-man battalion of Persian spearmen as the core of its garrison. He provides an account of how this rapid-reaction force functioned in describing how the Persians were able to fend off a raid on the countryside around Pergamum by rapidly summoning troops stationed in the vicinity. The Persians created a system of military land grants that provided a ready reserve force that could be mobilized swiftly to supplement the army. Estates were granted to Persian nobles, with the obligation of providing troops for royal service when summoned. There were also various types of military land grants given to ordinary soldiers, depending on the type of service and equipment that was expected. The three main types were horse-land, bow-land, and chariot-land. The grantees and their obligation were recorded in a royal census kept by army scribes at the main muster points in the satrapy. As the empire stabilized and the need for constant military call-ups declined, the descendants of the grantees were expected to pay a silver tax in lieu of their personal service.

During the last century of the empire's existence, mercenaries became a significant element in the Persian army. The most important source of mercenaries, at least in the western satrapies, was Greece. The Greek hoplite had demonstrated his superiority on the battlefield—and Greek mercenaries were plentiful, so their use was widespread. The Egyptians used them when they became independent. The rebel cities of Cyprus and the Levant used them, too. Apparently, during the 5th and 4th centuries, the Persians recruited mercenaries locally for their usefulness in local tactical situations. Xenophon indicates that mercenaries were recruited among the tribes of the Caucasus for use in the mountains there. Strabo indicates that Persia also recruited mercenaries in India for use on the eastern frontier. The Persian navy was always recruited from subject peoples. We hear of no native Persian squadrons, though we have no information about Persian fleets in the Gulf or the Indian Ocean. The main sources of naval recruitment were the Phoenicians, Egyptians, and Ionian Greeks. Their squadrons were commanded by native officers. There was no fixed organization that we can see for these naval squadrons.

The main warship was the *trireme*, which apparently was invented in Phoenicia or Egypt in the late 6th century. It had three stacked banks of oars and a crew of 170 rowers, plus marines. The designs varied. Phoenician *triremes* had high decks that made them good as archery platforms. Greek *triremes* had lower decks and were used primarily for ramming. In both cases, the final act was to grapple an opponent's ship and send over the marines. In assessing the effectiveness of the Persian army and navy, we shouldn't confuse size with strength. The Persian military suffered from real weaknesses. Its recruitment from a multitude of ethnic groups must have made communications very difficult. Were there translators posted with each ethnic contingent? How effective would one or two translators in a battalion of lasso-wielding Sagartian cowboys have been in the confusion and din of battle? Similarly, the bewildering array of ethnic tactical practices had to have complicated the effective employment of the army.

What do you do with lasso-wielding Sagartian cowboys on a battlefield, anyway? How would the Persians have handled drilling and training such a diverse force to fight cohesively? Did they even try? The army's most effective and cohesive force was the Iranian and Median regiments, but even they were hobbled by limitations. Their lack of heavy armor and long pikes made them dependent on their bows. If troops could close against them, as the Greeks did at Marathon and Plataea, they were doomed. The worst deficiency, though, may have been a failure to adapt, to find a way to best the phalanx without simply copying it. Perhaps the Persian army suffered from a failure of institutional culture, a deeply ingrained conservatism of thought that in the end brought it down.

But it's an open question whether any ancient army, no matter how innovative, could have triumphed in the face of the challenge that was posed by Alexander the Great.

Lecture Thirty-One
Alexander and the Fall of Persia

Scope:

In the 330s B.C., the Persian empire emerged from a period of rebellion and turmoil on the throne, only to find itself confronted by what it had so long worked to avoid: a Greece united and hostile to Persia. The agent of unification—Philip, King of Macedon—was soon assassinated, but his son and successor, Alexander, proved to be an even more lethal menace. At the head of a well-balanced army of seasoned veterans, he launched an invasion of Anatolia, crushing the Persian army there and marching on to Syria, where he crushed a larger Persian force under King Darius III's personal command. The Levant fell to him, then Egypt. Finally, in a hard-fought battle at Arbela in the old Assyrian homeland, he crushed the last army Persia could muster. Darius fled the field and was assassinated by a Persian nobleman. Alexander assumed the throne as King of Kings, and the Persian empire came to an end.

Outline

I. Persia, the greatest empire the world had yet seen, fell in a mere four years under the onslaught of the small Balkan principality of Macedonia, led by its young king, Alexander.

   A. Alexander's assault on Persia was in many ways the final episode in the Greco-Persian Wars.

   1. Depressed and impoverished by generations of internecine warfare, many Greeks saw a national crusade against Persia as a way to end Greece's infighting and restore the Greek soul.

   2. The Greeks knew that such a war was feasible. The March of the Ten Thousand had shown that Greek armies could march deep into Asia and come back alive.

   3. Alexander's father, Philip II, had already made preparations for a war against Persia before he was assassinated in 336 B.C.

B. But how was Macedonia able to do what no one had previously done and impose its domination on Greece? Why had Persia not taken steps to prevent Macedonia's rise, the way it had done with Sparta, Athens, and Thebes?

    1. One reason is that during the years when Macedonia rose from obscurity to the mastery of Greece, between 365 and 343, Persia had major problems of its own.

    2. The Egyptian and satrapal rebellions essentially cut Persia off from Greece during much of the mid-4th century, because they involved Persia's entire Mediterranean coastline, and that made it much more difficult for the Persians to gather intelligence and to conduct diplomacy in the Aegean.

    3. Effective action against Macedonia was also hampered by the bloody intrigues at the Persian court.

    4. It is also important to realize that prior to 350, no one would have believed that Macedonia could ever pose a threat to anyone, neither the poleis of Greece nor the Persian empire.

C. Macedonia's rise from obscurity was due entirely to one thing: the genius of Philip II, who forged Macedonia into a major power in a mere 20 years.

D. On the eve of their epic and fatal conflict, Macedonia and Persia seemed roughly balanced, at least on paper. Perhaps Macedonia's greatest advantage over Persia lay in the quality of their respective leadership.

    1. Royal authority within Persia itself was weak, thanks to decades of rebellion and repeated spasms of dynastic murder.

    2. In contrast, Macedonia had Alexander. Bold strategy was his forte; bold tactics were his trademark.

II. Alexander began his pursuit of empire in Anatolia in the spring of 334, where he met a spirited Persian defense.

A. His army numbered nearly 40,000 Macedonian and Greek troops. The invasion army was the sort of combined-arms force his father had perfected.

B. The Persian satraps were ready for Alexander's invasion. At the river Granicus, they met Alexander in a set-piece battle.

    1. The satraps' formation was faulty, with the cavalry on level ground behind the stream and the infantry in formation behind them.

    2. Alexander attacked, sending a squadron of light cavalry and one of heavy cavalry forward to secure the far bank of the stream while his infantry crossed.

    3. Persia lost 1,000 cavalry and almost all of its mercenary infantry at the Granicus; Alexander lost 90 Macedonians and an unspecified number of Greek allies.

C. After the destruction of its Anatolian field army at the Granicus, Persia tried to slow Alexander's advance by using its naval superiority to cut his supply lines and by using its gold to cause trouble in Greece.

D. But to counter Persia's naval superiority, Alexander adopted the novel strategy of defeating the Persian fleet by capturing its ports and marching down the Ionian coast, where the Greek cities welcomed him.

III. Late in 333, Alexander invaded Syria.

A. Darius III had mustered a large army at Babylon and marched to northern Syria to defend the Levant.

B. Darius III pulled off the remarkable feat of stealing a march on Alexander and got his troops behind Alexander's army as they marched down the coast. This forced Alexander to turn back to face the Persians, but it turned out that this worked to Alexander's advantage.

C. Instead of pursuing Darius and the remnants of his army, Alexander turned south and conquered the Levant, completely stripping the Persian fleet of its ports.

D. Darius tried both diplomacy and subversion to halt the Macedonian advance, but his efforts failed.

E. After destroying Gaza, Alexander arrived at the borders of Egypt. The Persian satrap surrendered without a fight, and the population welcomed the Macedonian as a liberator.

IV. Darius braced for Alexander's next move, which clearly would be an attack on Mesopotamia. Everyone knew that not only the possession of Mesopotamia but the fate of the Achaemenid empire hinged on the outcome of the inevitable battle.

    A. Darius mustered a large army to defend the empire's heartland, but it was of much lower quality than the armies that had fought Alexander before.

    B. Alexander's army was slightly larger than the one he'd had at the Granicus and Issus, but it was still heavily outnumbered by the Persians.

    C. Darius chose a battlefield in northern Mesopotamia, at Gaugamela, the site of the old Assyrian city of Erbil. This would keep Alexander away from the densely populated parts of Babylonia.

    D. The battle took place on October 1, 331. Once more, Darius chose to receive Alexander's attack. Once more, Alexander forced Darius into retreat.

V. Gaugamela marked the end of organized Persian resistance. In the weeks that followed, the Achaemenid empire came to an end and the empire of Alexander rose in its place.

    A. Babylon surrendered to Alexander without a fight. Alexander assumed the title King of Babylon and was hailed as a liberator.

    B. In 330, he invaded the Persian homeland. The Persian capitals of Susa and Persepolis surrendered to him without a fight.

    C. Darius fled north to the Caspian Sea and then east toward Bactria, closely pursued by Alexander. On the way, he fell victim to a plot among his courtiers.

    D. Alexander then assumed the Persian kingship, and with that the history of the Persian empire came to an end.

    E. The swiftness and brilliance of Alexander's victory obscures the determination of the resistance that the Persian empire offered to him.

        1. Darius's defensive strategy was reasonable and well planned: to use Persian naval superiority to cut off Alexander from his European base and to use Persian wealth and diplomacy to destabilize Greece.

2. We must also recognize that while Alexander won all his battles, in each of them the Persian army fought fiercely and bravely in defense of its king and its empire, especially at Gaugamela.

3. The Persian nobility remained loyal to Darius until the very end.

F. In the end, the solution to what one scholar described as "the enduring historical mystery"—how Alexander was able to destroy the mighty Persian empire—must be found in just three words: Alexander, the Great.

Suggested Reading:

Allen, *The Persian Empire*.

Cook, *The Persian Empire*.

Olmstead, *History of the Persian Empire*.

Questions to Consider:

1. Should we attribute Alexander's conquest of the Persian empire solely to Alexander's own genius, or were there significant advantages that the Macedonians and Greeks brought to the conflict that brought about Persia's defeat? What might the Persians have done to stop Alexander that they failed to do?

2. How did Alexander's army differ from the Greek armies that Persia had faced in the 5th century? How did Persia's army differ from the army that it had brought to Greece in the 5th century?

Lecture Thirty-One—Transcript
Alexander and the Fall of Persia

Persia, the greatest empire the world had ever known, fell in a mere four years before the onslaught of the small Balkan principality of Macedonia—led by its young king, Alexander. Alexander's conquest of Persia was in many ways the final episode in the Greco-Persian Wars. Depressed and impoverished by generations of internecine warfare, many Greeks saw a national crusade against Persia as the way to end Greece's in-fighting and restore the Greek soul. And eloquent voices like Isocrates were calling for a war of revenge to pay Persia back for the destruction caused by Xerxes's invasion in 480. The Greeks now knew that such a war was feasible. The "10,000" had shown that Greek armies could march deep into Asia and come back alive. Subsequently, Greek mercenaries had come to comprise the heart of Persia's armies, as well as those of rebel satraps and secessionist states like Egypt—and Greek officers had led Persian troops and commanded Persian fleets.

So, Greeks had served alongside Persians as well as against Persians; they knew Persian tactics, had served on Persian staffs, and knew how Persians thought. Which meant by the mid-4th century B.C, Persia held no fear for the Greeks; it offered only opportunities. Alexander's father, Philip II, had already made preparations for a war against Persia before he was assassinated in 336. He had achieved what no man had done before: Since 350, he had imposed his authority on the *poleis* of Greece and forged all of them but Sparta into an anti-Persian alliance—the League of Corinth, which he presided over as *hegemon*. He had already sent a Macedonian advance force to seize bridgeheads in northwestern Anatolia. But how was Macedonia able to do what no one had previously done and impose its domination on Greece? Why had Persia not taken steps to prevent Macedonia's rise—the way she had done with Sparta, Athens, and Thebes? One reason is that during the years when Macedonia rose from obscurity to the mastery of Greece, between 365 and 343, Persia had major problems of her own.

The biggest of these was the great satrapal rebellion, which broke out in Anatolia during the 360s—and for a while took Anatolia out of the empire. The rebellion prevented Persia from keeping an eye on Greece because it was the Anatolian satraps who, during the early 4th century, had provided the diplomatic energy and the resources that had kept the Greeks at each other's throats. With those satraps in revolt and often even drawing military and naval aid from the Greeks, that energy and those resources were unavailable. Another distraction Persia faced and a major drain on her energies was the threat posed by Egypt, which had seceded from the empire in 404. To protect itself from Persian attack, Egypt worked actively to destabilize Persian control over the Levant and Cyprus—fomenting rebellion after rebellion during the early and mid-4th century. Persia mounted expeditions to re-conquer Egypt in 373, 359, and 353, but they all failed. The failure of the last one led to even more rebellions in Phoenicia and Cyprus.

It wasn't until 343 that Persia finally re-conquered Egypt. Furthermore, the Egyptian and satrapal rebellions effectively severed Persian contact with Greece throughout much of the mid-4th century, because they involved Persia's entire Mediterranean coastline—and that made it much more difficult for the Persians to gather intelligence and to conduct diplomacy in the Aegean. Finally, effective action against Macedonia was hampered by the bloody intrigues that wracked the Persian court.

Artaxerxes III turned his attention to countering Macedonia once he had restored control over Persia's western territories in the late 340s. But then, in 338, he was assassinated—and his successor, Artaxerxes IV, was assassinated only two years later. With that sort of chaos on the throne, it was impossible to develop and pursue a coherent policy in Greece. It's also important to realize that prior to 350, no sane person would have believed that Macedonia could ever pose a threat to anyone—not the *poleis* of Greece and certainly not the Persian Empire.

Macedonia was an ethnically mixed, economically and culturally backward kingdom on the periphery of the Greek world. During the reigns of Darius I and Xerxes, it was nothing more than a weak pawn of Persia—a vassal state whose only role in the invasion of 480 and 479 was for her king, Alexander I, to skulk between the picket lines furtively passing messages between the opposing sides. Macedonia was freed of Persian authority after the collapse of the Persian satrapy in Thrace, but it remained weak and inconsequential. During the 5th and early 4th centuries, it was repeatedly pummeled by attacks from the Balkan tribes to the north—against which it seemed all but powerless to protect itself.

Macedonia's rise from obscurity was due entirely to one thing: the genius of Philip II—who, in a mere 20 years, forged Macedonia into a major power. It was something of a miracle that Philip even came to the throne in the first place. He was the youngest of King Amyntas III's three sons and in the normal course of things would've had no chance of becoming king—except that his two older brothers, as well as a pretender, all fell victim either to plots or invaders between 370 and 359. Even then, Philip was merely made regent for the proper king, his infant nephew, and had to defeat several other relatives who were jealous of his proximity to power, as well as a host of Macedonia's neighbors—who were eager to capitalize on her weakness. Once he had done so and proven his abilities, the infant king was deposed—and Philip was named king in his place.

Philip combined a high order of military and political genius with an unshakeable commitment to increasing his kingdom's power—and a clear-cut understanding of how to go about that. He quickly cemented the independent-minded hill clans and the low country *poleis* of Macedonia into a cohesive kingdom under his unchallenged authority. Building on the foundations laid by his predecessors, he forged a highly disciplined, professional citizen army that was completely devoted to him. He was absolutely willing to use whatever tools he needed—diplomacy, bribery, or war—to advance Macedonia's interests.

On the eve of their epic and fatal conflict, Macedonia and Persia seemed roughly balanced, at least on paper. The Persians had limitless financial resources. This was especially true after their re-conquest of Egypt—with its large annual grain surpluses, which generated huge profits. But the other provinces of the empire contributed immense quantities of tribute, too—and the king had hundreds of thousands of talents of gold and silver stockpiled in his treasuries. In contrast, Macedonia had only a collection of gold and silver mines it had recently acquired in Thrace, whose 1,000 talents of annual production were a pittance compared with what Persia had. Persia also had nearly complete control of the sea. The empire's fleet numbered nearly 500 first-line warships, most of them the new top-of-the-line *quinquiremes*. In contrast, the combined Greco-Macedonian fleet had only about 160 ships—mostly obsolete *triremes* and *quadriremes*. But on the other hand, Macedonia's army was now the finest in the Western world.

After Philip's reforms, Macedonian hoplites were less heavily armored than Greek ones—and, therefore, more mobile on the battlefield. They carried pikes that were much longer than Greek hoplites, which gave them greater range in combat. They fought in a deeper but more open and maneuverable phalanx. Philip had also developed an elite corps of light infantry, the peltasts, who could fight on rough ground and screen the flanks of the phalanx—yet were also able to fight in the line of battle when called on. Most important of all, Philip had made the heavy cavalry his main tactical striking arm, able for the first time in history to employ shock tactics. The cavalrymen wore armor and were equipped with long lances and swords. The Macedonians had bred large cavalry horses able to carry these armored riders at a gallop. Philip used the heavy cavalry to charge directly into an opponent's infantry battle line, scattering it.

The nucleus of the cavalry were the Companions—made up of the sons of the aristocracy, who were led in battle personally by their king. Philip had also created a corps of combat engineers, able to construct siege equipment and improvise tactics that made it possible to take fortresses quickly and efficiently. This army was highly disciplined, thoroughly professional, and absolutely loyal to their king and his house. The Persian army, meanwhile, relied heavily on Greek mercenary hoplites, but Philip's League of Corinth had cut off the supply of recruits—making it hard to replace any losses. Besides, Greek hoplites were inferior to Macedonian infantry on the battlefield. Only in their excellent cavalry could the Persians compare with the Macedonians, but even the Persian horse weren't equipped for shock tactics.

Perhaps Macedonia's greatest advantage over Persia lay in the quality of its leadership. Royal authority within Persia itself was weak, thanks to decades of rebellion and repeated spasms of dynastic murder. The satraps enjoyed nearly hereditary power, often passing on their provinces from father to son, and the damage from the great satrapal rebellions had yet to be repaired. The fact that bloodbaths or civil war had accompanied every change of ruler since 465 did nothing to bolster loyalty to the Persian throne. In contrast, Macedonia had Alexander. Where to begin in talking about Alexander? Some call him hero; some call him monster. Maybe all of them are right. But it's literally true that Alexander never lost a siege, a battle, or a skirmish—no matter the fortress, no matter the field, no matter the foe. Bold strategy was his forte; bold tactics were his trademark. He had an almost artistic intuition for the flow of battle, and a blood-chilling physical courage that put him in the forefront of his troops and in the thick of every combat. He had that certain something. A what? A divine madness? A dream, perhaps, that inspired men to follow him—across the sea and beyond the horizon, all the way to eternity. He was 21 years old.

Alexander began his pursuit of that dream in the spring of 334—leading his men into Anatolia, where he met a spirited Persian defense. His army numbered nearly 40,000 Macedonian and Greek troops. Anticipating that Persia might intrigue against him in Greece, he left a substantial force behind under a trusted general named Antipater. The invasion army was the sort of combined-arms force his father had perfected. There were 24,000 heavy infantry—half of them Macedonian and half of them Greek. There were also 8,000 light infantry and engineers. The core of its striking force was the 5,000 cavalry. This was the first Greek army the Persians had ever encountered that was strong in cavalry—3,600 of them were the Macedonian and Thessalian heavy cavalry, the finest in the world.

Always meticulous about supplies, Alexander had organized a sophisticated logistical service that brought food for 40,000 men and fodder for 6,000 horses, as well as the siege equipment—all carried in wheeled vehicles able to move swiftly on the imperial roads of Anatolia. But the Persian satraps were ready for Alexander's invasion. They had moved aggressively against the advance force Philip sent to Anatolia in 336 and penned it up at Abydos on the shore of the Hellespont. To face Alexander, they mustered an army equal to his in size, with 20,000 Greek mercenary hoplites and 20,000 Persian cavalry. They planned to fight him as far forward as possible, in northwestern-most Anatolia.

So, at the River Granicus, they met Alexander in a set-piece battle. The satraps' formation was faulty—with the cavalry on level ground behind the stream, and the infantry in formation behind them. Alexander deployed his army correctly—with the infantry in the center, along the stream, and the cavalry on either flank. Alexander attacked, sending a squadron of light cavalry and one of heavy cavalry forward to secure the far bank of the stream while his infantry crossed. The Persian cavalry met them with volleys of javelins that inflicted heavy casualties before Alexander intervened personally with the Companion Cavalry. The fighting became a close-quarters melee—more like hoplite combat on horseback than a typical cavalry battle.

Alexander unhorsed Darius III's son-in-law, Mithridates, in a personal duel, but then Alexander was nearly cut down when a Persian nobleman, Spithridates, rode to Mithridates's aid. History swayed in the balance when suddenly Alexander's friend, Cleitus the Black, cut off Spithridates's sword arm just as it was about to strike the king and saved Alexander's life. The Persian cavalry were forced to retreat. When the Greek mercenaries asked for quarter, Alexander refused—calling them traitors to Greece and had all but 2,000 of them slaughtered. The survivors were sent back to Greece as slaves. Persia lost 1,000 cavalry and almost all of its mercenary infantry at the Granicus; Alexander lost 90 Macedonians and an unspecified number of Greek allies.

After the destruction of its Anatolian field army at the Granicus, Persia tried to slow Alexander's advance by using its naval superiority to cut his supply lines and using its gold to cause trouble in Greece. The fleet captured the islands of Samos and Chios and brought support to Persia's coastal garrisons. But to counter Persia's naval superiority, Alexander adopted the novel but simple strategy of defeating the Persian fleet by capturing its ports—marching down the Ionian coast, where the Greek cities welcomed him. As the cities fell, Alexander boldly dissolved his own fleet—calling it a needless expense. He also won support by putting democracies in place of the oligarchic governments the Persians had imposed.

After he cleared the coast, Alexander turned inland to Gordium, where he cut the famous Gordian knot—thus, according to legend, guaranteeing himself the lordship of Asia—and then continued on to the coast of Cilicia in southeastern Anatolia. The Persians conceded him control of Anatolia and didn't contest his march. As he organized his new conquests, Alexander retained the basic outline of Persian administration. He named Macedonian noblemen as satraps and gave freedom to the Greek cities on the coast. But he was also generous to the native peoples and refused to place them under their Greek neighbors' control. These measures shrewdly placated both Greek and native elites and succeeded in winning them over to Alexander's rule.

Late in 333, Alexander invaded Syria. Darius III had mustered a large army at Babylon and marched to northern Syria to defend the Levant. The core of the Persian army was 30,000 Greek mercenaries—the largest Greek mercenary force Persia had ever fielded. The army also included the full infantry and cavalry levies of the Persian home territories of Media and Persis, also about 30,000 men—which gave Darius an overwhelming superiority in cavalry, even though he hadn't had time to wait for the crack heavy cavalry from Bactria to arrive. Alexander's army was about the same size as the one with which he'd invaded Anatolia. He had about 30,000 infantry. He also had about 5,000 cavalry, most of them the heavy cavalry from Macedonia and Thessaly.

Darius III pulled off the remarkable feat of stealing a march on Alexander and got into his rear as he marched down the coast, forcing Alexander to turn back to face him—but it turned out that this worked to Alexander's advantage. Alexander was able to force a battle in a narrow coastal plain, which neutralized the Persians' numerical superiority. Darius deployed his army along a shallow riverbed, facing south, posting himself in the center with the infantry. The cavalry lay on the wings—some in the foothills on the east end of the line, others along the shore to the west. Darius elected to await Alexander's attack, intending to flank the Macedonians as they moved forward. Alexander also positioned his infantry in the center and his cavalry on the wings—placing himself and the Companion Cavalry just to the right of the infantry. The Macedonians advanced slowly. Seeing that Darius intended to sweep along the beach and through the foothills to flank him, Alexander widened his line as he moved forward across the narrow plain.

Finally, the battle lines closed. The Persians unleashed clouds of arrows on the advancing Macedonians, but Alexander then led his infantry forward at a run—joined by the cavalry and infantry of the guard. This opened a gap in his line, and Persia's Greek mercenaries charged into it with great effect at the same time as the Persian heavy cavalry charged Alexander's flank on the shore. But Alexander's guard infantry and cavalry crushed the Persians facing them and then took the mercenaries in the flank—destroying the center of the Persian line. Caught up in the disintegration of his center, Darius fled the field in his chariot—and seeing him flee, his army fell apart. Still, the battle was closer than it first seemed: 10,000 of the Greek mercenaries fought their way through Alexander's army to freedom, and the Persian cavalry had nearly crushed Alexander's left flank. Alexander lost 450 dead and 4,000 wounded. Persian losses are unknown, but must have been in the tens of thousands—many of them dying in the rout. The battle had cost Persia an army and the

Levant. Alexander captured Darius's wife and daughter, whom he treated with royal honor. He also captured the mobile treasury that Darius carried with him—which had enough gold and silver in it to pay off all of Alexander's and Macedonia's debts and provide ample cash reserves for the future.

After Issus, instead of pursuing Darius and the remnants of his army, Alexander turned south and conquered the Levant, in order to completely strip the Persian fleet of its ports. Most Phoenician cities opened their gates to Alexander—but Tyre, the chief Persian naval base sitting secure on a fortified offshore island, defied him. So Alexander had his engineers build a mole out to the island, enabling him to bring his siege engines up to the walls. The siege engines broke through the fortifications. Alexander personally led the assault parties through the breach—8,000 defenders died, 2,000 were crucified along the coast, and the rest of the population was forcibly deported.

Alexander next met resistance at Gaza, which he took after a two-month siege—once more, slaughtering the defenders and depopulating the city. Darius tried both diplomacy and subversion to halt the Macedonian advance. He sent peace feelers to Alexander, but Alexander rejected them. Darius offered Alexander a ransom of 10,000 talents for the return of his captive family and offered to cede Alexander the western two-thirds of Anatolia. But Alexander had already conquered all that—and more. Darius also tried to stir up trouble in Greece. He dispatched agents to Athens and Sparta to encourage rebellion, but the agents were apprehended and captured. Nothing worked.

After he destroyed Gaza, Alexander arrived at the borders of Egypt. The Persian satrap surrendered without a fight, and the population welcomed the Macedonian as a liberator. To make an intentional contrast with how Artaxerxes III had acted in 343, Alexander took the time-honored Egyptian royal titles "King of Upper and Lower Egypt," "Son of Ra," and "Beloved of Amun"—and went out of his way to honor the traditional Egyptian deities. Then, after traveling 160 miles into the desert to visit the shrine of Amun at the Siwah Oasis, Alexander laid out the site of the first and greatest of his colonies, Alexandria. Then, Darius sent Alexander a last desperate peace offer. He upped his ransom to 30,000 talents and offered Alexander all the Persian territory west of the Euphrates River—in other words, the territory that Alexander had already conquered. This was territory in which the Greeks had long had political and commercial interests. It was also the territory that a Mediterranean power could effectively control, as Rome's later experience showed. Alexander's trusted general, Parmenio, said: "If I were Alexander, I would accept." Alexander replied: "If I were Parmenio, so would I"—because now Alexander aimed at nothing less than the throne of Persia itself.

Darius braced for Alexander's next move, which clearly would be an attack on Mesopotamia. Everyone knew that on the outcome of the inevitable battle not only the possession of Mesopotamia but the fate of the Achaemenid Empire itself would hinge. Darius mustered a large army to defend his empire's heartland, but it was of much lower quality than the armies that had fought Alexander before. Its numbers are uncertain, because the Greek sources exaggerate them to glorify Alexander, but Darius still had 6,000 Greek mercenary hoplites as well as the 10,000 Immortals—now trained and equipped as hoplites. He also had at least 40,000 excellent heavy cavalry and uncounted swarms of light cavalry. His trump card was 200 chariots equipped with scythes to mow down opposing infantry.

Alexander's army was slightly larger than the one he'd had at the Granicus and Issus, but it was still heavily outnumbered by the Persians. He had about 40,000 Greek and Macedonian infantry; most were hoplites—but there was a large corps of excellent light infantry as well. His cavalry corps had grown to about 7,000—all of excellent quality; most were battle-hardened Macedonians and Thessalians. Darius chose a battlefield in northern Mesopotamia at Arbela (or Gaugamela)—the site of the old Assyrian city of Erbil. This would keep Alexander away from the densely populated parts of Babylonia. He carefully prepped the field for the type of battle he intended to fight. The ground was leveled to optimize it for the massed charge of the chariots. Caltrops were strewn across the field to cripple Alexander's cavalry horses. The battle took place on October 1, 331. Once more, Darius chose to receive Alexander's attack. He deployed his army with the scythe chariots in the center, in front of the infantry, and his cavalry on both flanks.

The Persian line far overlapped Alexander's line—so Alexander advanced across the field in a formation that could easily be turned into a defensive square if it were attacked by Persian cavalry. His Macedonian and Greek phalanxes were in the center of the line, in a double-line formation so that the rear phalanx could about-face to defend the rear if necessary. His flank guards consisted of Greek cavalry on the left and Macedonian light cavalry on the right, supplemented by light infantry. Alexander posted himself with the Companion Cavalry and the other heavy battalions on the right flank of the phalanx. He approached the Persian line on the oblique, with his right advanced and himself in the lead. Seeing Alexander advance toward the left of the Persian line, Darius ordered his army forward, and the battle began. The cavalry fight on the Persian right was fierce. Darius's heavy cavalry pushed back the Greek cavalry, which then rallied and counterattacked. While the cavalry battle raged, Darius ordered his chariots to charge. They had mixed success. Alexander's light infantry eliminated most of them before they reached the line. Many of the rest passed harmlessly through the phalanx, which opened its ranks to let them through—but a few inflicted horrible carnage on the infantry facing them.

The Persian cavalry finally was able to pass around Alexander's flank, but at that moment, Alexander hurled his heavy cavalry against the Persian phalanx and smashed its formation—opening gaps that he immediately plunged into. The Persian battle line disintegrated—but the Bactrian heavy cavalry under the Persian nobleman Bessus had brought Alexander's left to a halt, and the battle now swirled into individual small-unit actions. The final moment came when, as the Macedonian lancers charged him, Darius turned and fled—just as he'd done at Issus. Alexander then turned his heavy cavalry against the Persian horse still battling Macedonian troops elsewhere on the field and around Alexander's camp, and they retreated. Darius fled with a small bodyguard to Ecbatana in Media. Losses were heavy on both sides. Although actual casualties on the Persian side were probably lighter than at Issus, the organization of the Persian army was destroyed. Only 2,000 Greek mercenaries and the royal guard and Bactrian cavalry escaped as cohesive units. Alexander's losses were also heavy—probably a couple of thousand dead, and many horses.

Gaugamela marked the end of organized Persian resistance. In the weeks that followed, the Achaemenid Empire came to an end, and the empire of Alexander arose in its place. Babylon surrendered to Alexander without a fight. He assumed the title "King of Babylon" and was hailed as a liberator. In 330, he invaded the Persian homeland. The Persian capitals of Susa and Persepolis surrendered to him without a struggle. The only resistance Alexander encountered was from the Zagros hill tribes, whom he suppressed. In Persepolis, Alexander burned Persian holy sites in retribution for Xerxes's destruction of the temples on the Athenian Acropolis. He confiscated the immense gold and silver reserves stashed in both places, relieving him of all fiscal concerns for the future. Finally, he declared the Greek crusade against Persia over.

Darius fled north to the Caspian and then east towards Bactria, closely pursued by Alexander. On the way, he fell victim to a plot among his courtiers. His cousin Bessus deposed Darius and imprisoned him in a wagon. Bessus claimed the throne in Darius's place, taking the name Artaxerxes V. When Alexander's pursuit drew near, some of Darius's entourage fatally wounded him and left him by the road, to die in the arms of a Macedonian cavalryman moments before Alexander arrived. Alexander gave Darius a state funeral at Persepolis, pursued Bessus to Bactria, captured him, cut off his nose and ears, and had him impaled for treason and regicide. Alexander then took the title "Lord of Asia"—and with that, the history of the Persian Empire came to an end. The swiftness and brilliance of Alexander's victory obscures the determination of the resistance that the Persian Empire offered him.

Darius's defensive strategy was reasonable and well-planned—to use Persian naval superiority to cut off Alexander from his European base, and to use Persian wealth and diplomacy to destabilize Greece. This strategy would've had an excellent chance of success against any other opponent, but Alexander wasn't any other opponent. We must also recognize that while Alexander won all his battles, in each of them the Persian army fought fiercely and bravely in defense of its king and its empire—especially at Gaugamela. The Persian nobility remained loyal to Darius until the very end. Its loyalties only began to waver when Darius became a fugitive after Gaugamela—and didn't swing to Alexander until Darius had been murdered. Even then, the nobles of eastern Iran continued to resist, and Alexander had to reduce their fortresses one by one. In the end, the solution to what one scholar described as "the enduring historical mystery"— how Alexander was able to destroy the mighty Persian Empire— must be found in just three words: Alexander the Great.

Lecture Thirty-Two
The Origins of Carthage and Its Empire

Scope:

Like the history of Persia, Carthage's history was written by its enemies. We have few Carthaginian inscriptions and no archives, but abundant writings from the Greeks, whom they fought in Sicily, and the Romans, who eventually destroyed them—writings that provide us with vivid but potentially partisan narratives. Archeology helps to fill in the gaps in those narratives. From it, we learn that Carthage was founded by Tyre around 800 B.C., near the end of a great wave of colonization that scattered Phoenician outposts throughout the western Mediterranean and down the coast of northwest Africa. Carthage seems to have remained under Tyrian authority until Tyre fell to the Neo-Babylonians in 573. Once independent, it moved swiftly to assert leadership over the other western Phoenician settlements. By the middle of the 5th century, it had established a thalassocracy that extended over western Sicily, the northwest coast of Africa, southern Spain, and the islands of the western Mediterranean.

Outline

I. The fall of Persia left only one Near Eastern state standing: Carthage, the westernmost outpost of the Near East. Founded by Tyre during a great wave of Phoenician colonization in the middle of the 1st millennium B.C., Carthage forged for itself a thalassocracy in the western Mediterranean—the greatest naval empire the world had ever seen, and the greatest it was to see for the next 2,000 years.

   A. In reconstructing the history of Carthage and its empire (which is called Punic, from the Latin for "Phoenician"), the available sources limit what we are able to know.

      1. The documentary sources for Carthaginian history and culture are very restricted, both in their nature and in their perspective.

      2. In the absence of Carthaginian sources, we are forced to rely on the ones provided by Carthage's rivals and enemies, the Greeks and Romans.

B. Archeology fills in some of the gaps in our knowledge, but there are the usual limits to what archeological evidence can tell us.

    1. The material remains recovered by archeologists can tell us that an object is present, or that something happened, but generally they cannot tell us how that object got there, or why that something happened.

    2. Furthermore, modern conditions often get in the way of exploring Carthaginian sites.

    3. But for all of its limitations, it is archeology that has provided us with most of our insights into Carthaginian history.

C. The fact that so much of what we know about Carthage comes either from archeology or from the writings of Carthage's opponents profoundly affects how we tell the story of Carthage and its empire.

    1. Our dependence on Greek and Roman authors, with their emphasis on narrative, means that the story of the rise and fall of Carthage's empire is long on storyline and short on the specifics of government and administration.

    2. Furthermore, since Greek and Roman texts reflect the interests of their authors and audiences, neither of which were Carthaginian, their accounts of the rise and fall of Carthage's empire tend to emphasize Punic relations with the Greeks and Romans at the expense of what was happening in other parts of Carthage's world.

II. Carthage was one of dozens of colonies founded in the western Mediterranean by the cities of Phoenicia during the early 1st millennium.

    A. Ancient writers differ regarding the dates of the colonization movement but tend to place it very early, several centuries before the Greek colonization of the rest of the Mediterranean.

    B. Archeological research has made it clear that Phoenician colonization was a gradual process, that it began in the eastern Mediterranean, and that it arrived in the various parts of the western Mediterranean at most a century or two prior to the arrival of the Greeks.

C. Phoenician colonization had a commercial purpose. Settlements were established as bases to support merchant ships by controlling choke points in the Mediterranean and by serving as trading posts.

III. Carthage was founded by Tyre and was given the Phoenician name Qart-Hadasht, meaning "new town."

A. The dates given by ancient authors for the foundation of Carthage sprawl across several centuries. The archeological evidence suggests that Carthage was founded in the 8th century.

B. Carthage is the only Semitic city that has a foundation legend comparable to the foundation legends of Greek and Roman towns.

C. For nearly three centuries after Carthage was founded, its ties with Tyre remained very close, both culturally and politically.
1. Tyre controlled Carthage's government, sending out governors to run the city.
2. Carthage annually sent a delegation back to Tyre to sacrifice at the temple of Melqart there. This sacrifice included the delivery of a tribute payment.

IV. The thalassocracy Carthage created embraced all of the Phoenician settlements of the western Mediterranean.

A. Carthage's move to create an empire for itself probably grew out of a combination of its own commercial interests, together with events back home in Phoenicia.
1. It was the largest and most prosperous of the Phoenician colonies in the western Mediterranean, the focal point of the most important trading network in the region.
2. But Carthage was only able to build its empire once it became independent of Tyre. The decisive moment in the process seems to have come when Tyre fell to the Babylonian empire in 573, after a 13-year siege.
3. As the largest and richest of their communities, Carthage took on the role of defender of the western Phoenicians.

B. The history of Carthage's transition from leadership of the western Phoenicians to empire over them is obscure, thanks to our lack of sources. Most of its imperial expansion seems to have taken place between circa 550 and circa 450.

1. The architects of the Carthaginian empire seem to have been the clan descended from an aristocrat named Mago. The Magonids dominated Carthage during the late 6th and 5th centuries.

2. Close by the location of Carthage itself, the Phoenician settlements on Malta and in western Sicily came under its authority during the last half of the 6th century.

3. Carthage got its first foothold in Sardinia by intervening to defend the Phoenician settlements there against the natives.

4. Corsica fell to the Carthaginians after 535, when they defeated the Greeks at Alalia, in alliance with the Etruscans.

5. While Carthage was establishing control in Sardinia and Corsica, the Balearic Islands were also becoming part of its thalassocracy.

6. The Phoenician settlements along the coast of southern Spain probably came under Carthage's authority in the late 6th century also.

7. The Phoenician outposts along the coastline of northwest Africa had been added to the empire by the early 5th century at the latest.

8. Carthage also extended its authority to the east of Tunisia, along the coast of Tripolitania.

9. It only extended its control into those interior territories, the hinterland of Carthage itself, during the mid-5th century.

C. By the end of the 5th century, Carthage had established itself as the sole power in the western Mediterranean, ruler of the largest, richest, and most successful thalassocracy the ancient world was ever to know.

Suggested Reading:

Lancel, *Carthage*.

Picard and Picard, *The Life and Death of Carthage*.

Warmington, *Carthage*.

Questions to Consider:

1. How does the fact that we know Carthage's history from the pens of its enemies affect our ability to understand Carthage objectively? What elements of the picture the Greeks and Romans give us of Carthage should we be suspicious of?

2. How did Carthage's acquisition of its empire differ from the way in which other Near Eastern empires acquired theirs? What were its motives? What means did it use?

3. Did Carthage attempt to expand its empire beyond the limits of Phoenician colonization in the western Mediterranean? Why or why not?

Lecture Thirty-Two—Transcript
The Origins of Carthage and Its Empire

After the fall of Persia, of the states of the ancient Near East, only Carthage was left—a lonely Near Eastern outpost in the western Mediterranean. But although she was lonely, Carthage was far from weak. Founded by Tyre during a great wave of Phoenician colonization, in the middle of the last millennium B.C., Carthage forged for herself a thalassocracy—which became the greatest sea-empire the world had ever seen, and ever was to see, for the next 2,000 years.

In reconstructing the history of Carthage and its empire (which are called "Punic," from the Latin word "Punus," or Phoenician), the sources we have available to us limit what we're able to know. The documentary sources for Carthaginian history and culture are very restricted—both in their nature and in their perspective. First of all, we have no archives from Carthage. The sorts of royal and municipal records libraries that are so common in the Near East are nonexistent. There are no cuneiform tablets. The Carthaginians apparently kept their records on perishable materials like papyrus, which didn't survive the Roman destruction of the city in the 2nd century B.C. There are plenty of Carthaginian inscriptions, but they tell us very little about Punic history and institutions. Most of them come from the 4th century. The vast majority are either funeral epitaphs or votive texts dedicated to various gods. There are no legal texts, no lists of magistrates, no dedications of monuments. The only historical information we can glean from the inscriptions is the titles some of the people give for themselves and for their ancestors.

There is also no Carthaginian literature. There's no question that the Carthaginians could write. After all, it was the Phoenicians who invented the alphabet. But if the Carthaginians had historians of their own, those historians' works have perished without a trace. Maybe it's just that they hadn't picked up Greek intellectual culture—which during the 5th century B.C. acquired the penchant for viewing the past through a naturalistic and rational interpretive lens, seeing it as "history" rather than legend. But then, we also don't have any Carthaginian poetry, or religious texts, or even law codes—which is not to say that poetry, religious texts, and law codes didn't exist at Carthage. They must have existed—but again, none of them seems to have survived the destruction of the city.

In the absence of Carthaginian sources, we're forced to rely on the ones provided by Carthage's rivals and enemies: the Greeks and Romans. Herodotus gives us a few passing mentions of Carthage. Aristotle includes passages on the Carthaginian constitution in Book II of his *Politics*, but what he says is hard to understand. The bulk of our information about Carthage is contained in the Greek writer Polybius and in the Augustan historian Livy. There's also material in Cicero, in Justin's summary of Pompeius Trogus, in Diodorus Siculus, and in Appian. For the most part, we have to rely on Livy and on Polybius—and their focus is on the wars between Carthage and Rome. They leave no doubt about whose side they're on.

Archeology fills in some of the gaps in our knowledge, but there are the usual limits to what archeological evidence can tell us. The material remains recovered by archeologists can inform us that an object is present or that something happened, but generally they can't tell us how that object got there or why that something happened. To know such things, we need documentary evidence. Furthermore, modern conditions often get in the way of exploring Carthaginian sites.

It's a testimonial to the Phoenicians' excellent eye for real estate that the most important Punic sites are still inhabited. Good examples are the city of Cadiz, founded by the Phoenicians as Gadir (the Romans called it Gades)—and Cartagena in Spain, which was founded as the Punic colony of New Carthage. The site of Carthage was itself overbuilt by a Roman colony founded by Caesar a century after the destruction of the Punic city. Today, Tunis lies nearby Carthage and little by little is encroaching on the location of the ancient settlement. Even those sites that are accessible have received only partial attention rather than a comprehensive and systematic excavation. This is probably because Carthage isn't really seen as central to the development of Western civilization, so Carthaginian projects are less attractive—and, therefore, generate less funding than projects at Greek and Roman sites or ones in the Holy Land. But for all of its limitations, it's archeology that's provided us with most of our insights into Carthaginian history. It's archeology that has told us what we know about the Phoenician settlement of the western Mediterranean. It's archeology that has told us what we know about the foundation and growth of Carthage—and about Carthaginian life and customs. It's archeology that has told us the bulk of what we know about the growth of Carthage's empire as well.

The fact that so much of what we know about Carthage comes either from archeology or from the writings of Carthage's opponents has a powerful effect on how we tell the story of Carthage and its empire. The Greek and Roman authors' emphasis on narrative means that the history of the rise and fall of Carthage's empire is delightfully long on storyline, but frustratingly short on the details of government and administration. Greek and Roman writers loved narrative, and they were both good at it and not above embellishing things for the sake of effect. But dragging your readers through a detailed analysis of constitutional minutiae is about as far as you can get from gripping narrative. Furthermore, since Greek and Roman texts reflect the interests of their authors and audiences, neither of which were Carthaginian, their accounts of the rise and fall of Carthage's empire tend to emphasize Punic relations with the Greeks and Romans at the expense of what was happening in other parts of Carthage's world. The shortcomings of our source material mean that we have to filter our history of Carthage's rise and fall to neutralize biases in our sources as well.

Just as the Greeks stereotyped the Persians as luxurious and degenerate, so also the Greeks—and especially the Romans—stereotyped the Carthaginians as greedy and devious. Polybius, for example, starkly contrasts the Roman emphasis on honesty with what he regards as the Carthaginian love of money. He says that in Carthage, public office was achieved by open bribery—and for the Carthaginians, nothing was regarded as disgraceful as long as it turned a profit. Cicero says that the most distinctive Carthaginian characteristics were craft, skill, industry, and cunning. He says that the Carthaginians, of all peoples, combined craft and cunning to an unusual degree. "Punic honor" and "Carthaginian cunning" were stock derogatory terms in Roman usage. But all they actually are is hostile opinions colored by the Punic Wars—and all they really say is that the Carthaginians were a commercial people who excelled as merchants and traders.

Carthaginians also had a reputation for cruelty, but we can't be sure whether this was a feature that permeated their entire culture, or only some aspects of it. Supposedly, Carthage often executed its defeated commanders—and not by lethal injection. They were either crucified or impaled. But then we have to wonder: If this were really the case, why would anyone agree to command a Carthaginian army or fleet? Was the aristocracy really that casually wasteful with the lives of its own leading members? What does seem apparent, through archeology, is that Carthaginian religion included infant sacrifice—offering up newborns to Baal Hammon and the goddess Tanit. What we don't know is why, or how the infants were chosen, or how many were sacrificed. In the end, what we have to bear in mind is that any account we give of Carthage can at best be only a partial one—based on incomplete and often biased texts, supplemented by whatever material remains archeology has been able to recover and interpret. With that caution in mind, let's begin our story.

Carthage was one of dozens of colonies founded in the western Mediterranean by the cities of Phoenicia during the early 1st millennium B.C. Greek and Roman writers differ regarding the dates of the colonization movement, but tend to place it very early—several centuries before the Greek colonization of the rest of the Mediterranean. They put the foundation of many of the most prominent Phoenician colonies in the late 2nd millennium. Velleius Paterculus places the foundation of Gadir (modern Cadiz) as early as 1110 B.C. Pliny the Elder places the foundation of Utica in north Africa in 1101. But archeological research has made it clear that Phoenician colonization was a gradual process, that it began in the eastern Mediterranean, and that the Phoenicians arrived in the various parts of the western Mediterranean at most a century or so prior to the arrival of the Greeks.

The earliest material evidence for Phoenician colonization is on Cyprus, Rhodes, and Crete in the 11th or 10th centuries B.C. The process seems to have begun on the east coast of Cyprus, at Citium, close by Phoenicia. It then proceeded to Ialyssos on the island of Rhodes—after that to the south coast of Crete, where there were at least two settlements, both of which the Greeks called Phoenix, meaning "Phoenicia." The archeology indicates that colonization in Spain and beyond the Pillars of Hercules (or Straits of Gibraltar) began after the establishment of the colonies in the eastern Mediterranean by about 200 or 300 years. The Phoenicians established a string of settlements along the southern coast of Spain, east of the Pillars—evidently during the early to mid-8th century. Their most important settlement in southern Spain was at Gadir, which seems to have been in existence by the 7th century. But the site has been inhabited continuously since its foundation—and the Phoenician levels have been disturbed or even destroyed by Roman, medieval, and modern construction.

What little we've been able to recover suggests that Gadir was a pretty small settlement until the 5th century—when it became part of the Carthaginian Empire and then began to prosper. The Phoenicians colonized the western and northwestern coasts of Sicily late in the 8th and early in the 7th centuries. Motya, an island settlement on the western tip of Sicily, was probably founded by Carthage herself around 700 B.C. Motya then went on to found Lilybaeum on the coast nearby. Panormus (the modern city of Palermo) appears to have been established sometime during the 7th century. The Phoenicians came to Sardinia in search of minerals. The focus of their colonization was on the southern and western coasts of the island. Phoenician contact with Sardinia was early. We have an inscription of around 800 B.C. from Nora, which is actually the earliest Phoenician text we've found in the entire western Mediterranean. But if there was a settlement at Nora that early, no traces of it have turned up. Instead, the earliest settlements on Sardinia only seem to date to the late 7th century. Settlement activity increased after around 600 with numerous outposts then being established. Many of these later settlements were founded by Carthage herself. Then, using the coastal enclaves as a base, in the 6th century the Carthaginians gradually pushed their control into the interior of the island. On the northwest coast of Africa, the first evidence of colonization dates to the early 7th century. This comes from Lixus, just down the coast from the Pillars of Hercules. The Phoenicians founded Tingis (the modern city of Tangier), just outside the Pillars—soon after they set up Lixus. The farthest south that evidence for Phoenician settlement extends on the Atlantic coast of Africa is the island of Mogador, 430 miles south of the Pillars. Mogador was settled by the middle of the 7th century, if not before—but it may have been only a seasonal trading post, rather than a permanent settlement.

Colonization along the coasts of Tunisia and Tripolitania (modern Libya) came both from Phoenicia and from Carthage itself. The earliest indication of foundation by Carthage is the presence of "tophets," cemeteries where sacrificed infants were buried. The practice of infant sacrifice had ceased in Phoenicia after the 8th century, but it continued at Carthage—so a tophet suggests Carthaginian colonization of a site. Utica, just west of Carthage, was founded from Phoenicia—probably in the 8th century, about the same time as Carthage. It had a preeminent place among Carthage's imperial possessions because of its antiquity and the fact that it grew to be a community of some size. Hadrumetum, south of Carthage on the Tunisian coast, was also founded from Phoenicia. It was intended to serve the return traffic from Spain to Phoenicia. Leptis, on the central Tunisian coast, was probably founded in the late 6th or early 5th century as a bar to any further Greek colonization. Since Phoenicia was under Persian rule at this point, it's likely to have been a Carthaginian settlement—although we have yet to find a tophet.

Along the coast of northwest Africa towards the Pillars of Heracles, Carthage established a number of her own settlements. Probably founded in the early 4th century, these were set up wherever the configuration of the coastline was suitable—at roughly 20- to 25-mile intervals, the distance sailed in a day by small coasting vessels. They were very small (probably no more than a few hundred people each) and are described by Greek authors as *emporia*, meaning that they served as markets and as way stations. The Greeks called their inhabitants the "Libyphoenicians." During the Roman period, some of these places grew into notable towns and cities—locations like Hippo, Rusicade, Tipasa, and Iol. All of this colonization activity was motivated by, and intended to serve, Phoenician commerce.

Phoenician merchant vessels sailed a regular circuit around the Mediterranean. First, they went west from Phoenicia along a northern route that took them through the western Mediterranean—stopping in at Sardinia and the Balearic Islands. Then, they picked up trade goods in Spain and Africa. They finally returned to Phoenicia along the coast of Africa, putting in at Carthage on the return voyage. The colonial settlements were established as bases to support these merchant ships by controlling chokepoints in the Mediterranean and serving as trading posts.

Most of what the Phoenicians were looking for was minerals. In Spain it was silver. In Sardinia it was silver, copper, lead, and iron. The Phoenicians preferred locations that were secure from the mainland. They were especially fond of coastal peninsulas joined to the mainland by narrow necks of land. Such places were easily defensible and had to be because colonizing parties were so small. Greek colonists tended to prefer similar locations for similar reasons. Greek colonies were founded as self-governing, independent communities—but Phoenician colonies weren't. They remained under the direct authority of their founding cities back in Phoenicia, which helped ensure that the merchant fleets received their full support. So, it's important to understand there was no program of imperial expansion behind Phoenician colonization. Phoenician colonies were not intended to relieve population pressure in the cities of Phoenicia, and Phoenician colonies were not founded as military bases for the conquest and consolidation of foreign territories.

During this wave of Western colonization, Phoenicia's leading city, Tyre, founded a settlement on the southern shore of the narrows of the central Mediterranean and gave it the Phoenician name *Qart-Hadasht*, meaning "New Town." We call it Carthage. The dates given by ancient authors for the founding of Carthage sprawl across several centuries. Several Roman writers and their Greek sources provide dates as early as the 13th century B.C. The 4th-century B.C. Greek historian Eudoxus of Cnidus and his contemporary, Philistos of Syracuse, both put Carthage's foundation in 1215. The 2nd-century A.D. historian Appian, on the other hand, gives a slightly earlier date—placing the foundation 50 years before the fall of Troy, or sometime around 1280. But the majority of ancient authors date the foundation to the end of the 9th century B.C.

Unlike the writers who place the foundation much earlier, these authors' dates were probably based on official records. We know that Tyre kept chronicles that included regnal lists with lengths of reigns and notices of important events. Greek historiography made use of these now-lost sources. Menander of Ephesus is known to have consulted Phoenician documentary sources, and he states that Carthage was founded in the seventh year of the reign of Pygmalion, King of Tyre. Timaeus of Taormina in Sicily had contact with Carthaginians in the 3rd century B.C. and evidently got some of his information through them. He says Carthage was founded in 814. That's virtually the same date that Cicero gives in his *Republic*. The date also appears in "Velleius Paterculus" and in St. Jerome's 4th-century A.D. *Chronicle*.

The archeological evidence suggests that Carthage was founded a bit later. The earliest pottery found at Carthage dates to somewhere in the early to mid-8th century, and the earliest tombs we've found date to the late 8th century. But this is close enough to the date of 814 to give the ancient authors some credibility—and, in one of history's many ironies, it also places Carthage's birth very close in time to the birth of her arch-nemesis: Rome.

Carthage is the only Semitic city that has a foundation legend comparable to the foundation legends of Greek and Roman towns. The story revolves around intrigues within the royal house of Tyre; the crimes of its king, Pygmalion; and the sufferings of his sister, Elissa. The precise details vary depending on who is telling it, but the gist of the story goes like this. Pygmalion, driven by greed, killed the husband of his sister, Elissa. She fled, accompanied by her loyal followers, who included a number of prominent citizens. Elissa landed first in Cyprus, and then after further journeys, she arrived in Libya. Her name—which is *Elishat* in the original Punic (Elissa being the Greek rendering)—is well attested at Carthage, but Dido is the name she's known by because it's the one that Virgil used for her in the *Aeneid*. Dido is actually a nickname or an epithet; it means "The Wanderer." Once she arrived in Libya, the local Libyan king, Hiarbas, wanted to marry Elissa—but in order to remain faithful to the memory of her dead husband, she committed suicide by climbing onto a pyre she had just lit under the pretense of carrying out an expiatory sacrifice (of course, Virgil tweaks this part of the story). This is actually an attested Phoenician practice, in which the king or queen would sacrifice themselves when their city faced a grave crisis.

A memorable feature of the foundation myth is the devious way that Elissa acquired land for her settlement from the natives. The Libyans agreed to give her as much land as she could cover with an ox hide, so she sliced the hide up into narrow strips and used those strips to lay out the settlement's boundaries—a circumference of 2½ miles. According to the legend, Elissa brought with her both a human and an institutional microcosm of Tyre. The settlers were a cross-section of Tyre's population. She also brought along the gods of Tyre, especially the cult of Melqart (whom the Greeks equated with Heracles), of which her murdered husband was supposedly a priest. For nearly three centuries after Carthage was founded, its ties with Tyre remained very close—both culturally and politically. Tyre controlled Carthaginian government, sending out governors to run the place. Carthage annually sent a delegation back to Tyre to sacrifice at the Temple of Melqart there. This sacrifice included the delivery of a tribute payment. Diodorus Siculus tells us that payment amounted to 10 percent of Carthage's revenues. When Carthage won victories she also gave a portion of the booty to the Temple of Melqart at Tyre. Had Carthage remained under Tyrian rule—that could have become a lucrative source of income for the god.

The Carthaginian thalassocracy embraced all of the Phoenician settlements in the western Mediterranean. Her move to create an empire for herself probably grew out of a combination of Carthage's own commercial interests together with events back home in Phoenicia. She was the largest and most prosperous of the Phoenician colonies in the western Mediterranean, the focal point of the most important trading network in the region. That meant that she had commercial interests that needed protection. It also gave her the resources to assert and expand her power in order to protect those interests. Maybe it also gave her ambitions, and it may have made her feel like the protector of the other Phoenician communities in the west—especially in the face of aggressive Greek colonization and commercial expansion. But Carthage was only able to build her empire once she and the other western settlements became independent of their founding cities back in the Levant. Carthage was subject to Tyre until the second half of the 6th century—and as a Tyrian subject, she was allowed no foreign policy of her own.

The decisive moment for Carthage seems to have come when Tyre fell to the Babylonian Empire in 573 after a 13-year siege. Then, 44 years later, after the fall of Babylonia—Tyre fell once more to Cyrus of Persia. After that, Tyre never regained her independence, but Carthage prospered in hers—and as the largest and richest of their communities she took on the role of defender of the western Phoenicians. The history of Carthage's transition from leadership of the western Phoenicians to empire over them is obscure, thanks to our lack of sources. Most of her imperial expansion seems to have taken place between about 550 and about 450 B.C. The architects of the Carthaginian Empire seem to have been the clan descended from an aristocrat named Mago. The Magonids dominated Carthage during the late 6th and 5th centuries.

Greek and Roman writers refer to the Magonids as "kings," though their position seems to have borne only an approximate resemblance to Greek and Roman monarchy. But it was the Magonids who forged links between Carthage and the other states of the Mediterranean—both great and small, Phoenician and non-Phoenician. They concluded an alliance with the Etruscans and together with them drove the Greeks from Corsica and Sardinia. When Rome drove out its Etruscan monarchs in 509, the Magonids pragmatically concluded a treaty with the new Republic—regulating Roman trade in the Carthaginian sphere of the Mediterranean. The Magonids also concluded a treaty with Persia—which around 500 B.C. was at the height of its power and seems to have regarded Carthage as some sort of vassal.

The Phoenician settlements on Malta and in western Sicily, which were nearest to Carthage geographically, came under her authority first—sometime during the last half of the 6th century. Establishing her dominance over Malta and western Sicily gave Carthage control over the strategic narrows of the Mediterranean Sea. Carthage got her foothold in Sardinia by intervening to defend the Phoenician settlements there against the natives. She first intervened on the island in the mid-6th century—when the Carthaginian general, Malchus, led a force to defend the Phoenician outposts against native attacks. The Carthaginians extended their control into the interior after the late 6th century by establishing a line of strongholds in the inland mountains—gaining control of their rich mineral resources, as well as founding new settlements on the coasts. Carthage's sovereignty over the island is made clear in her treaty with Rome in 509, which explicitly bars Rome from trading in Sardinia—a clause that was reaffirmed by a later treaty with Rome in 348. To the north of Sardinia, Corsica fell under Carthaginian domination toward the end of the 6th century.

In 535, the Carthaginians defeated the Greeks at Alalia in alliance with the Etruscans. Alalia was a hotbed of Greek pirates who preyed on Carthaginian and Etruscan shipping. The buccaneer stronghold had been founded from Massilia in 560—and about 20 years later received a massive influx of settlers from Phocaea in Ionia, fleeing the Persian conquest; this may have been what prompted the Etruscan-Carthaginian alliance. Carthage and the Etruscans each contributed 50 ships to the fleet that faced the Greeks at Alalia, while the Greeks could only muster 60 ships total. The result was a conclusive victory that drove the Greeks from the island and cemented the place of Carthage as the defender and protector of the western Phoenician settlements. While Carthage was establishing her control in Sardinia and Corsica, the Balearic Islands were also added to her thalassocracy. The Phoenician settlements along the coast of southern Spain probably came under Carthage's authority in the late 6th century also. The Phoenician outposts along the coastline of northwest Africa had been added to the empire by the early 5th century at the latest. Carthage also extended her authority to the east of Tunisia, along the coast of Tripolitania.

Herodotus tells us that Carthage exercised a protectorate over Leptis Magna in central Tripolitania. He relates that when Spartan refugees under Dorieus attempted to establish a settlement 12 miles southeast of Leptis around 515 B.C., Carthage reacted violently—and after three years expelled the Greeks, who then tried to establish another colony on Carthaginian territory in Sicily at Eryx. In alliance with Sicilian Phoenicians and native Elymians, the Carthaginians overwhelmed the colony—and Dorieus was killed. The episode at Leptis probably prompted Carthage to set the eastern frontier for her empire in the eastern Gulf of Sidra, where the coast turns north to Cyrenaica.

We don't know when this frontier was established, but according to Greek sources, it definitely existed by the mid-4th century B.C. Carthage's authority over the scattered Punic coastal settlements west of Leptis seems to have been in the nature of a loose suzerainty—but north of the Gulf of Gabes in southern Tunisia, in the area closest to the site of Carthage itself, her control was both close and direct. This coincided with the point at which she had established control over the interior territories as well. She only extended her control into those interior territories, the hinterland of Carthage itself, during the mid-5th century. The spur for this seems to have been her defeat at the hands of the Sicilian Greeks at Himera in 480. Carthage made good her naval losses and then turned her attentions to her environs in Africa. Her acquisition of these territories had the purpose of assuring the city of a reliable supply of food close at hand—one that wasn't vulnerable to interdiction by sea. The inhabitants weren't enslaved and were permitted to remain. The term "Libyan" was used to describe them. They were the only significant non-Phoenician population who were part of the Carthaginian Empire. So, by the end of the 5th century B.C., Carthage had established herself as the sole power in the western Mediterranean—mistress of the largest, richest, and most successful thalassocracy the ancient world was ever to know. How did she govern this remarkable empire, and how did she defend it against its enemies?

Lecture Thirty-Three
Ruling and Defending Carthage's Empire

Scope:

Carthage became independent of Tyre in the early 6th century B.C. By the early 5th century, an oligarchy of major merchant families dominated the city. Its organs of government were the same as those of other ancient oligarchies, consisting of magistrates, a council, and an assembly, with the real power lying with the council. The first city-state to create an empire, Carthage took a relaxed approach to imperial rule, leaving its subject communities considerable autonomy; its weakness was that it won the obedience of its subjects but not their loyalties. To defend its empire, Carthage relied on mercenaries drawn from the western Mediterranean, which provided it with an army varied in weaponry, talents, and language, which complicated command and control. Carthage recruited these mercenaries as needed, which impaired its ability to respond swiftly to threats. Its navy was a citizen fleet, equipped with the latest models of warships and employing the sophisticated tactics typical of other seafaring peoples of the Mediterranean, such as the Greeks.

Outline

I.   The Carthaginian thalassocracy was the product of commerce, and commerce shaped both Carthage's own government and the administration of its empire.

   A. For the first two centuries of its existence, Carthage was ruled by governors sent out each year from Tyre.

   B. The tradition that claims that Carthage began its independent life as a monarchy makes sense, but the tradition also claims that its government went on to evolve along the lines of Sparta's or Rome's.

   　　1. We get our information from Aristotle, who had very definite ideas about the evolutionary patterns in city constitutions, ideas that might color his account of Carthage's constitutional history.

2. The king's authority was carefully circumscribed. A king had military and religious duties but not the authority to take the city to war. There had to be a popular vote both authorizing the war and detailing the king's authority in conducting it.

3. Under the monarchy, the administration of the city was handled by officials called suffetes (a Latinization of *shophets*, "judges").

4. Monarchical Carthage also had a council, which probably consisted of the heads of the leading families and clans.

C. During the 4th century B.C., the monarchical model seems to have been discredited by Carthage's disappointments in its wars with the Sicilian Greeks, and that brought the monarchy to an end.

D. The postmonarchical constitution had three main branches: the magistrates, the council, and the people. They served both to counterbalance and to support one another.

II. Carthage was the first city-state to create an empire, and its empire was more successful than that of any other city-state besides Rome.

A. The Carthaginian empire was both long-lived and unwarlike. After it cemented its control over the Phoenician settlements of the western Mediterranean, Carthage showed no interest in further expansion.

B. The Carthaginians took a laissez-faire attitude toward imperial rule. For the most part, all that Carthage asked of its subject communities was political loyalty and the regular payment of tribute.

C. The subject communities were grouped into several different categories, reflecting their different levels of civilization and the varying ways in which they had become subject to Carthage.

D. The central weakness of Carthage's administration of its imperial possessions was that it failed to foster any sense of shared belonging and identity among its non-Phoenician subjects. In other words, it made no effort to "Punicize" them.

III. The army with which Carthage defended its empire was a mercenary force, but it was well-balanced and thoroughly professional, a multiethnic force that was highly flexible, able to employ a variety of weapons and tactics.

    A. The army had originally been a citizen levy like the armies of most other city-states, but it turned to mercenaries during the late 6th century, when the empire was born, and as it expanded.

    B. Carthage recruited its mercenaries from a broad spectrum of western Mediterranean peoples.

        1. The Libyans made up the largest contingent in the army.

        2. Mauretanian and Numidian mercenary cavalry were particularly important in the Carthaginian army.

        3. Spanish mercenaries served in Carthage's armies from the year 480 until the Second Punic War.

        4. Men from the Balearic Islands served as mercenary slingers.

        5. Gauls first appeared in Carthaginian service in 340, but they were most common in Hannibal's Italian campaign.

        6. In addition, Carthage also recruited Greek mercenaries, probably from the Sicilian poleis, who fought as hoplites in their customary phalanx.

    C. The elephant corps for which Carthage is famous was actually a minor element in the army.

    D. The army's senior commanders were almost always native Carthaginians.

IV. In contrast to the army, Carthage's navy was a citizen force.

    A. Being a mercantile state, Carthage had both a long seafaring tradition and a large seafaring element in its population.

    B. The navy consisted of three elements: warships, transports, and utility vessels.

    C. Naval battles mainly took place in coastal waters, where calmer seas made handling the slender, shallow-draught ships easier.

    D. Carthage rarely fielded all of its fleet at once. Much of it was kept in reserve for fiscal and commercial reasons.

V. Carthage's government and the structure of its mercenary army and citizen navy all reflected the commercial nature of its life and empire. But they were inadequate to the challenge posed by Rome.

    A. Its political and military institutions were very similar to those of its Greek neighbors.

    B. But if Carthage's political and military institutions were inadequate to the task of halting Rome, it must be said in its defense that nobody's political and military institutions proved adequate to that task. After the collapse of Carthage's empire, the Greek states of the eastern Mediterranean fell before the Roman advance like dominoes.

    C. Carthage was merely the first victim of what became the Roman Empire.

Suggested Reading:

Bagnall, *The Punic Wars*.

Goldsworthy, *The Fall of Carthage*.

Picard and Picard, *The Life and Death of Carthage*.

Warmington, *Carthage*.

Questions to Consider:

1. Did Carthage's character as a commercial city predispose it toward an oligarchic form of government? Why would this have mitigated against its becoming a democracy or a monarchy?

2. How did Carthage's commercial character shape its approach to ruling its empire? Would a different approach have been more effective in cementing the empire together? Why or why not, and what different approach might Carthage have taken?

3. What were the strengths and weaknesses of the sort of army that Carthage possessed?

4. Down through the First Punic War, Carthage routinely was defeated on land by its enemies, both Greek and Roman. What advantages did they have over Carthage? What did Carthage do to counter those advantages?

Lecture Thirty-Three—Transcript
Ruling and Defending Carthage's Empire

As we've seen, the Carthaginian thalassocracy was the product of commerce, and commerce shaped both Carthage's own government and the administration of her empire. For the first two centuries of her existence, Carthage was ruled by governors sent out each year from Tyre. She became independent—more or less of necessity—sometime after Tyre fell to the Babylonians in 573. We don't have any details about the Tyrian administration of Carthage during the period of direct rule. We have no idea how the annual governors were chosen. We don't know whether Carthage had some sort of municipal council or assembly that functioned alongside the governors—although on the whole it's likely that she did.

We do, of course, know that Tyre itself was a monarchy, which means that the tradition that Carthage began her independent life as a monarchy makes sense—but the tradition also claims that her government then went on to evolve along the lines of Sparta's or Rome's. We get our information from Aristotle, who had very definite ideas about the evolutionary patterns of city constitutions—ideas that might color his account of Carthage's constitutional history.

In the Aristotelian scheme of things, a city's constitution would begin as a monarchy, then evolve into an aristocracy, and finally into a democracy—with tyranny often interrupting the progress. But there's some question about whether Carthage ever actually was a monarchy. Phoenician constitutional terminology didn't translate very well into Greek or Latin, and Greco-Roman writers' ideas about Carthaginian monarchy may grow out of their confusion over the nature of Carthage's senior magistracies. Greek writers always use *basileus*, the normal Greek word for king, for the supposed kings of Carthage. Their actual Punic title is uncertain, but it was probably *milk*, a term we find once or twice on inscriptions. Roman writers often use the term "dictator."

The use of "dictator" suggests that the kings were chosen in military emergencies, like Rome's dictators were—which dovetails with Herodotus's statement that Carthage's kings were chosen for their valor. If, in fact, kings were chosen in military emergencies, they were probably subject to some sort of term limit—though it would've been longer of necessity than the six-month limit of Roman dictators. This picture of a limited kingship is supported by the fact that the king's authority was carefully circumscribed, particularly in the sphere of war. Although they had both priestly and military powers, they expressly lacked the authority to take the city to war on their own. There had to be a popular vote both authorizing the war and detailing the king's authority in conducting it.

Under the monarchy, the administration of the city itself was handled by officials called *suffetes*, which was a Latinization of *shophets* (or "judges"). We know very little about the *suffetes* of the monarchical era. There appear to have been multiple *suffetes* at any given time—at least two, but maybe several. We don't know how long they typically held office. We don't know how they were chosen. In addition, there were city managers who handled the technical details of running the city: things like revenues and accounting, street maintenance, market regulation and upkeep of public buildings, as well as maintaining law and order.

Monarchical Carthage also had a council, which probably consisted of the heads of the leading families and clans. Its main role would have been advisory, consulting with the king on military and diplomatic matters. It also would have supervised the municipal administration, and it probably played a central role in selecting new kings. During the 4th century B.C., the monarchical model seems to have been discredited by Carthage's disappointments in its wars with the Sicilian Greeks—and that brought the monarchy to an end. Although Carthage held her own against Syracuse and the other Greek communities, misfortunes—like repeated outbreaks of plague among her armies—robbed her of victory. Like other ancient peoples, the Carthaginians would have understood plagues as divine in origin—and may well have seen the ones that broke out when the armies were on the verge of triumph as divine punishment of the kings who led them.

The last known king came in the mid-4th century B.C., Hanno the Great. He was not a Magonid, and he's painted as a would-be tyrant. Hanno was filthy rich—even by Carthaginian standards, which is saying something. He appealed to the popular clubs and to the native Libyans for political support against the aristocracy, some of whom he accused of having tried to poison him during a banquet. An ardent nationalist, he had a leading noble condemned to death for advocating diplomacy with Syracuse, and even had the teaching of Greek outlawed—but when he asserted his own absolute power and tried to suppress the magistrates, he fell to a popular revolution. He was executed by torture, and the monarchy died with him. The post-monarchical constitution had three main branches: the magistrates, the council, and the people. They served both to counterbalance and support one another.

Executive authority lay with the magistrates—called the *suffetes*. In post-monarchical Carthage there were two of them. They were elected for one-year terms on the basis of both a wealth and a birth requirement. They presided over the Senate, and in all civil matters their authority was superior. The main limitation on that authority was that they were barred from exercising command over the army. In emergencies, military authority was bestowed on generals. At any given time, there might be several of these generals in the field. But we never hear of any one man exercising supreme command over all of the armies.

As in other aristocracies and oligarchies, the real focus of power lay in the council. Roman writers call it the "Senate"; Greek ones call it the *gerousia*. The council consisted of several hundred members— said to be distinguished on account of their age, birth, wealth, and experience. They served for life. The council was both a deliberative and a legislative body. It served as the main venue for public debate. It heard complaints, received ambassadors, and declared war. Within the Senate, there were subcommittees consisting of five members— responsible for particular legislative activities and for vetting appointments. If the council's vote was unanimous, there was no appeal from its decision—but when the vote was divided, issues were referred to the people. Being jealous of its authority, the council usually avoided this course.

A supervisory body of 104 council members formed a separate Council of Judges. This body was designed to counter excessive aristocratic power and at the same time to suppress any rebellion against the established order. It oversaw the actions of the generals and the *suffetes*. The Judges seem to have wielded near-despotic power. The effectiveness of their oversight is probably why Carthage never fell under a tyranny. The popular assembly was the most broadly representative body in Carthage. Normally, it was only consulted in the event of an irreconcilable disagreement within the council. The assembly was an elected body, but it isn't clear how its members were chosen. Slaves, foreigners, and those below a certain income level are known to have been excluded from voting. Over time, the assembly became more assertive, hinting at a slow evolution towards democracy—but then it became divided into factions and cabals, which crippled its ability to expand its role in government.

Carthage was the first city-state to create an empire, and her empire was more successful than that of any other city-state, besides Rome. The Carthaginian Empire was both long-lived and unwarlike. It lasted 300 years—from the mid-6th century to the late 3rd. Athens's empire, by contrast, lasted barely more than 50. After she cemented her control over the Phoenician settlements of the western Mediterranean, Carthage showed no interest in further expansion. The main focus of her imperial policy seems to have been maintaining her dominance of western Mediterranean trade, rather than expanding that dominance into other areas. She maintained her trading monopolies by the simple expedient of sinking any foreign ships that ventured inside her commercial territory. Apparently this wasn't regarded by other states as a warlike act. They evidently had treaties with Carthage that recognized her monopolies—and their ship captains intruded at their own risk.

The Carthaginians took a laissez-faire attitude towards imperial rule. For the most part, all that Carthage asked of its subject communities was political loyalty and the regular payment of tribute. Local matters were left in local hands. But loyalty meant Carthaginian control over her subjects' foreign affairs. This included their trade relations as well since, after all, her empire was a commercial one. The subject communities were grouped into several different categories, reflecting their different levels of civilization and the varying ways in which they had become subject to Carthage. The most favored were the Phoenician colonial settlements in Spain and the Carthaginians' own colonies in north Africa (the so-called "Libyphoenicians"); their relations with Carthage were presumably governed by mutual treaties. The evidence from Malta and Gadir indicates that some of these old Phoenician colonial settlements had local institutions and officials similar to those of Carthage, but it isn't clear whether Carthage imposed those institutions or not.

Polybius says that the Libyphoenicians had the same laws as the Carthaginians, which could either mean that they had the same civil rights or that they had the same organs of government. Carthage exacted customs duties at these towns, and some at least also paid direct taxes. Once in awhile, Carthage levied troops from the

Libyphoenician communities, and now and then they provided crews for warships. The condition of the subject communities in western Sicily was less privileged than that of the Libyphoenicians and the Phoenicians of Spain, but still relatively favorable. They were left to live according to their own laws and institutions. Carthage regulated their economic relations less tightly than she did most of her possessions elsewhere. Their close proximity to the Greek communities on the island made tight control both more difficult and more injurious to trade.

During the 5th century B.C., they were given the privilege of issuing coins, probably out of recognition of their close proximity to—and need to trade with—neighboring Greek communities. In consequence, these communities' coins were strongly modeled on Greek coins, with only modest Phoenician elements. The tribute paid by the Sicilian towns is unknown, and most modern estimates are extrapolated from subsequent Roman practice—which required a tenth of the produce. Some of the towns were garrisoned by Carthaginian troops—but more for their own defense against sudden attacks than for the purpose of forcing them to remain under Carthaginian rule. The Libyan natives who lived in Carthage's Tunisian hinterland were more intensively exploited than any of the rest of her imperial subjects.

Carthage divided the Tunisian territories into districts under governors whom she appointed directly. According to Polybius, who is scarcely a sympathetic source, Carthage encouraged the governors to oppress their Libyan subjects. He says that she honored and admired not those governors who treated them with justice and humanity, but rather those who extorted the most tribute from their subjects and treated them most ruthlessly. He claims that during the exigencies of the First Punic War, the Libyans were forced to pay tribute amounting to half of their produce. He says that the Libyans joined the mercenaries' revolt after the First Punic War because their hatred of Carthage was so deep.

The central weakness of Carthage's administration of its possessions was that it failed to foster any sense of shared belonging and identity among its non-Phoenician subjects. In other words, it made no effort to "Punicize" them. This failure was particularly apparent among the Tunisian Libyans. Admittedly, Punicizing the Libyans would have been a daunting task given the disparity in cultural levels and outlook between Carthage and the native population. Still, it looks as though Carthage bore a real prejudice against the Libyans. She exploited them both economically and militarily, and she made little or no effort to encourage development of Libyan culture and the Libyan economy. Carthage seems to have been mostly interested in using the native population as a breadbasket—extracting the maximum amount of foodstuffs out of their farms and villages—to support the commercial population of the privileged city itself. This failure to foster shared identity and common loyalty left Carthage vulnerable when defeat finally called her authority into question.

The army with which Carthage defended her authority was a mercenary force, but it was well-balanced and thoroughly professional—a multi-ethnic army that was highly flexible, able to employ a variety of weapons and tactics. The Carthaginian army had originally been a citizen levy like the armies of most other city-states, but she turned to mercenaries during the late 6th century B.C., when the empire was born and began to expand. Her population was too small to meet all of the merchant, naval, and military manpower demands of a growing empire. It's unlikely that that population topped 200,000 in the 5th century B.C. So, it was more practical and expedient to use state revenues to hire an army than it was to withdraw scarce citizen manpower from commercial activity to fill the army's ranks.

By the end of the 4th century, citizen units had all but vanished from the Carthaginian army. Small contingents still participated in expeditions to Sicily in the 5th and 4th centuries, but their last recorded appearance in a Carthaginian army outside of Africa was in 311. The Carthaginians did organize an elite citizen force called the "Sacred Band," perhaps modeled on that of Thebes in Greece. Approximately 3,000 in number and trained to fight as Greek hoplites, we first hear of this unit in 339. It was also used as an officer training pool, where Carthage gave its prospective commanders battle experience and the experience of comradeship.

Although it was expedient given Carthage's scanty citizen manpower resources, the use of mercenaries carried with it some real disadvantages. In order to keep costs down, Carthage kept relatively few mercenaries under arms on a permanent basis. This meant that mercenary armies were usually recruited for specific campaigns, and that meant that Carthage lacked the ability to react swiftly to threats. It typically took a year for her to hire troops and organize them into an army before she could mount a campaign in response to an attack. Furthermore, Carthage was careful not to use mercenaries in the vicinity of their own homelands, and that complicated both recruitment and deployment. Finally, since her mercenaries spoke a lot of different languages and dialects of languages, command and control on the battlefield was a very complicated matter—not just between Carthaginian commanders and the armies they led, but between the units within those armies, which came from very different areas and cultures. To Carthage's credit, though, her commanders kept their polyglot armies well in hand—maybe this was because discipline was so severe. Capital punishment was a normal punishment for infractions.

Carthage recruited her mercenaries from a wide spectrum of western Mediterranean peoples. The Libyans made up the largest contingent in the army. In the 4th century, Libyan communities may have been required to provide troops in addition to their other tribute. But by the 3rd century, Libyans show up as mercenaries—so perhaps by this time the Carthaginians were extracting cash tribute from their Libyan subjects in lieu of troops, and then using the money to recruit and pay volunteers from those same communities. The Libyans were particularly valuable as light infantry because the Carthaginians felt that Libyans could tolerate the sun's heat better than other peoples, and because their native style of fighting consisted of light infantry-style ambushes and hit-and-run attacks. But Libyans could be used as frontline heavy infantry as well and turned out to be very effective in that role during Hannibal's invasion of Italy.

Mauretanian and Numidian mercenary cavalry were particularly important in the Carthaginian army. The Numidians were light cavalry: nimble, bold, and impetuous—equipped with spears and javelins, lightly clad, riding without benefit of either saddle or bridle. They could fight with equal ease on flat land or in hill country, and it was said that they maneuvered like flocks of starlings—wheeling and turning as if by instinct. Hannibal had over 6,000 of them in the army he led to Italy, and he suffered his only defeat, at Zama, when they were no longer available. Spanish mercenaries served in Carthage's army from 480 down to the Second Punic War.

During the period of Punic dominance in Spain, from 237 down to 210, they were compulsorily enrolled—but then paid as mercenaries. Most of them were Iberians or Celtiberians from the hill tribes of the interior. These peoples had no social unit larger than the clan, which resulted in constant clan warfare that turned them into excellent military material. They were temperamental, though, which made them hard to discipline and meant that they gave their loyalty to their particular commander rather than to Carthage itself. The heavy infantry recruited from the Iberian tribes of interior Spain used a large, oblong shield—like the Roman *scutum*—which covered their otherwise lightly protected bodies. Their main weapon was either a curved, single-edged sword with a two-foot blade called a *falcata*, excellent for cut-and-thrust fighting at close quarters; or a straight, double-edged sword with a two-and-a-half-foot blade, which became the model for the Roman legionary *gladius*.

Carthage's heavy cavalry came mostly from Spain, too. Almost as mobile as the Numidians because of their weaponry, they were usually employed as heavy cavalry. Their primary weapon was a long lance with an iron head a foot-and-a-half in length. They also carried the *falcata* sword as a sidearm—together with a small, round shield for protection. Men from the Balearic Islands served as mercenary slingers. Famous for their savage way of life, rumor had it that the Balearic islanders were paid in women rather than gold. They were organized in a corps of 2,000—armed with two types of sling: one for long-range engagements with close-packed infantry formations; the other for close-quarter use against individual targets. They were trained to whirl their slings once about their heads and then release the slug inside and were able to hit a man-sized target 200 hundred yards away—better than a smoothbore musket could do 2,000 years later.

Gauls first appear in Carthaginian service in 340, but they were most common in Hannibal's Italian campaign. They wore little, if any, armor—and sometimes no clothing at all. For protection, they relied on a large shield. Their main weapon was a javelin similar to the Roman *pilum* and a sword with a blade about two-and-a-half-feet long. They were famed for the impetuosity of their attacks and were organized in small companies under their own chieftains. Although they were employed as heavy infantry, they preferred individual combat to fighting in formation. Their individual style and impetuosity meant they could be unreliable, especially when hard pressed. But in the hands of Hannibal, they were solid and true.

In the 4th century, Carthage also used Campanian mercenaries from Italy. Employed as heavy infantry, they had a terrible reputation for treachery and barbarism—but like the Normans of the 11th and 12th centuries A.D., their effectiveness in combat was out of all proportion to their small numbers. In addition, Carthage also recruited Greek mercenaries, probably from the Sicilian *poleis*, who fought as hoplites in their customary phalanx. Modeled on Macedonian usage, the 4th-century phalanx would've been a formation of 256 files—each 16 men deep—yielding a body of 4,000 infantry. The men would've been equipped with metal helmet, and greaves, and a linen cuirass—plated with metal for the men in the front ranks. Each would've carried a shield about 2 feet in diameter. Their weapons were a pike 16 to 23 feet long and a short sword. The use of mercenaries doesn't seem to have caused Carthage many problems. Mercenaries made up in experience for what they lacked in patriotism, and battlefield desertions were rare. The only major problem was the mercenary revolt after the First Punic War, and that came about because Carthage hadn't been able to pay their salaries.

Chariots were used down to the end of the 4th century. Although the numbers are probably inflated, Diodorus Siculus says that in 345 the Carthaginians could deploy 300 four-horse chariots and 2,000 two-horse chariots. But the Carthaginians seem to have abandoned the chariot altogether by the time of their first war with Rome. The elephant corps for which the Carthaginian army is famous was actually a minor element. Carthage originally used the now-extinct African forest elephants that during the 3rd century still lived in the foothills of the Atlas Mountains in the coastal country of northern Africa. African forest elephants were smallish creatures, though—too small to carry a tower on their backs. Their main value was psychological: They struck terror into any troops and horses that weren't accustomed to them. But it's possible that Hannibal acquired some of the larger and heavier Indian elephants from the Ptolemies. The drawback to elephants was that they were prone to terror themselves—when they panicked and stampeded, they often caused more damage to friendly troops than they did to enemies.

The army's senior commanders were almost always native Carthaginians. Generals were drawn from families with long military traditions, such as the Magonids, and wielded considerable political power. The Barcas were another great military clan who made themselves into nearly independent powers in Spain, carving out an empire that was as much theirs as Carthage's. Greek generals were also employed by Carthage, usually with great success. The most prominent example is the Spartan Xanthippus, whose generalship saved the Carthaginians from defeat when the Romans landed in north Africa during the First Punic War.

In contrast to the army, Carthage's navy was a citizen force. Being a mercantile state, Carthage had both a long seafaring tradition and a large seafaring element in its population. The navy consisted of three elements: warships, transports, and utility vessels. Its warships were long and slender shallow-draught vessels. They had a length-to-beam ratio of about 7-to-1. They carried two masts in addition to their oars. The central mainmast provided propulsion, while the auxiliary foremast was used for steering in crosswinds. The sails were used for normal traveling and for getting to the battle area, but they were lowered and stowed before battle was joined. Each warship had three officers, one of whom was the navigator, and a crew of about 40 charged with handling the rigging.

Warships came in three classes: *triremes*, *quadriremes*, and *quinquiremes*. As we know from our discussion of the Greco-Persian wars, *triremes* had three banks of oars arranged vertically. *Quadriremes* (which were invented by Carthage) and *quinquiremes* (which were invented either in Phoenicia or Egypt) either had four and five banks of oars, respectively, or they had four or five men pulling on each oar. The debate over which it was rages among modern scholars and naval architects. The number of oarsmen varied with the size of the warship: There were about 150 for a *trireme*, 240 for a *quadrireme*, and 300 for a *quinquireme*. A *quinquireme* would have also had 120 marines, which means that a fleet of 200 ships would've carried a complement of 60,000 rowers and 24,000 troops. Slaves weren't used—except in 204 B.C. when Hasdrubal bought 5,000 slaves for use as rowers in anticipation of Scipio's final invasion of Africa. The basic tactical unit was the squadron of 12 ships, which could be grouped together into fleets of varying size—though the norm seems to have been 10 squadrons or 120 ships.

Carthaginian transport vessels were deep-hulled and broad-beamed. They had a length-to-beam ratio of about 4-to-1, and they were propelled by sails—not oars. Fleet utility vessels were smaller and were used for tasks like reconnaissance and communications. We've found the wrecks of two of them—which show that they were made of prefabricated wooden components that were later put together in a naval dockyard.

Naval battles mainly took place in coastal waters—where calmer seas made handling the slender shallow-draught warships easier. There were two basic battle tactics, in both of which the fleet was deployed initially in line-ahead formation—but that were adapted subsequently according to the enemy's dispositions. If there was enough space, the Carthaginian ships would maneuver alongside the enemy's vessels—then turn suddenly and ram them, Greek-style. If there wasn't enough space, the Carthaginian ships would maneuver through gaps in the enemy's line and then turn sharply to take them from the rear. In the meantime, the small utility vessels maneuvered near the battle scene to assist damaged vessels or to take captured enemy vessels in tow.

Carthage rarely fielded all of her fleet at once. Much of it was kept in reserve for fiscal and commercial reasons. Carthage apparently liked to keep a 200-ship active fleet, to which more ships could be quickly added if necessary. In our sources, the typical strengths of Carthaginian war fleets at sea range either side of 200. Carthage constructed a large, circular harbor that served as a navy yard—with sheds for about 190 *quinquiremes*. Maintenance and repair could be carried out there, and ships could also be laid up there in reserve when they weren't in use. A major problem for the cost-conscious Carthaginians was that it was expensive to pay the large crews needed for the warships when they weren't needed for active campaigning. Keeping them tied up in naval service also made them unavailable for service in the merchant fleet—and Carthage was always worried about the bottom line.

Carthage's government and the structure of her mercenary army and citizen navy all reflected the commercial nature of her life and empire, but they were inadequate to the challenge posed by Rome. Her political and military institutions were very similar to those of her Greek neighbors. Aristocratic and oligarchic constitutions were common in the Hellenistic world. Mercenary combined-arms armies were also the Hellenistic norm. Their multi-ethnic composition mirrored the armies of Philip and Alexander and permitted the employment of a variety of weapons and tactics on the battlefield—which gave their commanders flexibility. Mercenary recruitment reduced the burden on the subject peoples of Hellenistic cities and kingdoms. But if Carthage's political and military institutions were inadequate to the task of halting Rome, it must be said in her defense that nobody's political and military institutions proved adequate to that task. After the collapse of Carthage's empire, the Greek states of the eastern Mediterranean fell before the Roman advance like dominoes. Macedon was defeated in a series of four wars and was absorbed as a province by the Romans in 148. The city-states of Greece became a Roman province in 146, when Rome also annexed Africa. The great empire of the Seleucids was humiliated in a brief war in the 190s and never challenged Rome again. So let's not fault Carthage for her failure. She was merely the first victim of what became the Roman Empire.

Lecture Thirty-Four
The First War with Rome

Scope:

At the beginning of the early 3rd century B.C., Carthage was the sole great power in the western Mediterranean, but by 270, a second great power had emerged as Rome established its control over the Italian peninsula. There was only room for one great power in the confines of the western Mediterranean, and a confrontation between Carthage and Rome soon developed, sparked by Carthage's conflict with the Greeks of Sicily. Carthage and Rome both possessed important advantages, Rome on land and Carthage at sea. The First Punic War tested those advantages. Rome adapted to naval warfare and devised novel tactics that enabled it to best the more experienced Carthaginians at sea, though it suffered terrible losses to storms. Ultimately, the Carthaginians were able to stymie the Romans on land in Sicily. After more than 20 years of warfare, the two concluded a peace that cost Carthage its possessions in Sicily.

Outline

I. Carthage's confrontation with Rome was the outgrowth of a centuries-long struggle with the Greek city of Syracuse over dominance in Sicily.

   A. Arriving on the scene soon after the Phoenicians, the Greeks established hundreds of colonies in the western Mediterranean during their great colonial expansion in the 8th, 7th, and 6th centuries B.C. The area the Greeks colonized most intensively was southern Italy and Sicily, to which the Romans gave the name Magna Graecia, or Greater Greece.

   B. By arriving first, the Phoenicians managed to frustrate further Greek colonization in some areas.

   C. The first open conflict between Carthage and the Sicilian Greeks broke out the early 5th century. It culminated in 480 at the Battle of Himera.

      1. The generation of Greek tyrants who seized power in Sicily in the early 5th century posed a direct threat to the Punic position on the island.

> **2.** Carthage saw Xerxes' assault on Greece in 480 as a chance to neutralize the Greek threat to western Sicily.
>
> **3.** The Battle of Himera was a crushing military defeat for Carthage, but it did not do much to alter the strategic situation on the island.

D. For 70 years after Himera, there were little more than skirmishes between the two sides. Then, in the late 5th century, the Carthaginians resumed the offensive and were finally able to neutralize the power of Syracuse.

> **1.** Hostilities began when Carthage became embroiled in the intercity strife that broke out following Athens's disastrous attempt to crush Syracuse during the Peloponnesian War.
>
> **2.** Initial victories held out the hope that Carthage might be able to conquer all of Sicily, and for a time its prospects looked bright, until bad luck, in the form of a plague, struck its army and navy.
>
> **3.** Victorious but crippled by disease, Carthage dictated terms to Syracuse, terms that isolated and neutralized it but that it had no choice but to accept.

E. Syracuse struck back at Carthage in the early 4th century, but without much effect on the balance of power.

F. After the wars in the early 4th century, there were no more major conflicts on Sicily between Carthage and the Greeks, though occasional flare-ups continued down through the 4th century.

II. Despite local challenges from the Greeks in Sicily, from the late 6th to the early 3rd century. Carthage remained the preeminent power in the western Mediterranean. But then a new power arose to challenge that preeminence: Rome.

A. The ultimate origin of the Punic wars lies in the geopolitics of the western Mediterranean.

> **1.** By the early 3rd century, Carthage's thalassocracy encompassed all the islands of the western Mediterranean and most of the coastal areas.
>
> **2.** But during the late 4th and early 3rd centuries, the city of Rome suddenly vaulted to control over the Italian peninsula, which elevated it to great power status too.

3. The geopolitical problem caused by the rise of Rome was that in the confined space of the western Mediterranean, there was not enough room for two great powers to exist side by side. Sooner or later, conflict was inevitable.

B. Carthage and Rome each brought advantages to their confrontation.

1. Carthage had the advantage of its dominance at sea and the professionalism of its navy and its mercenary army.
2. Rome had the advantage of immense manpower resources. In simple terms, Roman soldiers were expendable, Carthaginian soldiers were not.

III. The clash between Carthage and Rome began very soon after Rome cemented its authority over southern Italy. A minor incident sparked the first of what would ultimately be three wars between the two powers. This First Punic War lasted 23 years, from 264 to 241, but it failed to resolve the basic geopolitical issue.

A. The immediate cause of the First Punic War was an internal dispute in the northeast Sicilian town of Messana (the modern Messina).

B. The first two years of fighting centered around Roman efforts to establish control over eastern and central Sicily. It seesawed back and forth.

C. In 261, Rome figured out that to defeat Carthage, it needed to build a navy. This shifted the main arena in the fighting to the sea.

D. Frustrated with the stalemate in Sicily, in 256 the Romans decided to take the war to Africa, so they sent an army into Tunisia.

1. This led to a climactic naval battle at Ecnomus, when the Carthaginians intercepted the Roman invasion fleet off the southern coast of Sicily.
2. The Roman fleet sailed on and landed the troops south of Carthage, where they ravaged the countryside and settled in for the winter. But the Carthaginians called in foreign talent to help them repel the Roman invasion.

3. A Roman fleet of 210 ships was sent to Africa. It crushed the 200-ship Carthaginian fleet that stood in its way and rescued the remnant of the army in Africa, but on the voyage back to Italy, it was wrecked by a storm, losing hundreds of warships and transports and as many as 100,000 men.

4. Although a disaster to the Romans, the invasion of North Africa sparked widespread rebellions in Tunisia against the now-weakened Carthage, which Carthage suppressed once the Romans left.

E. Following Rome's withdrawal from North Africa, the action shifted back to Sicily, where the fighting was savage but again inconclusive.

F. In 247, Carthage appointed Hamilcar Barca to command in Sicily. Under his leadership, the Carthaginians took the initiative. Hamilcar established a fortified base near Panormus and used it to prosecute a mobile war of harassment against Rome in Sicily.

G. The war finally ended after 23 years, when both parties had exhausted their resources.

H. The terms of the peace represented a defeat for Carthage but did nothing to resolve the underlying geopolitical cause of the war.

Suggested Reading:

Bagnall, *The Punic Wars*.

Caven, *The Punic Wars*.

Goldsworthy, *The Fall of Carthage*.

Questions to Consider:

1. Do you find the geopolitical interpretation of the underlying cause of the wars between Carthage and Rome persuasive? Why or why not? What role do you think geography plays in the relations between countries, and especially in conflicts?

2. "Rome won the First Punic War because Rome was able to innovate and Carthage was not." Do you agree or disagree with this statement? What role does national psychology (for want of a better term) play in conferring advantages on nations?

Lecture Thirty-Four—Transcript
The First War with Rome

Carthage's confrontation with Rome grew out of her centuries-long struggle with the Greek city of Syracuse over dominance in Sicily. Arriving on the scene not long after the Phoenicians, the Greeks established hundreds of colonies in the western Mediterranean during their great colonial expansion in the 8th, 7th, and 6th centuries B.C. The area the Greeks colonized most intensively was southern Italy and Sicily, to which the Romans gave the name *Magna Graecia* (or "Greater Greece"). The Greeks came in search of the mineral wealth of central Italy, the same way the Phoenicians had come to southern Iberia. The first Greek colonies were founded at Ischae and Cumae on the west-central coast of Italy in the early 8th century. Next, they established colonies on the Straits of Messina, between the northeastern tip of Sicily and the toe of Italy, to secure the shipping routes between central Italy and Greece. These were the settlements of Rhegium and Zancle, founded in the late 8th century. The name of Zancle was later changed to Messana, the modern Messina, from which the Straits take their name. With the Straits under their control, between the late 8th century and the early 6th century, the Greeks colonized the eastern and southern coasts of Sicily. Thucydides said that they encountered and expelled small settlements of Phoenicians from these areas. Syracuse, which became the greatest of all the Greek colonies in Sicily, was founded by Corinth around 730.

One of the last areas that Greek colonists penetrated was the western Mediterranean. Massalia, or Marseilles, was founded by Phocaea around 600. Ampurias on the Catalonian coast of Spain was set up soon afterwards in the early 6th century. The farthest limit reached by Greek settlement in the west was at Hemeroskopeion, at the southern end of the Gulf of Valencia. By arriving first, the Phoenicians managed to frustrate further Greek colonization in some areas. It was the Phoenician presence that blocked further Greek expansion down the east coast of Spain. Acting as the defender of the Phoenicians in western Sicily, Carthage barred Greek attempts to expand into that part of the island—and set up colonies of her own there to cement her hold. The first open conflict between Carthage and the Sicilian Greeks broke out in the early 5th century B.C. It culminated in 480 in the Battle of Himera.

The generation of Greek tyrants who seized power in Sicily in the early 5th century threatened the Punic position on the island. The most important tyrants were Gelon of Syracuse and Theron of Agrigentum, who seized control of Himera in 483—expelling Carthage's ally, Terillos. Gelon was a thug who made Syracuse into the most populous city in Sicily by forcibly resettling it with half the population of his native city of Gela—as well as all the people of Camarina and the upper classes of the Sicilian cities of Megara and Euboea. He then sold the lower classes of the latter two cities into slavery overseas to raise money for his armament programs. Carthage saw Xerxes's assault on Greece in 480 as a chance to neutralize the Greek threat to western Sicily. The massive Persian invasion tied down the resources of the mainland Greeks and made it impossible for them to send aid to their brethren in Sicily. So, Carthage dispatched an expeditionary force to the island under the command of a general named Hamilcar, with the aim of restoring Terillos and neutralizing the tyrants' threat. There may even be some truth to the rumors that the expedition was coordinated with Xerxes.

According to legend, the Carthaginian force consisted of 200 warships, 3,000 transports, and 300,000 men assembled from Africa, Spain, Sardinia, Corsica, Gaul, and Liguria. Hamilcar sailed from Carthage with about 50,000 infantry and 5,000 cavalry—to which he added levies from Carthage's Sicilian allies that raised his army to about 100,000 men all told. Gelon had created an army of 20,000 hoplites—with additional 2,000-man brigades of heavy cavalry, light cavalry, archers, and slingers, as well as a division of 10,000 mercenaries. His cavalry was particularly high quality, composed of aristocrats mounted on specially bred horses. Presumably, Gelon had his entire army present, as well as levies from his own allies. Hamilcar landed at Panormus and marched to Himera, where he camped outside the city—beaching his fleet and fortifying both its anchorage and the camp he built for his army outside the town. The Battle of Himera was a crushing defeat for Carthage, but it didn't do much to alter the strategic situation on the island.

During the pre-battle maneuvering, Gelon exploited his great superiority in cavalry to round up Hamilcar's foraging parties and impose a blockade on the Carthaginians. Then, he got lucky. His cavalry intercepted a Carthaginian message summoning cavalry aid from Selinus. Gelon sent his own cavalry to pretend to be the Selinan horsemen. The Carthaginians unwittingly admitted them to the stockade—once inside they burned the ships, and in the confusion Hamilcar was killed. The fighting was bitter and prolonged. The Carthaginians were driven back into a last strongpoint, where lack of water finally compelled them to surrender at nightfall. Their entire army had been wiped out, either killed or captured. Diodorus claims that Hamilcar's defeat was so complete that only a single ship with a few fugitives made it back to Carthage. According to the Greeks—who were famous for their love of symmetries, whether real or imagined—the Battle of Himera took place on the same day as Salamis. Still, Gelon gave Carthage generous terms: They had to pay an indemnity of only 2,000 talents and underwrite the construction of two temples, in which the terms of the treaty were engraved.

For 70 years after Himera, there were little more than skirmishes between the two sides. Then, in the late 5th century, the Carthaginians resumed the offensive and were finally able to neutralize Syracuse's power. Hostilities began when Carthage became embroiled in the inter-city strife that followed Athens's disastrous attempt to crush Syracuse during the Peloponnesian War. In 409—during a war with Selinus, which was now Syracuse's ally—Segesta asked Carthage for aid. Carthage mustered an army of citizen troops—Libyans, and European mercenaries—under the command of Hamilcar's grandson, Hannibal. Hannibal took Selinus by assault and massacred its population. He then outwitted a Syracusan force sent to confront him and took Himera, where he avenged his grandfather's death by first torturing, then executing, 3,000 prisoners—after which he returned triumphant to Carthage, leaving mercenaries behind to garrison Carthage's much-expanded holdings on the island. These initial victories held out the hope that Carthage might be able to conquer all of Sicily. For a time, her prospects looked bright until bad luck, in the form of a plague, struck her army and navy.

Recruiting in Spain, the Balearic Islands, and Campania in central Italy, Carthage raised a mercenary army that allegedly numbered over 100,000 men and sent them to Sicily under Hannibal and Himilco. They attacked the number-two Greek city in Sicily—Acragas—but the garrison there, commanded by the Spartan mercenary captain Dexippus, held off the assault. A plague then struck the besieging Carthaginian army, killing Hannibal. A Syracusan relief force arrived, but soon evacuated the city, after which the Carthaginians took the place and massacred the population. The Carthaginians then laid siege to Gela. The tyrant of

Syracuse, Dionysius I, sent a relief force to Gela—but it was defeated, and Gela was evacuated. Sicily seemed within Carthage's grasp, but the plague got worse and worse—raging through the Carthaginian army until half the troops were dead. Victorious but crippled by disease, Carthage dictated terms to Syracuse—terms that isolated and neutralized her, but which Dionysius had no choice but to accept. She ceded possession of western Sicily to Carthage. Leontini, Messana, and the native Sicel communities were to be autonomous. Selinus, Acragas, Gela, and Camarina on the south coast were to be demilitarized tributaries of Carthage, as was Himera on the north coast. The Syracusans struck back at Carthage in the early 4th century, but without much effect on the balance of power.

Stung by defeat, Dionysius undertook an ambitious and innovative rearmament program. He built a mercenary force of 20,000 specialist troops, supplemented by levies from the population. His engineers invented the catapult, a large mechanically strung bow with a range of 200 yards, as well as numerous types of siege engines. Some sources claim that his shipwrights, rather than those of Egypt or Phoenicia, invented the *quinquireme*—with five men on each oar. In any case, Dionysius built a fleet of 200 of them.

In 398, once he had rearmed, Dionysius renewed the war. He sent Carthage an ultimatum demanding that it evacuate all Greek cities in Sicily. Carthage rejected the ultimatum and began to muster its own mercenary forces, but the time lag involved in doing so enabled Dionysius to strike. The Greek cities rose up in support of Syracuse, and he marched into Carthage's territory in western Sicily at the head of an army of more than 80,000 men and a fleet of 200 warships. Despite his overwhelming strength, Dionysius failed to take any of the Carthaginian cities in the west, but he did lay siege to the island settlement of Motya.

Himilco came to its relief, but although he was able to cripple Dionysius's supply ships, he wasn't able to defeat his navy. As Alexander would later do at Tyre, Dionysius built a mole (or causeway) from the mainland to the island on which Motya lay—and while his battering rams went to work on its walls, his new catapults swept the defenders from the parapets. The walls were breached, but the defenders fought back in vicious street-fighting, block by block, from rooftops and down barricaded alleyways—until finally the Greeks overwhelmed them by sheer weight of numbers. Dionysius tried in vain to prevent the massacre that followed. The few survivors were sold into slavery. In 397, Carthage counterattacked—driving Dionysius back to Syracuse, but the siege of Syracuse failed. Himilco retook Motya and won the native Sicels over to his side. He then advanced along the north coast while his fleet sailed east to take Messana. Dionysius was deserted by everyone but his mercenaries. The Carthaginian fleet—under Mago—crushed the Syracusan fleet, and Himilco laid siege to Syracuse itself. But plague, again, struck the Carthaginians—and Dionysius, with reinforcements from Sparta, broke the siege, inflicting severe defeats on both the Carthaginian fleet and army. Himilco withdrew to Carthaginian territory in the west. In 393, the Carthaginians attacked again, but once more met with frustration. Mago landed and raised an army of Sicels with which he advanced on the eastern part of the island. He was beaten, but advanced again in 392. That campaign was inconclusive, but a peace was finally arranged between the exhausted parties that established a neutral zone between the eastern part of the island, dominated by Syracuse, and Carthage's territory in the west.

After the wars in the early 4th century, there were no more major conflicts in Sicily between Carthage and the Greeks—though occasional flare-ups continued down through the 4th century. The most noteworthy was Carthage's failed intervention in a Syracusan civil war in 343 and 342. One of the rival contestants for the tyranny in Syracuse summoned Carthaginian aid—and the Punic fleet sailed into, and occupied, the Grand Harbor at Syracuse on his behalf, but soon had to return to western Sicily. The next year, the Carthaginians sent an army of 80,000 mercenaries and citizen troops to Sicily, but it was defeated by the Syracusans in the Battle of the Crimisus River and nearly annihilated when a violent storm broke in the Carthaginians' faces during the fighting. A treaty between Syracuse and Carthage in 341 once more confirmed the division of the island between them.

Throughout these conflicts with the Greeks in Sicily from the late 6th to the early 3rd century B.C., Carthage had remained the preeminent power in the western Mediterranean. But then a new power arose to challenge her preeminence: Rome. The ultimate origin of the wars between Carthage and Rome lies in the geopolitics of the western Mediterranean. By the early 3rd century, Carthage's thalassocracy encompassed all the islands of the western Mediterranean and most of the coastal areas: western Sicily, Sardinia and Corsica, the Balearic

Islands, the southern coast of Spain, the coast of northwest and north Africa from the Atlantic Ocean to Libya—all were under Carthage's control. But during the late 4th and early 3rd centuries, the city of Rome had suddenly vaulted to control over the Italian peninsula—which elevated her to great power status, too. Founded in the mid-8th century B.C., for several centuries Rome was little more than a hamlet on the hills above the marshy south bank of the Tiber River.

During the 6th century, while Carthage was building her empire, Rome was dominated by Etruscan clans. Casting off Etruscan rule at the end of the 6th century, Rome remained a local power until the end of the 4th century—when the Romans defeated their neighbors the Samnites and won control over central Italy. Then, during the first three decades of the 3rd century, Rome conquered the Greek cities of southern Italy and defeated their would-be rescuer—Pyrrhus, King of Epirus—and advanced its frontier to the northern Apennines, making itself master of nearly all of the Italian peninsula.

The geopolitical problem caused by the rise of Rome was that in the confined space of the western Mediterranean, there wasn't enough room for two great powers to exist side-by-side. Conflict was all but inevitable. The cramped geography of the western Mediterranean was exacerbated by the fact that, because the eastern coast of Italy is mountainous and lacks good harbors, Italy is oriented more toward the western Mediterranean than toward the Adriatic and the Balkans. The likeliest flash point between a great power on the southern and western shores of the Mediterranean and one on the Italian peninsula was the islands of the region—and especially Sicily, which bridges the narrows of the central Mediterranean. Carthage and Rome each brought advantages to their confrontation. Carthage had the advantage of her dominance at sea and the professionalism of her navy and her mercenary army. Control of the sea gave the Carthaginians strategic mobility. Her navy was large and manned by highly skilled and dedicated citizens. Her mercenary army, though relatively small, consisted of seasoned professionals who possessed a wide array of military skills. Rome had the advantage of immense manpower resources. Though the population of Roman Italy may have been no more than several million, Rome used conscription—the draft—to fill the ranks of her legions. This meant that although man-for-man, Roman troops might not be the equal of Carthaginian mercenaries, there were a lot of Roman troops. So, Rome could field several armies at once—and she could afford to lose them, too, because she could draft hundreds of thousands more men and put them into new armies. In simple terms: Roman soldiers were expendable; Carthaginian soldiers were not.

The clash between Carthage and Rome began very soon after Rome cemented her authority over southern Italy. A minor incident sparked the first of what would ultimately be three wars between the two powers. This First Punic War lasted 23 years, from 264 to 241 B.C., but it failed to resolve the basic geopolitical issue. The immediate cause of the war was an internal dispute in the town of Messana, the old Zancle. As we've just seen, Messana occupies a very strategic location because it controls the Straits of Messina, between the northeast tip of Sicily and the toe of the Italian peninsula. The Straits were especially important because Carthage controlled the coasts of the Mediterranean narrows and all the commerce that passed through them—making the Straits of Messina important to Rome and her Greek subjects and allies because they were the only route by which sea traffic could move east and west free of Carthaginian oversight.

The Mamertines, a mercenary band from Campania in central Italy, had seized control of Messana in 289 and begun plundering northeast Sicily. In 265, the tyrant of Syracuse, Hieron II, defeated them. The Mamertines then appealed to both Carthage and to Rome for aid. Recognizing the strategic importance of Messana and seeing an opportunity, both Carthage and Rome responded to the Mamertines' plea. For Carthage, this held out the prospect of gaining a foothold at the most strategic point in all of eastern Sicily. But Rome saw the threat in that, and the result was a confrontation—and then the outbreak of war. Carthage's aid came by sea, so it arrived first. The Carthaginians installed a small garrison in Messana. The Mamertines may not have expected this, though it's difficult to believe they didn't realize how much merchant powers like Carthage disapprove of pirates like the Mamertines. So the Mamertines soon came down with buyer's remorse about accepting Carthage's help and drove the Carthaginians out—as a result of which, when the Romans arrived, they were welcomed with open arms. There had been a lot of debate in the Roman Senate about the morality of aiding a bunch of piratical thugs like the Mamertines and the possibility of a confrontation with Carthage. But the Romans' concerns over allowing Carthage to control the Straits and establish a foothold adjacent to the Italian mainland won out, and the issue was referred to one of the popular assemblies for a vote—where the appeal of the distinguished Senator

Appius Claudius Caudex carried the day, and aid was dispatched to Messana under Caudex's command.

Faced with Roman intervention on the island—for the first time in their history, Carthage and Syracuse allied and laid siege to Messana. But Carthage and the Syracuse failed to coordinate their attacks, so the Romans were able to survive intact. Thus, began the First Punic War, on which the future of the ancient world hinged. Its first casualty was the Carthaginian commander, Hanno, who was crucified for getting run out of Messana and then getting beaten by Rome. The first two years of fighting centered around Roman efforts to establish control over eastern and central Sicily. It seesawed back and forth. The Romans sent an army of 40,000 men to Sicily in 263, commanded by both of Rome's senior magistrates—the consuls. They besieged Syracuse, which surrendered when they offered it generous terms. Supposedly, 67 other towns then quickly submitted, too. Next, in 262, the Romans besieged the main Carthaginian base at Acragas. A Carthaginian relief effort failed, and the city fell. Carthage sent out a force of 50,000 men and 50 elephants to lift the siege, but this was the first time they'd used elephants in battle—so their attack was poorly coordinated, and the Romans were able to defeat it. This was one of Rome's few successful sieges. The Romans lacked experience and equipment for taking cities swiftly and couldn't afford to sit and starve them out. The Romans treated Acragas brutally, sacking it and enslaving the inhabitants. But this turned out to be counterproductive because it stiffened resistance and alienated many of Rome's Sicilian supporters.

In 261, Rome realized that in order to defeat Carthage, she needed to build a navy. This shifted the main arena of the fighting to the sea. Rome lacked shipbuilding expertise and expertise at naval warfare because she had never had a fleet before. The story is that the Romans found a Carthaginian *quinquireme* stranded on a beach, dismantled it, and reverse-engineered a *quinquireme* of their own. They seem to have done this on their own, rather than relying on their Greek subjects in southern Italy, who had miniscule fleets and evidently none of the advanced *quinquiremes*. To overcome Carthage's superior naval tactical skill, the Romans introduced a tactical innovation: the *corvus*, a boarding grapple. The idea was to grasp Carthaginian ships, immobilizing them and pulling them alongside Roman ones so that Roman marines could board.

The *corvus* was erected at the bow of a ship. It consisted of a round 24-foot pole, with a pulley at the top through which ran a rope attached to the top of a 36-foot-long, 4-foot-wide gangway that leaned out from the base of the pole. The gangway could swivel to starboard or port and had a long, heavy iron spike at the far end. When dropped on the deck of a nearby ship, it held the ship in place and allowed marines to swarm over onto its decks. In other words, the *corvus* turned a sea battle that Carthage could win into a land battle that Rome could win. In 260, using the *corvus*, the Romans won the Battle of Mylae—off the north coast of Sicily. Confident of their superiority and unaware of the *corvus*, 130 Carthaginian *quinquiremes* under an admiral named Hannibal rashly attacked a Roman squadron of 145 ships under the consul Gaius Duilius; half of the Carthaginian ships were either sunk or captured.

Meanwhile, back on land, Carthage dispatched an army to Sicily under a new commander, Hamilcar—who defeated the Romans at Thermae, but then got penned up in the western part of the island. Stalemate ensued for several years. Carthage used Corsica and Sardinia as bases from which to raid the Italian coast. Roman efforts to neutralize the islands bore little fruit. Frustrated with the stalemate in Sicily—in 256, the Romans decided to take the war to Africa, so they sent an army to Tunisia. This led to a climactic naval battle at Ecnomus, when the Carthaginians intercepted the Roman invasion fleet off the south coast of Sicily. With 360 warships on each side, Ecnomus was one of the largest sea battles in antiquity. The Romans arranged their fleet in four squadrons, with their troop transports protected behind the warships. The Carthaginians also arranged their ships in four squadrons and relied on their superior naval skills. They feigned flight before the Romans—then turned back suddenly to attack.

At first, the Romans were taken by surprise—but they rallied, and the fighting became general. The Romans eventually won. Each side lost about 25 to 30 ships sunk, but thanks to the use of the *corvus*, the Carthaginians lost more than 60 ships captured—which the Romans repaired and added to their fleet. The Roman fleet sailed on and landed the troops south of Carthage, where they ravaged the countryside and settled in for the winter. But the Carthaginians called in foreign talent to help them repel the Roman invasion. The Roman force numbered about 15,000 men. It seized 20,000 slaves in the region outside Carthage and defeated a Carthaginian force sent against it—so the defenders retreated within their walls. Then, the Romans recalled their fleet to Italy because of supply shortages, leaving the army in Africa. Carthage brought in a Spartan general, Xanthippus, with a small force of Greek mercenaries as reinforcements.

Xanthippus proved that it was bad generalship, not poor troops, that had cost Carthage victories before—because at Bagradas in 255, he crushed the Romans in battle. He recruited citizen troops, reorganized the Carthaginian army in Macedonian-style phalanxes, and restored their morale. He placed 100 elephants in the center of his line, with his phalanxes behind the line and light troops and cavalry on the flanks. The elephants trampled the Romans facing them, while the Carthaginian cavalry drove the Roman horse from the field. Only 2,000 Romans survived the battle. A Roman fleet of 210 ships under the two consuls for the year was sent to Africa to rescue the survivors. It crushed the 200-ship Carthaginian fleet that stood in its way and rescued the remnant of the army in Africa—but on the voyage back to Italy, it was wrecked by a storm, losing hundreds of warships and transports and as many as 100,000 men. The losses were due in part to amateur Roman seamanship, but they were also due to the *corvus*, which made the ships top-heavy and dangerously unstable in rough seas. Although a disaster to the Romans, the invasion of north Africa sparked widespread rebellions in Tunisia against the now-weakened Carthage, which Carthage suppressed once the Romans left.

Following Rome's withdrawal from north Africa, the action shifted back to Sicily—where the fighting was savage, but again inconclusive. In 254, the Romans captured the Carthaginian town of Panormus and brutally slaughtered the inhabitants. The Carthaginians regained the initiative in Sicily under Hasdrubal, but he was defeated by the Romans when he tried to lift the siege of Panormus and was recalled and impaled. After Hasdrubal's defeat, Rome laid siege to the main Carthaginian base in Sicily—Lilybaeum, but because of a lack of experience and equipment, the siege dragged on unsuccessfully for years. Repeated weather-caused naval disasters finally led Rome to abandon the *corvus*, but this gave the advantage back to the Carthaginian navy. The *corvus* was probably eliminated after the loss of 150 ships to a storm in 253. Even Rome couldn't sustain continuous losses on this scale. Roman naval construction lost momentum, and she replaced only half of the lost ships. Following Rome's abandonment of the *corvus*—in 249, the Carthaginians were able to inflict a disastrous defeat on the Roman navy at Drepana during the siege of Lilybaeum.

The Roman fleet of 120 ships had taken a beached Carthaginian squadron by surprise, but swift reaction and superior seamanship enabled the Punic ships to turn the tide, costing Rome 93 vessels. Poor Roman seamanship remained a mortal threat to Roman fleets, and shortly after Drepana, Rome lost another fleet of 120 warships and 800 transports to a storm as they were coming to the aid of the force besieging Lilybaeum. This effectively wiped out the Roman navy. But distracted by problems closer to home with the Libyan tribes of Tunisia, Carthage was unable to exploit her naval advantage. In 247, Carthage appointed Hamilcar Barca to command in Sicily. Under his leadership, the Carthaginians took the initiative. Hamilcar established a fortified base near Panormus and used it to prosecute a mobile war of harassment against Rome and Sicily. He also launched numerous raids on the Italian coast. Most of them were focused on Lucania and Bruttium in southern Italy—but he also struck coastal towns as far north as Cumae, prompting Rome to establish defensive colonies along the coastline.

The war finally ended in 241, after 23 years, when both parties had exhausted their resources. Thanks to the Roman census, we have statistics for the effect of the war on Rome's male citizen population: During the 20 years after 264 it fell 17 percent. She was bleeding herself white. Rome raised a last fleet, with great difficulty, and defeated Carthage's last fleet, raised with equal difficulty, at the Aegates Islands in 241. Financially drained, Carthage instructed Hamilcar to negotiate peace. The terms of the peace represented a defeat for Carthage, but did nothing to resolve the underlying geopolitical cause of the war. Carthage evacuated Sicily. Carthage agreed to pay Rome an indemnity, or reparations, of 3,200 talents over the course of 10 years. The war had ended as a nominal victory for Rome—but with Carthage still powerful and her empire shaken but largely intact. But since Rome was now stronger, it was inevitable that the issue would be joined again—and with Rome's organization of Sicily as her first overseas province, the Roman Empire was now born.

Lecture Thirty-Five
Hannibal and the Fall of Carthage

Scope:

After the First Punic War, Carthage lost Sardinia and Corsica to Rome, thanks to a rebellion among its mercenary troops on the islands. In compensation, the Barca family led an aggressive expansion of Carthage's empire in Spain. The ultimate origins of the Second Punic War lay in the unresolved geopolitical issues that had caused the first, but the immediate causes were Roman claims that Carthage was impinging on its interests in Spain. Anticipating war, the brilliant Hannibal Barca led a Carthaginian army overland to Italy and inflicted a series of annihilating defeats on the Roman armies sent against him. Simultaneously, the Romans sent armies to Spain to destroy Carthage's empire there. Ultimately, the Romans were able to isolate and neutralize Hannibal in southern Italy and to drive the Carthaginians from Spain. Hannibal returned to Carthage when the Romans landed in North Africa and was defeated decisively at Zama. In the peace, Carthage was forced to surrender its empire.

Outline

I. After the First Punic War, Carthage's empire teetered on the brink of collapse.

    A. A massive rebellion erupted in 241 B.C. and lasted for four exhausting years, the so-called Truceless War.

    B. Rome capitalized on the Truceless War to seize control of Sardinia and Corsica, which it then organized as another province of its new empire.

    C. The Truceless War and Rome's seizure of Sardinia and Corsica produced a shakeup in Carthage's oligarchy and a restructuring of its empire.

        1. Hamilcar Barca's faction ousted the peace party led by Hanno and began rebuilding Carthage's strength in anticipation of a new war with Rome.

        2. The centerpiece of the Barcid program was the expansion of Carthage's territories in Spain.

3. Accompanied by his young son, Hannibal, and his son-in-law, Hasdrubal, Hamilcar conquered southern and southeastern Spain before his death in 229.

4. He was succeeded in command by his son-in-law, Hasdrubal, who expanded Carthage's territory north along the Spanish coast.

5. Rome was concerned about Carthaginian expansion in Spain but was unable to do anything because of an invasion of Italy by Gallic tribes from the north. Instead, the Romans came to an agreement with Hasdrubal by which he agreed not to advance beyond the Ebro River.

6. Then, in 221, Hasdrubal was assassinated. The Carthaginian army in Spain held an election and chose the 25-year-old Hannibal to succeed him in command.

II. The Second Punic War was a very different proposition from the first one, thanks to the brilliant generalship of Hannibal Barca. The war earned him military immortality and nearly destroyed Rome, but in the end it was Carthage's empire that lay in ruins.

A. The underlying cause of the Second Punic War was still the geopolitics of the western Mediterranean.

B. The immediate cause was a dispute over the Spanish coastal town of Saguntum.

C. Each side intended to target the other's military and economic resources.
1. The Roman plan was to conquer Carthaginian Spain and deprive Carthage of its resources.
2. Hannibal's plan was to invade Italy, force Rome to fight on its own soil, and break up the alliance system that bound the communities of Italy to Rome.

D. Both sides moved quickly, and their armies passed one another in transit to their destinations.

E. Once he was in Italy, Hannibal immediately displayed his genius as a commander and dramatically reversed Carthage's history of defeat at the hands of Roman armies.
1. His first battle was a victory over Roman cavalry at the Ticinus River near Pavia in November 218.
2. Then, in late December, Hannibal crushed the combined forces of both Roman consuls at the Trebia River.

3. Hannibal spent the winter in northern Italy, then in the spring of 217 marched south, crossed the Apennine Mountains, stole past a Roman army guarding the way, and ravaged Etruria. There, Hannibal met and destroyed another Roman army at Lake Trasimene.

4. After Trasimene, the Romans appointed a dictator, Q. Fabius Maximus, who swiftly raised an army of four legions and pursued Hannibal but was careful not to meet him in battle.

F. Hannibal's greatest triumph, and Rome's greatest defeat, came in 216 at the Battle of Cannae.

1. Hannibal had marched to southern Italy, where most of Rome's allied communities were located.

2. The two Roman consuls raised four new legions to join the four legions that had served under Fabius Maximus. Their army heavily outnumbered Hannibal's.

3. The armies arrived near the town of Cannae and faced each other for several days, until looming supply shortages finally forced them into action.

4. The Romans' battlefield dispositions were flawed. In contrast, Hannibal deployed his army so as to maximize its tactical flexibility.

5. The battle proceeded almost exactly as Hannibal planned. The result, a masterpiece of battlefield tactics, was the annihilation of the largest army Rome had ever put in the field.

G. But strategic failures robbed Carthage of victory.

1. The flaw in Hannibal's crushing success at Cannae was that he failed to go on to take Rome itself, which would have ended the war.

2. He also failed to seize any major port, which could have opened up supply lines to Africa.

3. Instead, Rome retained command of the sea and could supply besieged ports with impunity.

H. Gradually, Carthage's hopes of victory dimmed as Rome defeated its allies and slowly reestablished control over Italy and its empire.

I. Meanwhile, the Carthaginians fought to hold off the Romans in Spain.

J. Back in Italy, Hannibal found himself first frustrated, then isolated. The Carthaginians tried to send reinforcements to Hannibal, but the Romans intercepted and destroyed them.

K. The war's final campaign took place in Tunisia.

    1. Sailing from Sicily, Scipio landed a Roman army in Africa in 204.

    2. A peace faction of landowners and merchants in Carthage overthrew the Barcid party and asked Scipio for terms. He granted them.

    3. But Hannibal then returned from Italy with his troops and reinvigorated the war party, which undermined the peace.

    4. Late in 202, in Zama, Hannibal and Scipio finally met in battle. With two great generals facing one another, the result was a slugging match, which the Romans finally won.

    5. On Hannibal's advice, Carthage again sued for terms, which this time were much less generous.

    6. After Zama, Hannibal remained active in public life at Carthage for several years, but internal politics forced him into exile, and he committed suicide in 183.

III. After the destruction of its empire, Carthage prospered as a commercial city-state, but the fact that its treaty with Rome barred it from even defending itself eventually led to its destruction. The final act came in the Third Punic War.

A. The Numidians had capitalized on Carthage's defenselessness by encroaching on its remaining territory.

B. Carthage pleaded with Rome to defend it, or to allow it to defend itself, but the Senate turned a deaf ear.

C. Finally, in desperation, Carthage violated its peace with Rome and raised an army, which the Numidians destroyed. In response, Rome sent an army to Tunisia.

D. Carthage agreed to unconditional surrender, but when the consul commanding the Roman army ordered them to abandon the site of the city and move 10 miles inland, wrecking them as a commercial power, they resolved to fight.

E. Finally, Scipio Aemilianus took the city in seven days of fierce house-to-house combat. The city was completely demolished, and the entire population was sold into slavery.

IV. The fall of Carthage's empire had a simple cause: military defeat.

   A. There were no signs of internal rot in the empire prior to the Punic Wars.

   B. Carthage's one weakness was its military. Carthage never succeeded in creating an army equal to the armies of its enemies.

Suggested Reading:

Bagnall, *The Punic Wars.*

Caven, *The Punic Wars.*

Goldsworthy, *The Fall of Carthage.*

Questions to Consider:

1. Given that his army was the same as previous Carthaginian armies and that Roman armies had not changed either, what advantages did Hannibal have over the Romans that enabled him to defeat them on the battlefield, where previous Carthaginian generals had consistently suffered defeats?

2. What might Hannibal have done differently to turn his tactical success on the battlefield into strategic success by defeating Rome decisively in Italy?

3. What enabled Rome finally to defeat Carthage?

Lecture Thirty-Five—Transcript
Hannibal and the Fall of Carthage

After the First Punic War, Carthage's empire teetered on the brink of collapse. A massive rebellion erupted in 241 and lasted for four exhausting years, the so-called "Truceless War." The rebellion began among frustrated mercenaries at the end of the war with Rome. Carthage was nearly bankrupt by the war's end, so their pay was deeply in arrears. To make matters worse, when troops were sent to Sardinia to put down the revolt, they joined the rebels—then crucified their Carthaginian officers and tortured and murdered all the Carthaginians on the island. Then, the subject cities on the African coast began joining the revolt. They'd been hit hard by taxes to cover the endless expenses of maintaining and rebuilding the fleet and army after all of Carthage's defeats. The native peoples of Libya saw their opportunity—and they rose up against Carthage, too. But Carthage's reaction was swift and decisive.

Hamilcar Barca joined with his political rival, Hanno, to crush the Libyans and the rebel mercenaries in a campaign that was marked by atrocities on both sides. The rebel cities in north Africa then wisely gave in without a fight—except for Utica and Hippo, which were taken after short sieges and lost their privileges. Rome capitalized on the Truceless War to seize control of Sardinia and Corsica, which she then organized as another province of her new empire. Rome had initially stood aloof—but saw her chance and seized control of the islands when the mercenaries were driven out by the natives and appealed to Rome for aid. Rome had no legal justification for taking the islands—Carthage had been guaranteed possession of them in the peace treaty. So what this did was convince the Carthaginians that despite the peace, Rome remained hostile towards Carthage. The Truceless War and Rome's seizure of Sardinia and Corsica produced a shakeup in Carthage's oligarchy and a restructuring of her empire. Hamilcar Barca's faction ousted the Peace Party, led by Hanno, and began rebuilding Carthage's strength in anticipation of a new war with Rome.

The centerpiece of the Barcid program was the expansion of Carthage's territories in Spain. Spain was rich in silver, which could quickly restore Carthage's wealth. Spain was also a fertile source of mercenary manpower. So accompanied by his young son, Hannibal, and his son-in-law, Hasdrubal, Hamilcar conquered the southern and southeastern parts of Spain before his death in 229. Hannibal himself told the story that before leaving for Spain, his father made him swear an oath never to be a friend of Rome. When the Romans sent an embassy to Spain to investigate, Hamilcar told them that he was conquering Spain so that he could get money to pay off the indemnity that Carthage owed to Rome under the peace treaty. But then, lured by a false promise of aid from a treacherous Spanish chieftain, Hamilcar was ambushed and then drowned while riding to safety across a river. He was succeeded in command by his son-in-law, Hasdrubal, who expanded Carthage's territory north along the Spanish coast. He also founded a city to serve as the capital of Carthage's expanded province: Carthago Nova (the new Carthage, the modern Cartagena).

Rome was concerned about Carthaginian expansion in Spain, but unable to do anything about it because of an invasion of Italy by Gallic tribes from the north. Instead, the Romans came to an agreement with Hasdrubal by which he guaranteed that he would not advance beyond the Ebro River. The Romans don't seem to have regarded this treaty as constraining their activities south of the river. The Carthaginians saw matters differently. Then, in 221, Hasdrubal was murdered by a Gallic slave in revenge for the execution of his master. The Carthaginian army in Spain held an election and chose the 25-year-old Hannibal to succeed him in command. The assembly in Carthage retroactively approved the army's choice. Hannibal immediately proved himself to be an outstanding commander, crushing rebellions among the Spanish tribes and expanding Carthage's territory deep into the interior of the peninsula.

The Second Punic War was a very different proposition from the first one, thanks to the brilliant generalship of Hannibal Barca. The war earned him military immortality and nearly destroyed Rome—but in the end, it was Carthage's empire that lay in ruins. The underlying cause of the Second Punic War was still the geopolitics of the western Mediterranean. Since Rome had now created an empire of her own, the western Mediterranean was even more crowded than it had been in 264. The events following the First Punic War—like Rome's seizure of Sardinia and Corsica, and Carthage's expansion in Spain—had only exacerbated Rome and Carthage's mutual suspicions. The immediate cause of the Second Punic War was a dispute over the Spanish coastal town of Saguntum. Saguntum had clashed with Spanish tribesmen who were Carthaginian allies.

Hannibal came to the tribesmen's defense. Saguntum appealed to Rome. Rome sent an embassy to Hannibal to protest his intervention. Saguntum lay more than 100 miles south of the Ebro River, well within what Carthage regarded as its sphere of influence.

So, backed by the government of Carthage, in 219, Hannibal laid siege to Saguntum—which fell after eight months—and so the war began. Each side intended to target the other's military and economic resources. The Roman plan was to conquer Carthaginian Spain and deprive Carthage of its minerals and manpower. Hannibal's plan was to invade Italy, force Rome to fight on its own soil, and break up the alliance system that bound the communities of Italy to Rome. Those allies provided Rome with about half of its manpower and almost all of its naval expertise. Both sides moved quickly, and their armies passed one another in transit to their destinations.

Leaving his brothers, Hasdrubal and Mago, in command in Spain, Hannibal set out from Carthago Nova in May of 218 with a large army—conquering the area between the Ebro and the Pyrenees during the summer. The army numbered 90,000 infantry, 12,000 cavalry, and 37 elephants, but he left 40,000 infantry and 3,000 cavalry behind with Hasdrubal. Marching through southern Gaul, Hannibal had to fight hostile Gauls, but avoided combat with the Roman army marching to Spain under the consul Publius Cornelius Scipio. Arriving at the Alps, Hannibal's army crossed the mountains in a harrowing 15-day ordeal. The pass that Hannibal used is still hotly debated. The two best possibilities are the steep, 9,000-foot-high Col de la Traversette—or the nearly equally inhospitable Col du Clapier. Tens of thousands of Carthaginian soldiers died during the passage due to accidents, weather, and attacks by Alpine tribesmen. When Hannibal finally arrived in northern Italy in mid-October, less than half of the army remained—a mere 26,000 men and seven of the elephants.

Once he was in Italy, Hannibal immediately displayed his genius as a commander and dramatically reversed Carthage's history of defeat at the hands of Roman armies. His first battle was a victory over Roman cavalry at the Ticinus River near Pavia in November of 218. Then, in late December, Hannibal crushed the combined forces of both Roman consuls, Scipio and Tiberius Sempronius Longus, at the Trebia. He had been reinforced by Gallic mercenaries, bringing his army to a strength of about 40,000—roughly equal to that of the Romans. The Romans got cocky after winning a skirmish between two foraging parties. Hannibal used his Numidian cavalry to tire out the Roman horse and lure the aggressive-minded Longus into crossing the Trebia—where the Roman deployed his 36,000 infantry and 4,000 cavalry with the river at their backs.

Hannibal had 29,000 infantry and 11,000 cavalry, When the Roman legions advanced toward him, he used his superiority in cavalry to sweep the Roman horse from the field—exposing the infantry's flanks. Then Hannibal turned his cavalry, his light troops, and his elephants loose on the Romans' flanks at the same time that 2,000 picked troops under his brother, Mago, sprang from ambush and attacked the Romans from the left rear. The Romans' flanks disintegrated, and the fugitives were pinned against the river and annihilated—but the Roman center was able to break through the Punic line, and 10,000 of them escaped to safety within the walls of nearby Placentia (the modern city of Piacenza). There are no figures given by our sources for either side's losses, but Roman losses must have been close to 50 percent.

Hannibal spent the winter in northern Italy—then in the spring of 217, marched south, crossed the Apennine Mountains, stole past a Roman army guarding the way, and ravaged Etruria north of Rome. There—on June 21, 217—Hannibal met and destroyed another Roman army at Lake Trasimene. This battle was basically a giant ambush. Hannibal had increased his army to some 60,000 men; the Roman consul Gaius Flaminius had only 25,000. Flaminius had expected Hannibal to attack Rome itself and failed to intercept Hannibal as he passed through Etruria. He now set off in pursuit, without waiting for reinforcements to join him under his fellow consul, Gnaeus Servilius Geminus.

Taking advantage of Flaminius's rash advance, Hannibal lured the incautious Romans onto a road that ran along the north shore of the lake, with high wooded ground above it. Hannibal posted his Spanish and Libyan infantry in the open on a ridge ahead of the Roman army, where Flaminius could see them. The trap was baited. Meanwhile, his Balearic slingers and light infantry were hidden on the reverse slopes of the hills above the lakeshore road—with the cavalry concealed near the entrance to the ambush site to seal off the Roman escape route. Flaminius advanced from his camp at dawn and took the bait Hannibal put before him. When the bulk of the Roman force had entered the ambush, Hannibal sprang the trap. Confused by enemies attacking out of the woods in the early morning mist, the Romans were slaughtered on the shore of the lake—15,000 of them were killed, including Flaminius; nearly 10,000 more were taken prisoner. Hannibal lost about 2,000 men. He tried to find Flaminius's corpse to give it an honorable burial, but the bodies had been looted of their armor and equipment, and it couldn't be identified. Meanwhile, rushing to join Flaminius, 4,000 of Geminus's cavalry were intercepted by Hannibal's Numidian horse. They crushed the Romans, killing or capturing all of them.

After Trasimene, the Romans appointed a dictator, Quintus Fabius Maximus, who swiftly raised an army of four legions and pursued Hannibal—but was careful not to meet him in battle. His strategy—known ever since as the "Fabian strategy"—involved staying just out of Hannibal's reach while the Carthaginians marched south. This curtailed Hannibal's freedom of movement and restricted his ability to live off the land by making it dangerous to send out small detachments to forage. At the end of his six-month term, Fabius stepped down as dictator, and regular government resumed. The Fabian strategy would eventually prove decisive, but first the advocates of direct confrontation with Hannibal would have one more try.

Hannibal's greatest triumph—and Rome's greatest defeat—came in 216 at the Battle of Cannae. Hannibal had marched to southern Italy, where most of Rome's allied communities were located. The two consuls for 216, Marcus Terrentius Varro and Lucius Aemilius Paullus, raised four new legions to join the four legions that had served under Fabius Maximus. Their army heavily outnumbered Hannibal's. The combined strength of the Roman forces was about 80,000 infantry and 6,000 cavalry. Hannibal had about half the infantry of the Romans, but nearly twice as much cavalry—10,000 of superior quality. The armies arrived near the town of Cannae in the eastern coastal plain and faced each other for several days, until looming supply shortages finally forced them into action. The Romans' battlefield dispositions were flawed. Varro and Paullus placed their cavalry on the flanks—with eight legions in the center, and the light troops in front. The presence of the river Aufidus on the right flank limited the mobility of the Romans' right-flank cavalry. The infantry were cramped—turning the open formation of their legions into a dense mass and robbing them of the flexibility that gave their army its tactical superiority. In contrast, Hannibal deployed his army so as to maximize its tactical flexibility. He placed his cavalry on the flanks, facing the Roman horse. He thinned out his center, which consisted of Spanish and Gallic infantry, screened by light forces. This gave his center room to bend, if needed, under Roman assault. He positioned himself there, in personal command at the most vulnerable spot. He positioned combat-hardened Libyan infantry on either side of his center—drawn up in deep formation, giving his flanks great strength.

The plan was that his center would slowly yield and draw the densely packed Roman infantry forward—while his cavalry chased off the Roman horse and the Libyan infantry pressed the Romans' flanks back. Finally, the cavalry would wheel around and strike the Roman infantry from the rear. In other words, Hannibal planned to carry out a double envelopment of a numerically superior force—a tactical tour de force almost unimaginable in its audacity, and almost never again repeated in all the history of warfare. The battle proceeded almost exactly as Hannibal planned. The Romans attacked, and Hannibal's center slowly fell back, drawing them inward—while his flanks either held or pressed forward, overlapping the Romans' flanks, then turned against the Romans in the center. Meanwhile, his cavalry routed the weaker Roman horse and, having driven them from the field, turned and fell on the Roman infantry's rear—completing their encirclement. The trapped Romans were so densely packed that they lost all formation, were unable to maneuver, and could no longer respond to commands. Still, they fought back fiercely, and the slaughter went on for hours— Hannibal's troops rotating in and out of the melee to rest.

According to Polybius, 70,000 Romans were killed, 10,000 were taken prisoner, and only 3,500—mostly cavalry—escaped. The largest army Rome had ever put in the field was all but annihilated, but they sold their lives dearly. Hannibal lost one-eighth of his men, more than 6,000—an impossibly high figure for a victorious army in antiquity. Victory now seemed within Carthage's grasp. War fever swept the city. Allies flocked to her side. Philip V of Macedon allied himself with Carthage. Hieronymus of Syracuse came over to Carthage's side, and an anti-Roman rebellion broke out in Sardinia— but strategic failures robbed Carthage of victory.

The flaw in Hannibal's crushing success at Cannae was that he failed to go on to take Rome itself, which would've ended the war. Instead of marching immediately on the city, he remained in southern Italy—pursuing his goal of breaking up Rome's alliance system. Many of the south Italian allies did defect, but the ones in central and northern Italy remained loyal. Now he found that he had to defend the Italian cities that had gone over to him against Roman counterattack, which robbed him of his freedom to maneuver. Hannibal also failed to seize any major port, which would have opened up his supply lines to Africa. Instead, Rome retained command of the sea and could supply besieged ports with impunity. Carthage had never rebuilt her fleet after the First Punic War. Carthage frittered away her resources in peripheral campaigns instead of concentrating all of them in support of Hannibal.

In 215, 13,500 men with elephants and ships intended for Hannibal were sent instead to Spain; another 13,500 were sent to Sardinia in 215 in a doomed bid to regain the island. In 213, 28,000 men with elephants were dispatched to Sicily. Gradually, Carthage's hopes of winning the war dimmed as Rome defeated her allies and slowly reestablished control over Italy and her empire. Philip V was beaten, and the Adriatic coast was secured. In 214, the Carthaginians were driven from Sardinia. In 212, the Romans defeated the Carthaginian army in Sicily and recaptured Syracuse—then, in 210, finally drove the Carthaginians from the island entirely. Meanwhile, the Carthaginians fought to hold off the Romans in Spain.

In 217, Rome sent an army to Spain under the brothers Gnaeus and Publius Cornelius Scipio. The Romans hoped that if the Scipios couldn't conquer Spain, at least they would be able to prevent the dispatch of reinforcements from Spain to Hannibal—and divert support from Carthage to Hannibal. The Scipios swiftly defeated a Carthaginian force under Hanno in northern Spain. At Ibera near the Ebro in 215, Hasdrubal attempted to repeat Cannae against the Scipios, but his center broke, and his army was destroyed—enabling the Romans to recover Saguntum. This was what prompted Carthage to divert the reinforcements intended for Hannibal. But the Scipios couldn't exploit their success because they were short of reinforcements due to the losses that Rome was suffering in Italy at Hannibal's hands. In 211, Carthage recovered the initiative when Mago and Hasdrubal Gisgo managed to destroy the Roman army and kill both Scipios at Amtorgis in the Tader Valley. But in 210, Publius Cornelius Scipio's young son and namesake, Publius Cornelius Scipio, was given extraordinary pro-consular powers by the Roman

Senate and quickly restored Rome's fortunes. In 209, following a forced march from the Ebro, he captured Carthago Nova by a daring ruse and then won over the tribes of the interior. In 208, he defeated Hasdrubal at Baecula in southern Spain—after which Hasdrubal left Spain for Italy, taking the remainder of his troops. In 206, he defeated Mago at Ilipa, north of Seville. Mago failed in an attempt to retake Gadir and Carthago Nova, abandoned Spain to Scipio, tried to retake the Balearic Islands, but failed in that as well—and finally sailed off to Italy himself.

Meanwhile, back in Italy, Hannibal found himself first frustrated, then isolated. The Romans could put multiple armies into the field, while Hannibal had only one—so they avoided battle with Hannibal and slowly retook whatever areas he wasn't occupying. This put Hannibal on the defensive, unable to protect even the most important cities that had come over to his side. Despite marching on Rome itself in 211, Hannibal couldn't break the Roman siege of Capua—which was the most important city to defect to him. In punishment for its disloyalty, Rome executed Capua's leaders and stripped it of its territory and its rights.

The Carthaginians tried to send reinforcements to Hannibal, but the Romans intercepted and destroyed them. In 207, Hasdrubal attempted to march overland from Spain to reinforce Hannibal, but his army was brought to bay and crushed on the Metaurus River in Umbria. In 205, Mago landed in northern Italy with 14,000 men—but accomplished nothing and was finally defeated in 203. Little by little, Hannibal was forced into smaller and smaller parts of Italy—at first Bruttium and Lucania; then, by 207, just Bruttium itself; finally, by 203, just the vicinity of the port of Croton. Finally, after 15 years in Italy, Hannibal was recalled to north Africa and managed to extricate both himself and his troops. The war's final campaign took place in Tunisia. Sailing from Sicily, Scipio landed a Roman army in Africa in 204. He failed to take Utica, but defeated a Carthaginian force sent to oppose him, and began ravaging the agricultural lands that fed the city.

A peace faction of landowners and merchants in Carthage overthrew the Barcid party and asked Scipio for terms. He granted them: All Roman POWs and deserters were to be handed over; a large indemnity was to be paid; and Carthage's navy was to be reduced to only 20 warships. Realizing that the terms were generous, the

Carthaginians accepted them. But Hannibal then returned from Italy with his troops and reinvigorated the war party, who undermined the peace. They seized beached Roman ships and waylaid vessels bearing envoys from Rome. Although the Roman Senate had accepted the terms of the negotiated peace, provocative acts like these persuaded Scipio of the need to crush Carthage's spirit—and so the war resumed.

Late in 202 at Zama, 100 miles southwest of Carthage, Hannibal and Scipio finally met in battle. With two great generals facing one another, the result was a slugging match—which the Romans finally won. The armies were roughly equal in strength. Hannibal had 36,000 infantry, 4,000 cavalry, and 80 elephants. Scipio had 29,000 infantry—and for once was superior in cavalry, with 6,000 horse. Hannibal opened the battle with his elephants, but Scipio skillfully countered them. He left lanes open in his infantry formation to channel the elephants through, or else drove them out to the flanks—where they collided with, and disrupted, Hannibal's cavalry, making it easy prey for the Roman horse. When the infantry battle was joined, the Romans defeated Hannibal's first three infantry lines, but they then re-formed on his third line—which was composed of the veterans of his Italian campaign. The Roman and Carthaginian infantry then became locked in close-quarters combat. The issue was decided when the Roman cavalry returned from its pursuit of the Carthaginian horse and fell on the rear of Hannibal's infantry formation—which finally broke.

On Hannibal's advice, Carthage again sued for terms—which this time, were much less generous. It was allowed to retain its pre-war territories in Tunisia—but it had to surrender all Roman deserters and POWs, all of its warships, and all of its elephants. It had to agree to pay 10,000-talent indemnity over a 50-year period. It had to return to Masinissa—the King of the Numidians and a Roman ally—all that had in the past belonged to him or his ancestors. Most crippling of all, it was not allowed to rearm or to make war without Roman approval. After Zama, Hannibal remained active in public life at Carthage for several years—but, in 195, internal politics forced him into exile at the courts of various Greek monarchs—until finally, still hounded by the Romans, he committed suicide in 183. After the destruction of her empire, Carthage prospered as a commercial city-state, but the fact that her treaty with Rome barred her from even defending herself eventually led to her destruction.

The final act came in the Third Punic War. The Numidians had capitalized on Carthage's defenselessness by encroaching on her remaining territory. She pleaded with Rome to defend her, or to allow her to defend herself, but the Senate—dominated by a conservative faction bitterly hostile to Carthage—turned a deaf ear. That faction was led by Cato the Elder, who used to end every speech—regardless of its subject—with the words: "*Delenda est Karthago!*" ("Carthage must be destroyed!"). Finally, in desperation, in 150, Carthage violated her peace with Rome and raised an army— which the Numidians destroyed. Carthage abased itself before Rome, but Rome had already decided on war and sent troops to Tunisia. Carthage agreed to unconditional surrender, but when the consul commanding the Roman army ordered them to abandon the site of the city and move 10 miles inland—wrecking them as a commercial power—they resolved to fight. For three years, the Carthaginians defeated every Roman effort to take the city. Finally, in 146, the Romans sent out a new commander, Scipio Aemilianus, who took the city in seven days of fierce house-to-house combat. The story that the Romans sowed the site of Carthage with salt is a modern invention, but the truth is harsh enough: The city was completely demolished, and the entire population was sold into slavery.

The fall of Carthage's empire had a simple cause: military defeat. There are no signs of internal rot in the empire prior to the Punic Wars. Carthage had created a stable imperial system. There are no hints of revolt, other than the mercenary rebellion after the First Punic War. There are no hints of political instability in Carthage itself. Taxation doesn't seem to have been oppressive, except at the end of the First Punic War. The empire wasn't aggressive itself. It encompassed the Phoenician settlements of the western Mediterranean, and aside from the Libyan tribes of her own hinterland, Carthage showed no interest in adding other peoples to her empire. The empire functioned smoothly, like a business, focused on its commercial interests. Carthage's one weakness was its military. Carthage never succeeded in creating an army equal to the armies of her enemies. The Carthaginian army nearly always met defeat at the hands of the Greeks of Sicily.

Roman armies routinely defeated Carthaginian armies in the First Punic War. Only under Hannibal—one of history's great military geniuses—was a Carthaginian army consistently victorious. But why was Carthage's army so ineffective? It's tempting to blame it on the multi-ethnic and mercenary character of the army. But nothing indicates that those factors caused problems on the battlefield. There are no reports of garbled orders—and no reports of disloyalty, except when pay was in deep arrears. The troops seem to have fought effectively and tenaciously. Perhaps it was faulty tactical formations or equipment. The Carthaginians borrowed the heavy infantry phalanx from the Greeks—256 men wide and either 8 or 16 men deep, equipped with long thrusting spears—which should have been effective against Greek phalanxes in Sicily.

Carthaginian troops seem to have worn fairly light armor, and that may have put them at a disadvantage against heavily armored Greek hoplites. Furthermore, the Romans had already abandoned the phalanx and adopted a more open and flexible formation for their legions. Based on the maniple of two centuries, it enabled Roman commanders to maneuver their troops efficiently and rotate troops in and out of the front line. It's worth noting that after the Second Punic War, using the maniple-based legion, Roman commanders routinely defeated outstanding Greek commanders—like Philip V and Antiochus the Great, who were still using the phalanx.

But the problem may also have been faulty leadership. Hannibal was a brilliant commander on the battlefield. His father, Hamilcar Barca, was also capable. Xanthippus the Spartan was able to defeat Roman troops using a Carthaginian army in the First Punic War. But the rest of Carthage's commanders were failures. This suggests that Carthage's system of preparing men for military command was faulty. The Carthaginian fleet also had a disappointing record. Although manned by citizens and using cutting-edge warships, the Carthaginian fleet was only rarely able to defeat Roman fleets commanded and crewed by landlubbers. Of course, the Romans used a novel tactical device—the *corvus*—but professional Carthaginian seamen ought to have been able either to outmaneuver Roman ships trying to close and board, or figure out a tactical counter to the *corvus*. So maybe the basic flaw in the Carthaginian military was a lack of adaptability. Hannibal is said to have rearmed and restructured his army after Trasimene so as to give it the flexibility of the Roman legions. Xanthippus is said to have reorganized the Carthaginian infantry after he received command of the army in the First Punic War. But it would appear that most Carthaginian commanders were afflicted with a rigidity of mind that deterred them from seeking novel solutions to novel military problems. So we should ask ourselves: Was it lack of imagination in the end that brought down the Carthaginian Empire?

With Scipio's triumph on the field of Zama, the story of Near Eastern empire comes to a dramatic close. Within the next 200 years, the story of Greek Empire would come to a close as well. In the end, there would be but one empire—the greatest of them all: Rome.

Lecture Thirty-Six
Ancient Empires before Alexander, and After

Scope:

The two millennia between the rise of Sargon and the fall of Hannibal saw a dozen empires come and go on the stage of the ancient Near East. They were strikingly diverse in their origins, in their approach to imperial rule, in their extent, and in their longevity—a diversity that reflects their varied environments, historical circumstances, and cultures. They anticipated much that was to come in the empires of later ages. This was particularly true in imperial administration; we find Near Eastern elements both in the empires of Alexander's successors and in Rome. It is also true in military organization; the Assyrian army set the standard for the Persians, and through them for the Parthians and Sassanids, and for the heavy cavalry of Rome, which in turn inspired the armored knights of medieval Europe. But the most enduring legacy may be the idea of empire itself, which has endured and still endures to the present day.

Outline

I.   What have we learned about this grand but elusive thing called empire? Given the sheer number of them that we have explored and the span of time and space they occupied, it comes as no wonder that the first thing about these empires that grabs our attention is their diversity.

  A.   They came in all sizes. Even by modern standards, some of them were huge. But others were modest in size, even small.

  B.   Some were by land; some were by sea.

  C.   Some of these empires were created by great conquerors, while others were painstakingly assembled by generations of leaders who were often just as capable.

  D.   The motives that lay behind the creation of these empires have proven to be as diverse as the empires themselves.

  1.   In several cases the motives are pretty clear. Carthage's empire, for example, came into being because of its commercial concerns.

2. But what motivated the conquest of other empires is pretty much a mystery. For instance, we have no idea what lay behind the formation of Mitanni or Kassite Babylonia.
3. But much of the time it looks as though the driving force lay within the psyches of individual conquerors—the dream of empire.

E. These empires' forms of government were as diverse as the impulses that led to their creation. Some were tightly centralized tyrannies; others were loosely knit webs of vassals.

F. The empires had very diverse life spans, too: Some seemed to last little longer than a dusting of spring snow; others endured for centuries.

G. And finally, the ends of these empires were as diverse as everything else about them. Some were laid low by the sudden onslaught of unforeseen enemies, while others, weak and feeble, collapsed in the face of rebellion or attack.

II. As diverse as these empires were, there are common threads that link them together.

A. The Near Eastern ones had "royal ideologies," and those royal ideologies had strikingly similar features.
1. At the top of the list was the association of kingship with the qualities of a warrior.
2. In all of the royal ideologies, the king was also the guarantor of justice, and especially of social justice.
3. We have seen that religion was central to Near Eastern kingship. The royal ideologies universally espoused what we today would call "divine-right monarchy." But as we have seen, the kings were almost never regarded as gods themselves.
4. Although Near Eastern kings were not gods, royal ideologies often regarded them as superhumanly wise.
5. Finally, Near Eastern royal ideology saw the king as the great bulwark standing between order and chaos.

B. Another common thread was the instability of royal power. Violence ran through the internal politics of many of these empires like a river of blood.

C. In their political cultures, we can detect a sharp divergence between the empires centered in the great river valleys and the ones outside.

    1. The empires of Mesopotamia looked back to Sargon as their model and lavished immense resources on maintaining the cultural traditions of the past, to exhibit a degree of continuity in their political culture.

    2. Elsewhere, political authority was typically much less centralized.

  D. Regardless of their political culture, stability eluded the empires of the ancient Near East. Very few ever solved the problem of how to maintain loyalty and order among the subject peoples of their empires.

III. In their military institutions, our empires exhibit more similarity than diversity.

  A. They typically consisted of a mix of professional, full-time troops and native levies.

  B. The empires' armies were strongly conservative. They avoided innovation.

IV. We said at the beginning of the course that the empires that rose and fell across the ancient world during the 2,000 years before Alexander blazed trails that he and future conquerors would tread. So how much did the conquerors of the Greek and Roman world consciously borrow from their Near Eastern predecessors?

  A. Alexander probably borrowed more from his Near Eastern predecessors than any subsequent rulers did.

    1. He presented himself to his various subject peoples in ways that were familiar to them.

    2. He borrowed much, including ceremonial rites and administrative practices, from the Persians.

  B. When Alexander's generals carved up his empire and set themselves up as kings, they were more sparing in taking on Near Eastern elements.

  C. The Romans borrowed even less from the Near Eastern imperial past than did Alexander and the Hellenistic kings.

  D. Cultural factors may explain why the Greeks and Romans borrowed so little from the empires that went before them.

    1. First of all, the Greeks do not seem to have known very much about the ancient Near East.

2. After their victory in the Persian Wars, the Greeks formed a stereotype of corrupt "Oriental" despotism that mitigated against Hellenistic monarchs borrowing from their Near Eastern predecessors.

3. The Romans then inherited the Greeks' stereotypes about the East.

E. The main inheritors of the great imperial tradition that preceded Alexander were the empires that arose in the Near East during and after the collapse of the Hellenistic kingdoms founded by his successors.

F. What the West retained was an image of the East as alien and threatening—a source of menace and the home of despotism, not the birthplace of civilization and the cradle of empire.

V. It is time to offer a final reflection on the question we posed at the beginning of the course: Why should we study the ancient empires that came before Alexander?

A. It is not because of the impact that they had on our world as empires. The ancient Near East has given us a great deal, including civilization itself, but its great empires were all but forgotten, all the way from antiquity down to the 19th century A.D.

B. But maybe there is one thing that the empires of the ancient Near East gave us that does descend in a direct and unbroken line all the way from antiquity to the present day, even if we have forgotten where it comes from. That one thing is the dream of empire.

1. It was in the ancient Near East that this grandiose dream, which has driven so many conquerors across so many millennia, was born: the dream of a power that spans the world.

2. The dream came to Greece in the vision of Alexander, then traveled to Rome, where it found its name: *imperium*.

3. In the Middle Ages, it inspired Charlemagne, Otto, and Henry II.

4. In the modern world, empires that truly did span the world finally came into being, but while those empires have passed into history, the dream that gave them birth has not.

Suggested Reading:

Bowman, *Egypt After the Pharaohs*.

Brosius, *The Persians*.

Green, *Alexander to Actium*.

Millar, *The Roman Near East*.

Questions to Consider:

1. "The more things change, the more they stay the same." How relevant is this observation to the relationship between the empires of the ancient Near East and the ones that followed?

2. What similarities do you find between the empires of the ancient Near East and other empires with which you are familiar, whether ancient, medieval, or modern?

3. Is empire an unavoidable fact of human political life? Why or why not?

Lecture Thirty-Six—Transcript
Ancient Empires before Alexander, and After

What a long, strange trip it's been: from Sargon to Scipio, from Akkad to Zama—a dozen ancient empires, some of them famous, some of them forgotten, spread across 20 centuries in time and 5,000 miles in space. So, what have we learned about these empires during our journey? What have we learned about this grand but elusive thing called "empire" itself?

Given the sheer number of empires that we've explored and the span of time and space they've occupied, it comes as no wonder that the first thing that grabs our attention about them is their sheer diversity. They came in all sizes. Even by modern standards, some of them were huge. Persia spanned the entire Near Eastern world, from Libya to India. The empire of New Kingdom Egypt stretched 1,500 miles, from Nubia to Syria. But others were very modest in size, even small. Mitanni never included more than northern Syria and northern Mesopotamia. Minoan Crete's thalassocracy may not even have included all of the Aegean—and certainly didn't extend outside of it. Some were by land; some were by sea. Most of our pre-Alexandrian empires were landlubbers. This is only to be expected, since the Near East was bounded by seas, rather than centered on them. But the thalassocracy was invented almost 4,000 years ago by Crete and perfected 1,500 years later by Carthage—and both of their sea empires preceded the most famous one of all, that of Athens.

Some of these empires were created by great conquerors, while others were painstakingly assembled by generations of leaders who were often just as capable. The roster of great conquerors begins with the very first conqueror of all: Sargon the Great, and it goes on through Hammurabi down to Cyrus. But then recall the names of all those kings and commanders who merely collaborated in building their empires, rather than doing it all themselves, names like Suppiluliumas, Tiglath-pileser, Thutmose III, Ramesses II—and, of course, Hannibal. Perhaps we should pause a moment to reflect on the fickleness of historical memory. Who was it that conquered the sea for Crete? Who spread Carthage's authority across the shores of the western Mediterranean? We all remember the names of the heroes of Troy, but who remembers the names of the men who built the kingdoms from which they set forth in search of plunder and glory?

The motives that lay behind the creation of these empires have proven to be as diverse as the empires themselves. In several cases, those motives are pretty clear. Carthage's empire, for example, came into being because of her commercial concerns. Most of it consisted of settlements that had been founded to serve Phoenician commerce; all she did was establish her leadership over them after Phoenicia lost its independence. The shadowy Minoan thalassocracy, assuming there was one, would have also been born out of commercial concerns. The motive behind Egypt's conquest of her empire, at least in the Levant, is equally clear: It was to create a defensive glacis that would protect the Egyptian heartland in Upper and Lower Egypt against a repetition of the humiliating Hyksos invasion. But what motivated the conquest of other empires is pretty much a mystery. Maybe with Assyria it was religion: a determination to overcome the forces of chaos and bring order to the world in the service of Ashur—or maybe that was just a rationalization born out of living in a place without natural defenses and surrounded by hostile neighbors. Of course, given that we know so little about them, we have no idea what lay behind the formation of Mitanni or Kassite Babylonia—nor do we know why the Hittites, alone among the peoples of Anatolia, took it upon themselves to expand their rule beyond the confines of their homeland.

But as I suggested in the first lecture, a lot of the time it looks as though the driving force lay within the psyches of individual conquerors: that dream, the dream of empire, the longing for power, the hunger for glory, the thirst for fame. What else can we see that binds together the exclusive membership of the Conquerors' Club? Sargon, Hammurabi, Nabopolassar, David, Cyrus, even Alexander—none of them had a compelling reason to embark on their careers of conquest; they simply did it.

Our empires' forms of government were as diverse as the impulses that led to their creation. Some were tightly centralized tyrannies; others were loose-knit webs of vassals. The vassal empires have an eerily medieval quality. Hatti feels a lot like Germany in the High Middle Ages, with its king always battling restive vassals and hostile neighbors. But the centralized ones feel frighteningly modern. You get the sense that Josef Stalin would have been right at home in Third Dynasty Ur, with its central planning and *gurush* (as opposed to Gulag) labor gangs. All that's missing was the secret police. But some combined different styles of administration—like Egypt, with its tight control over Nubia, but looser rule in the Levant, even though tighter control might've kept the Levant more secure.

The empires had very diverse life spans, too. Some lasted little longer than a dusting of spring snow, historically speaking. Conquered in 10 years, Hammurabi's empire was gone in 30. How long did the Neo-Babylonian Empire endure? Two generations? Two generations is all that David's empire lasted. But others endured for centuries. Egypt's empire in Nubia and the Levant lasted more than 300 years—so did the Neo-Assyrian Empire. The all-but-forgotten Babylonian Empire of the Kassites lasted longer still, almost as long as the Roman Empire lasted in western Europe.

Finally, the ends of these empires were as diverse as everything else about them. Some were laid low by the sudden onslaught of unforeseen enemies—while others, weak and feeble, collapsed in the face of rebellion or attack. The fates of Carthage and Persia prove that in history, luck counts. Carthage's empire was as healthy as ever when, in the space of a half-dozen decades, Rome burst upon the scene and swept it away—and pity the poor Persians. Persia had endured a long period of rebellion and dynastic upheaval, but had recovered and gotten back on its feet, when suddenly there was Alexander. Now, that's bad luck. But we've also seen plenty of examples that would lead us to wonder whether some empires may have almost biological life expectancies. Hatti lost its vigor during the 13th century and collapsed like a house of cards in the upheavals at the century's end. Mycenae seems to have yielded to some violent new culture that eroded its internal stability and destabilized its civilization. Assyria overstretched its resources, exhausted itself, and finally was swept away like autumn leaves by Nabopolassar and the Medes.

But as diverse as these empires were, there are common threads that link them together. The Near Eastern ones had "royal ideologies," and those royal ideologies had strikingly similar features. At the top of the list was the association of kingship with qualities of a warrior. The king was supremely skilled with weapons. He was the finest charioteer. He was the deadliest archer. He was a cold-blooded spearman.

Please note that these are the qualities of a warrior—not of a commander. The ideal king was, in other words, more hero than general. In fact, the cool, calculating qualities of a strategist and battlefield tactician are nowhere to be found in these ideologies. But because prowess as a warrior-hero was associated with victory, the ideology of kingship, of course, portrayed the king as victorious. This was because war was seen as individual combat between nations—and since the king is the ruler of the nation, the nation's corporate conflicts are his personal combats. In all of the royal ideologies, the king was also the guarantor of justice—and especially of social justice. He was sometimes the font of law, sometimes its transmitter, but always its overseer. Everywhere, he was the supreme judge—and he was the defender of the weak and helpless against their greedy and grasping wealthy neighbors. The irony of this, of course, is that no one was more-wealthy than the king. No one made greater demands on the persons, and property, and produce of the common people than the king. No one could, or did, oppress ordinary folk more than their defender, the king. Do you suppose that irony was lost on his subjects?

We've seen that religion was central to Near Eastern kingship. The royal ideologies universally espoused what we today would call "divine right monarchy." Since the gods were believed to be sovereign over the heavens and the earth, they were believed to be the source of human sovereignty as well. So, kings held their power by the favor of the gods and were answerable for their kingship only to the gods—and that made the king the mediator between the gods and us mortals: tending the temples, leading the sacrifices, doing their will. But as we've seen, the kings were almost never regarded as gods themselves. The only certain case of divine kingship was Sargon the Great's grandson, Naram-Sin, and that was both self-declared and poorly received.

Most of the time, kings were portrayed as the human subordinates of the gods. New Kingdom pharaohs were called the "image" of the god, or the "son" of the god—which did not mean that they were gods. Likewise, the King of Israel was often called the "son of God," which didn't mean that he was a god, either. The title of early Assyrian kings was the most expressive of all. They were simply the "viceroys of Ashur."

Although Near Eastern kings were not gods, royal ideologies often regarded them as superhumanly wise. Solomon's wisdom was celebrated in the memory of David's empire. Like the old comic book superhero "The Shadow," pharaoh was able to divine men's innermost thoughts—and like Solomon, he was the epitome of wisdom, in whom the people could place their unswerving trust.

Finally, Near Eastern royal ideology saw the king as the great bulwark standing between order and chaos. This is what ties together many of the other elements of royal ideology. Deep down, everyone worries that the normalcy and order that make everyday life manageable may suddenly disintegrate into chaos—but in the violent and insecure world that was the ancient Near East, this deep-rooted anxiety had real substance. The threats from foreign armies, robbers and bandits, marauding tribesmen, wild animals, and political rebels were very real and very common. You got no warning that these things were on their way, except maybe a pillar of smoke in the sky from the village up the road as it vanished in flames. So, it was the king's duty as the gods' anointed one—their chosen deputy on earth—not just to fend off, but to destroy, these threats. So, the king is a great hunter, eradicating the beasts that threaten the flocks in the pastures and the crops in the fields. He's the defender of the realm against the enemies who would disturb its peace and threaten its order—and he's the punisher of rebels, who violate their oaths to the king and to the gods from whom he received his sovereignty. As we've seen, no one took this obligation to uphold divinely ordained order more seriously than did the kings of Assyria—who brutally punished rebels because they had violated their sacred oaths of loyalty, and by doing so imperiled the very order of the cosmos.

Another common thread was the instability of royal power. Violence runs through the internal politics of many of these empires like a river of fresh blood. It was almost a coronation ritual that rebellions would break out following the accession of a new king. Figuring that a new ruler would need time to get a firm grip on power, any of his subjects who longed for freedom were apt to figure that now was the time to go for it. Disgruntled vassal rulers would see an opportunity to negotiate better terms for themselves and made their point by not renewing their oaths of loyalty. But the reason for these rebellions also lies in the little-noticed fact that loyalty was personal in nature: Subjects and vassals were loyal to a king—not the king. When the person with whom they shared bonds of loyalty died, those bonds dissolved. This says something about Near Eastern political psychology. "Institutional consciousness" had not yet developed. People still thought very much in terms of individual persons like kings—rather than institutions and abstractions like "the throne" or "the crown."

Then, there's the matter of dynastic bloodshed. Intramural slaughter was almost as common as coronation rebellion. Though much revered in biblical memory, the House of David was notably savage in its purging of rivals—real or potential, both inside and outside the dynasty. There were also royal bloodbaths in Hatti, despite Telepinus's laws, as well as in Assyria. In Persia's 200-year history the only royal transitions that did not involve dynastic butchery or civil war were when Cambyses succeeded Cyrus and when Xerxes succeeded Darius.

In their political culture we can detect a sharp divergence between the empires centered in the great river valleys and the ones outside. The empires of Mesopotamia looked back to Sargon as their model and lavished immense resources on maintaining the cultural and political traditions of the past. Both there and in New Kingdom Egypt, political authority tended to be centralized—but elsewhere, political authority was often much less centralized. Hatti and Mitanni were basically vassal-state empires. What we can discern of the political structure of Mycenaean Greece gives a picture of almost anarchic decentralization under a titular high king. Though not a vassal empire, Persia granted her subject communities autonomy over their local political and economic affairs. Like Persia, Carthage seems to have left her Phoenician subject communities free to run their own business, too.

Regardless of their political culture, stability eluded the empires of the ancient Near East. Only a couple of them, like Carthage and the Kassites, ever solved the problem of how to maintain loyalty and order among their subject peoples. If it adopted a loose vassal system, an empire faced the prospect of rebellions—particularly when new rulers came to the throne. Vassals were tempted either to switch their allegiance to competing empires or to seek better terms for themselves. But attempting to coerce loyalty by imposing central control was expensive, and it still didn't eliminate unrest. The Assyrians progressively tightened their control over their empire, converting vassal states into provinces and punishing rebellion with infamous brutality—but rebellions persisted nonetheless. Even the widespread use of deportation wasn't enough to ensure internal peace.

If there's a great deal of diversity in the political cultures of these empires, there's a great deal of similarity in their military institutions. Their armies typically consisted of a mix of professional full-time troops and native levies. None of the empires maintained a purely citizen army—like the Greek *poleis* that defeated Xerxes or like the legions of the Roman Republic that faced Hannibal. Typically, native levies were used as a supplement to the standing army that was built around the royal guard. But none of them maintained a large, purely professional standing army either, like that of the Roman Principate. Maybe the problem was that without a monetary economy, it's very hard to pay such an army. You have to either pay them in supplies or pay them in land. Of course, the availability of money by the 5th century B.C. made it possible for Carthage to field a professional army of mercenaries, but this was never a standing army. Instead, to hold costs down, the businessmen who ran Carthage recruited a fresh army of mercenaries at each new crisis.

The empires' armies were also strongly conservative. They avoided innovation. Over the course of 2,000 years, the armor and basic arms of Near Eastern infantry changed very little. They remained lightly armored, if they were armored at all. Their basic arms remained a short spear and short sword, with a lightweight shield of something like wicker. The main innovations were the introductions of chariots (around 1800 B.C.), cavalry (about 1,000 years later), and elephants (at the beginning of the 3rd century). Their commanders also exhibited little adaptability. Near Eastern armies lost to Greek and Roman armies with depressing regularity. The fact that a Near Eastern army like Carthage's could win when it was commanded by a mercenary captain like Xanthippus—or by a native commander like Hannibal, who grew up in Spain, not in Carthage itself—shows that command problems were probably the decisive handicap for the armies of the ancient Near East. Nor was the problem of ineffectiveness confined to the armies: Phoenician and Carthaginian naval forces typically lost, too, when they were confronted by Greek and Roman fleets—again, probably because of problems with their commanders.

We said at the beginning of the course that the empires that rose and fell across the ancient world during the 2,000 years before Alexander blazed trails that he and future conquerors would tread. So, how much did the conquerors of the Greek and Roman world consciously borrow from their Near Eastern predecessors? Alexander probably borrowed more from his Near Eastern predecessors than any subsequent rulers did. He presented himself to his various subject peoples in ways that were familiar to them. In Egypt, he became pharaoh. In Babylonia, he became King of Babylon. In Persia, he became lord of Asia. But except in Persia, this was posturing meant for public consumption—a matter of artistic style rather than royal substance. He borrowed a lot from the Persians themselves. In Persia, he adopted Persian court ceremonial and the practice of *proskynesis* (or prostration before the monarch). More importantly, he took over the administrative framework of the Persian Empire (though whether he would've changed it had he lived longer we don't know). There is no indication, though, that other than Persia, and Babylonia, and Egypt, Alexander was aware of the mighty empires that had once ruled the lands he conquered. In the accounts of Alexander's exploits we hear nothing of Assyria, of Hatti, of Ur, or Akkad. There is nothing to suggest that Alexander ever heard the names of Tiglath-pileser, or Suppiluliumas, Naram-Sin, or the great Sargon.

When Alexander's generals carved up his empire and set themselves up as kings, they were more sparing in taking on Near Eastern elements. Ptolemies in Egypt merely placed an Egyptian façade on their otherwise Greek regime. They adopted Egyptian styles in presenting themselves to their Egyptian subjects, but that was mere show and had nothing to do with any adoption of Egyptian ways. Their subjects knew it, too—and at the end of the 3rd century B.C. launched a great insurgency that lasted half a century, and only ended when the Ptolemies gave them a share in power. The Seleucid kings who took over Anatolia, Syria, Mesopotamia, and Iran continued to use the outline of Persian administration, but they adopted little else. Like the Persians, they allowed their subjects cultural and local autonomy, but that had less to do with direct imitation of Persia than with imitation of Alexander and accepting the realities of ruling an awkwardly large and culturally diverse empire. It was, in the end, an Iranian resurgence that together with Roman pressure destroyed the Seleucid Empire.

The Romans borrowed even less from the Near Eastern imperial past than did Alexander and the Hellenistic kings. Like the Persians, the Romans, from Augustus on, allowed their subjects almost complete cultural autonomy—but there's no evidence that suggests Augustus modeled his policy on that of Darius. Instead, it appears that Augustus's reforms grew out of a sober reflection on the staggering price Rome had paid for adopting a more despotic approach towards its provinces under the Republic. From the mid-1st century A.D. on, the Romans actively sought to integrate their provincials into the imperial army and administration—with so much success that by the end of the 2nd century, a Carthaginian, Septimius Severus, sat on the throne, culminating his lifetime of service as a Roman general, governor, and senator. But the Romans tended to learn from their own experience rather than that of others, and their orientation was always towards the Mediterranean and Europe rather than towards the East.

I think that cultural factors probably explain why the Greeks and Romans borrowed so little from the empires that went before them. First of all, the Greeks don't seem to have known very much about the ancient Near East. Herodotus provides a thorough, though not unbiased, ethnographic survey of the Persian Empire—but his knowledge of earlier Near Eastern empires is shaky at best. We now know that he basically invented the notion that a Median Empire preceded the Persians. He knew of the Neo-Babylonian Empire, but his understanding of its history was pretty vague. He'd heard of the Assyrian Empire, too, and even promised to discuss its history—but seems to have forgotten his promise, because nothing about Assyria ever appears in his book. Besides Herodotus, the Greek physician Ctesias wrote a history of Persia that survives in fragments but seems to be less reliable than Herodotus's information.

That's basically it. It looks as though Greek intellectuals just weren't interested in Near Eastern history. The reason probably lies in their biases: After their victory in the Persian Wars, the Greeks formed a stereotype of corrupt Oriental despotism that mitigated against Hellenistic monarchs borrowing from their Near Eastern predecessors. The experience of victory left the Greeks convinced of their own cultural and moral superiority. After all, they'd handily beaten the largest empire the Near East—and the world—had ever known. They saw themselves as "free" men (Greek women certainly weren't free) and manly men—while Near Easterners were effeminate battlefield losers with a legacy of enslavement to despotic masters, to luxury, and to the pleasures of the flesh. This stereotype permeates Greek writing about the Near East from the mid-4th century B.C. on.

The Romans then inherited the Greeks' stereotypes about the East. From a Roman perspective, even the masculinity of the Greeks was suspect. After all, just as Greek armies had handily beaten the Persians, so also had Roman armies handily beaten the Greeks. Roman attitudes were intensified by their experience with Carthage in the Punic Wars. The Second Punic War was the one time that a Near Eastern—or at least semi-Near Eastern—army had enjoyed more than temporary success against a Western army on the battlefield. But the

Romans also were so scarred by the shock that Hannibal administered to their self-confidence that they painted a stereotype of Carthaginian deceit and dishonesty that they applied to their subsequent dealings with other Near Eastern peoples and cultures.

So, Octavian successfully cast his war against Marc Antony for supremacy in the Roman world as a crusade against the Oriental despot Cleopatra—who, he said, aimed at enslaving the free peoples of Rome. Cleopatra was actually a purple-blooded Macedonian Greek, but popular prejudices against the Near East were so strong that the campaign was a brilliant success. The East became identified in the Roman mind with all things dark, and alien, and threatening. The main inheritors of the great imperial tradition that preceded Alexander were the empires that arose in the Near East during and after the collapse of the Hellenistic kingdoms founded by his successors.

The first of these were the Parthians. A people from northern Iran, the Parthians drove the Macedonian Seleucids from the Iranian Plateau and Mesopotamia during the 3rd and 2nd centuries B.C. and established an empire that endured until the early 3rd century A.D. Their empire was a loose collection of vassal states, similar in outline to Hatti or Mitanni. But it was the Parthians who formed the bulwark against Roman expansion further east into Mesopotamia. The Parthians were then followed by the Sassanids. The Sassanids were a dynasty from the old Persian homeland in southwestern Iran who overthrew the Parthians. Their empire endured until the Muslim conquest of the 7th century A.D. The Sassanid Empire was much more centralized and far more aggressive than the Parthians. Its monarchs identified with Persia's imperial past and took Achaemenid names like Ardashir (or Artaxerxes) and Khurush (or Cyrus). They also openly proclaimed their goal of re-conquering the territories in the West once ruled by Darius, and in the early 7th century A.D., nearly did so—regaining Anatolia, the Levant, and Egypt and laying siege to Constantinople, driving the East Roman Empire to the brink of extinction. But these empires and the others that have arisen in the Middle East took—as their model—Persia. The empires that had gone before—the Neo-Babylonians, the Assyrians, the Hittites, Third Dynasty Ur, even Akkad—were all forgotten. What the West retained was an image of the East as alien and threatening, a source of menace and the home of despotism—not the birthplace of civilization and the cradle of empire.

It's time to offer a final reflection on the question we posed at the beginning of the course: Why should we study the ancient empires that came before Alexander? It isn't because of the impact that they had on our world as empires. The ancient Near East has given us a great deal, including civilization itself—but its great empires were all but forgotten, all the way from antiquity down to the 19th century. It's pretty hard to be directly influenced by something that's been forgotten. But maybe there is one thing that the empires of the ancient Near East gave us that does descend in a direct and unbroken line all the way from antiquity to the present day—even if we've forgotten where it comes from. That one thing is the dream of empire.

It was in the ancient Near East that this grandiose dream that has driven so many conquerors across so many millennia was born: the dream of a power that spans the world. A foundling child conceived that dream and made it real—and so won fame as Sargon the Great. His grandson proclaimed it in the title he took for himself: "king of the four corners of the universe." The dream inspired Hattusilis, and Tiglath-pileser, and Thutmose. It went by the name of Hatti, and Mitanni, and Israel. It drove Persia's armies to India, to Russia, and to Thermopylae. The dream came to Greece in the vision of Alexander and then traveled to Rome, where it finally found its name: *imperium*. In the Middle Ages it inspired Charlemagne, and Otto, and Henry II. In the modern world—in Spain, and France, and Britain—empires finally came into being that truly did span the world, but while those empires have passed into history, the dream that gave them birth has not.

It's a grand dream, the dream of empire—a dream of glory, a dream of fame, a dream with the power to inspire and the power to destroy. It's a dream that will endure as long as human ambition endures, but its origins will forever lie in the plains of Mesopotamia—in the heart of a foundling child, 2,000 years before Alexander.

Timeline

All dates are before the common era (B.C.).

c. 2334–2278...............................Reign of Sargon, creator of history's first empire, Akkad (or Agade).

2255–2218...................................Sargon's grandson, Naram-Sin, conquers states along the Persian Gulf as far as Oman and campaigns into Armenia.

2217–2193...................................Akkadian empire disintegrates under Sharkalisharri; Gutians seize much of Mesopotamia.

c. 2119–2112..............................Utuhegal of Uruk expels the Gutians.

2112–2047...................................Ur-Nammu defeats Utuhegal, founds Third Dynasty of Ur (Ur III), and conquers all of Mesopotamia. He and his son Shulgi create a strongly centralized state.

2028–2004...................................Ur III empire collapses under Ibbi-Sin.

c. 2000.......................................Ashur becomes an independent city-state after collapse of Ur III empire, develops network of merchant colonies in Anatolia; first great palaces appear on Crete; Greeks conquer the Balkan peninsula; Hurrians settle throughout northern Mesopotamia.

c. 2000–1770..............................Mesopotamia reverts to a patchwork of city-states; Isin and Larsa compete for supremacy.

c. 1808–1776..............................Shamshi-Adad creates short-lived kingdom of Upper Mesopotamia, centered on Ashur.

c. 1800–1750	Pitkhana and Anitta of Kussara create kingdom in central Anatolia that Hittite rulers view as ancestral.
c. 1800–1450	Period of supposed Minoan naval empire (thalassocracy) in Aegean.
1792–1750	Reign of Hammurabi.
c. 1765–1755	Hammurabi conquers Mesopotamia.
c. 1760	Ashur becomes a vassal state of Hammurabi's empire.
c. 1730–1670	Hammurabi's empire disintegrates following his death.
c. 1650–1620	Hattusilis I of Kussara founds the Hittite Old Kingdom by conquering central and southern Anatolia.
c. 1650–1500	Hittite Old Kingdom.
c. 1640	Massive eruption of the volcanic island of Thera, north of Crete; substantial damage is done to the palaces on the island, but they are rebuilt.
c. 1630–1600	Founding of Mycenae; Mycenaeans take a leading role in Aegean trade.
1620–1590	Reign of Hittite king Mursilis I, who conquers northern Syria.
c. 1620–1580	Hittite sources report Hurrian attacks on eastern Hittite kingdom.
16th century	Emergence of the Kassite kingdom in Babylonia.
1595	Mursilis I sacks Babylon.
c. 1590–1550	Hurrian kingdom of Mitanni emerges in the power vacuum in northern Mesopotamia.

c. 1590–1525 .... After Mursilis I's assassination, Hittite kingdom falls into chaos and contracts into central Anatolia.

c. 1550–1450 .... Merchant princes of Grave Circles B and A rule from the great palace of Mycenae; other ancient dynasties of Mycenaean Greece founded.

c. 1530 .... Ahmose founds Egypt's Dynasty 18 and drives Hyksos from Lower Egypt, conquering southern Palestine.

c. 1530–1525 .... Ahmose advances Egyptian frontier into Nubia, to second cataract of the Nile.

c. 1525 .... Telepinus becomes king of the Hittites and restores order, but the Hittite realm remains weak for another century.

1525–1504 .... Reign of Amenhotep I, who expands Egyptian control 100 miles deeper into Nubia.

c. 1500 .... Ashur briefly conquered by Mitanni; Thutmose I advances Egyptian frontier to third cataract of the Nile.

c. 1495 .... Thutmose I leads an Egyptian army to the Euphrates and expands the empire into central Palestine.

1479–1425 .... Thutmose III conducts 33 Levant campaigns, conquering northern Palestine and southern Syria.

1457 .... Battle of Megiddo; Thutmose III defeats coalition of Mitanni vassals.

c. 1450 .... Wave of destruction sweeps Crete; Minoan civilization ends. Mainland Greeks take over the island and palaces, colonize the Aegean.

c. 1450–1350	Tholos-Tomb Dynasty rules from the great palace at Mycenae.
c. 1430–c. 1410	Tudhaliyas II founds Hittite New Kingdom and expands Hittite frontiers into eastern and western Anatolia, as well as northern Syria, but after his death, the kingdom again lapses into chaos.
1427–1400	Reign of Amenhotep II. Egypt and Mitanni fight to a standstill in their contest for control of Syria.
c. 1410	The Gasga of northern Anatolia sack Hittite capital of Hattusas; "Atarissiya, the man of Ahhiyava" raids Cyprus in alliance with the Hittite renegade Madduwatta.
c. 1395	Increasingly alarmed by the rise of Hittite power, Mitanni and Egypt make peace. (Syrian frontier remains quiet until the late 14th century.)
c. 1370–c. 1330	Suppiluliumas I aggressively expands Hittite empire, conquering northern Syria and crushing Mitanni.
c. 1350	Dynastic civil war in Mitanni following defeat at the hands of Suppiluliumas I.
after 1350	Assyria begins its rise to power in vacuum left by Mitanni's defeat.
c. 1354–934	Middle Assyrian empire.
c. 1350–1300	Signs of rising insecurity in Greece; merchant princes give way to warrior hero dynasties; massively fortified citadels replace many earlier palaces; Mycenaean trade empire shrinks.

c. 1330...Ashur-uballit of Assyria briefly places an Assyrian puppet on the throne of Kassite Babylonia; Mitanni is reduced to a vassal principality of Hittite empire.

c. 1330–c. 1295 ....Hittite Mursilis II conquers Arzawa in western Anatolia, suppresses rebellions in northern Syria, and temporarily subdues the Gasga.

c. 1325...Mursilis II crushes an Egyptian army at Amki, near Kadesh in southern Syria.

c. 1320–1295...............................Massive rebellion among Syrian and Palestinian vassals nearly destroys the Egyptian empire in the Levant.

c. 1295–c. 1271 ....Muwatallis II expands Hittite control in Syria.

1295–1264....................................Adad-Nirari I expands Assyrian power into northern Syria and pushes the Kassites back into central Mesopotamia.

1294–1279....................................Pharaoh Sety I suppresses rebellion in the Levant but fights an inconclusive war with Muwatallis for control of southern Syria and the key fortress of Kadesh.

c. 1285...For the first time, Egypt is attacked from the west; Sety I defeats the Libyan incursion.

c. 1280...Muwatallis II abandons Hattusas as the Hittite capital in the face of incessant Gasga raids.

1279–1213....................................Reign of Ramesses II.

1278 ....Sea Peoples attack Egypt for the first time.

1274	Battle of Kadesh, a tactical victory for the Egyptians but a strategic one for the Hittites, who push their control south to Damascus.
1271–1270	Ramesses II campaigns in Syria to regain territory lost after Kadesh.
c. 1265	Hittite power weakened by dynastic civil war.
c. 1264–c. 1240	Under Hattusilis III, Hittites' peripheral territories begin to fall away.
1258	Hattusilis III concludes formal peace treaty with Ramesses II.
mid-13th century	Final collapse of the Mycenaean trade empire. Pottery exports from Greece cease soon after 1250.
c. 1250–c. 1230	The Trojan War.
c. 1240–c. 1210	Hittite disintegration accelerates under Tudhaliyas IV; Assyrian Tikulti-Ninurta I conquers eastern Anatolia; western Anatolia falls away.
c. 1230	Elamites devastate Kassite Babylonia.
1225	Tikulti-Ninurta I deposes Kassite king Kashtiliash IV and installs an Assyrian puppet in Babylon.
c. 1220	The Exodus.
c. 1220–c. 1180	Mycenaean civilization collapses violently. Waves of destruction sweep the citadels on the mainland and the palaces of Crete.
c. 1210	Libyans instigate a rebellion against Egypt in Kush; Israelites settle in Canaan.

1207	Second, massive attack on Egypt by the Sea Peoples, coming through the Levant; Merneptah crushes them and campaigns in Palestine against Israel.
1203–1184	Dynastic chaos in Egypt following Merneptah's death.
c. 1200	Hittite empire vanishes.
c. 1200–c. 1180	Waves of destruction sweep over coastal zone of the Levant.
c. 1200–1030	"Judges" rule the autonomous Israelite clans in Canaanite hill country.
early 12th century	Elam expels Assyrian puppet king from Babylon; brief Kassite resurgence.
1197	Tikulti-Ninurta I is assassinated; Assyria falls into chaos for a century and loses most of its conquests.
1179	Massive Libyan attack on Lower Egypt, defeated by Ramesses III.
1176	Third and greatest attack of the Sea Peoples on Egypt. Ramesses III decisively defeats them in the Nile Delta, and they vanish from history.
c. 1175	Ramesses III settles the Philistines on the southern coast of Canaan.
1173	Final Libyan attack on Egypt, defeated by Ramesses III.
1155	Elamites invade Babylonia and destroy the Kassite kingdom.
c. 1150–1140	Egypt loses the last remnants of its empire in the Levant.
1125–1103	Nebuchadrezzar I of Isin destroys the Elamite kingdom.

1114–1076	Under Tiglath-pileser I, Assyria begins its recovery; he sacks Babylon and campaigns as far west as Phoenicia.
c. 1080	Egypt loses control of Nubia and retreats to the first Nile cataract; the Egyptian empire is finished.
c. 1030	Philistines begin to expand into the interior of Canaan, putting pressure on the Israelite clans of the hill country.
c. 1025–1000	Uniting against the Philistines, the Israelite clans anoint Saul as the first king of Israel.
late 11th century	Egypt disintegrates into feuding principalities.
c. 1000–960	David becomes king of Israel following Saul's death. He expands his power east of the Jordan River and north of Damascus.
c. 960–920	Solomon reigns as king of Israel.
c. 945	Solomon begins construction of the Temple.
934–612	Neo-Assyrian empire.
c. 920	Northern clans of Israel reject Solomon's son Rehoboam and anoint Jeroboam as their king; Israel disintegrates into northern (Israel) and southern (Judah) kingdoms.
883–859	Under Ashurnasirpal II, Assyria becomes a great power once more.
858–824	Shalmaneser III cements Assyrian authority in the Levant.
c. 850–c. 600	Phoenician colonization of the western Mediterranean.

823–745.....................................Internal unrest weakens Assyria.

c. 800...Carthage is founded by Tyre.

8th–early 6th centuries ....Medes dominate western Iran.

744–727.....................................Tiglath-pileser III reasserts Assyrian power in the Levant, defeats the Caucasus kingdom of Urartu, and annexes Babylonia.

744–630.....................................Zenith of the Assyrian empire.

722 ....Shalmaneser V conquers the kingdom of Israel.

721–705.....................................Sargon II expands Assyrian power into southeastern Anatolia.

705 ....Sargon II dies in battle with the Cimmerians.

704–681.....................................Rebellions greet the accession of Sennacherib; he fights all his reign to maintain Assyria's frontiers and to maintain control of Babylonia.

681 ....Sennacherib assassinated.

680–669.....................................After putting down rebellions following his accession, Esarhaddon defends Assyria's northern frontier against Scythian and Cimmerian attacks.

678 ....Esarhaddon launches Assyrian conquest of Egypt.

673 ....Egyptians defeat Assyrian invasion.

671 ....Assyrians besiege and capture the Egyptian capital of Memphis; Lower Egypt falls to Assyria.

669–668.....................................Following Esarhaddon's death, Egyptians expel Assyrians from Lower Egypt.

667	Ashurbanipal regains control over Lower Egypt and installs an Egyptian puppet ruler as his vassal.
664–663	Ashurbanipal returns to Egypt to put down rebellions, capturing Thebes and taking control of Upper Egypt.
656	Assyria's puppet king in Egypt, Psammetichus I, declares himself independent of Assyria. Assyria loses control over Egypt.
652–648	Ashurbanipal's brother, Shamash-shum-ukin, viceroy of Babylonia, rebels; it takes four years to suppress the revolt.
648–646	Ashurbanipal devastates Elam in punishment for its support of Shamash-shum-ukin's rebellion; Elam never recovers from this blow.
c. 645	After its king is defeated and killed by the Cimmerians, the kingdom of Lydia submits to Assyria as a vassal.
late 7th century	Under Teispes, a Persian dynasty establishes itself in the former territory of Elam.
c. 630	Death of Ashurbanipal.
627	Kandalanu, Assyrian ruler of Babylonia, dies.
626	Nabopolassar takes power in Babylonia; it takes him 10 years to expel the Assyrians. He founds the Neo-Babylonian empire.
616	Nabopolassar invades the Assyrian heartland.

612	Aided by the Medes, Nabopolassar captures Ashur and Nineveh, destroying the Assyrian empire.
608	Nabopolassar destroys last Assyrian outpost at Harran in eastern Syria.
605	Nebuchadrezzar defeats the Egyptians at Carchemish, driving them out of the Levant and annexing it to the Neo-Babylonian empire.
601	Nebuchadrezzar defeated when he attempts to invade Egypt.
597	Nebuchadrezzar takes Jerusalem and plunders the Temple following a rebellion against Neo-Babylonian authority. He deposes king Jehoiachin and places Zedekiah on the throne.
591	Psammetichus II of Egypt invades the Levant. King Zedekiah of Judah rebels against Nebuchadrezzar.
587	Nebuchadrezzar drives the Egyptians from the Levant and besieges Jerusalem.
586	Jerusalem falls to Nebuchadrezzar. The Temple is destroyed, and thousands are deported to Babylonia, beginning the Babylonian Captivity.
584–573	Nebuchadrezzar besieges and ultimately captures Tyre; with the fall of Tyre, Carthage becomes independent.
after 573	Carthage establishes control over the Phoenician settlements of the western Mediterranean.

570	Neo-Babylonians are defeated again in an attempt to invade Egypt. A border is agreed upon.
562–556	Dynastic chaos in Babylonia following Nebuchadrezzar's death.
559	Cyrus becomes king of Persis/Anshan.
555–539	Reign of Nabonidus in Babylonia.
553–543	Nabonidus removes himself from Babylonia, taking up residence at Teima in northern Arabia. His son Belshazzar rules Babylonia as viceroy.
550	Cyrus destroys and annexes the Median kingdom.
546	Cyrus conquers Sardis and annexes the kingdom of Lydia, giving Persia control of Anatolia.
539	Cyrus crushes the Neo-Babylonian army at Opis, ending the empire.
535	Carthage defeats the western Greeks at Alalia, off Corsica, establishing itself as defender of the Phoenician communities against Greek aggression.
530	Cyrus dies in battle with the Massagetae.
526–525	Cyrus's successor, Cambyses, conquers Egypt.
522	Cambyses dies under suspicious circumstances. Darius I succeeds him as king of Persia.
522–520	Widespread rebellions greet Darius's accession.

513–512	Darius launches an expedition into the Ukraine against the Scythians. It fails, but he retains a Persian foothold in Europe.
509	Carthage concludes a trade treaty with Rome after Rome expels its Etruscan kings.
499	Ionian revolt breaks out, beginning the Greco-Persian wars.
494	Persians crush Ionian rebels at Lade.
492	Persian expedition against Athens and Eretria to punish them for aiding the Ionian rebels is destroyed by a storm in the northern Aegean.
490	Persians besiege and destroy Eretria but are badly defeated by the Athenians at Marathon.
486	Egypt unsuccessfully rebels against Persian rule, distracting Darius from mounting another expedition against Greece. Darius dies and is succeeded by Xerxes.
480	Xerxes leads a massive land and sea assault on Greece. Greeks are defeated at Thermopylae, but the Persian fleet is crushed at Salamis. War erupts between Carthage and Sicilian Greeks. Carthage is badly defeated by Gelon of Syracuse in the Battle of Himera.
479	In a hard-fought battle at Plataea, Greeks rout the large Persian army left behind in Greece.
478–465	Athenian-led Delian League captures remaining Persian outposts in Europe.

465–464	Xerxes murdered and succeeded by Artaxerxes I.
460–453	Egypt rebels against Persia, briefly winning independence.
453	Persians annihilate an Athenian expeditionary force sent to aid Egypt against the Persian counteroffensive.
451	Cimon of Athens captures Cyprus from the Persians.
449	Following Cimon's death, Pericles of Athens makes a truce with Persia.
424–405	Reign of Darius II of Persia.
412	Darius II capitalizes on Athens's disastrous defeat in Sicily to funnel aid to Sparta, beginning a period of active Persian diplomatic intervention in Greek affairs.
409–397	Renewed war between Carthage and Sicilian Greeks.
404	Egypt rebels; remains independent of Persian control for 60 years.
401	Aided by a large force of Greek mercenaries, Cyrus the Younger challenges his brother Artaxerxes II's succession to the throne. He is killed in the Battle of Cunaxa. Greek troops fight their way home across northern Mesopotamia and Anatolia.
395	Sparta turns on Persia; Artaxerxes redirects Persian aid to Athens, rebuilding its navy and walls.
387	To counter Athens's revival, Artaxerxes switches Persian aid back to Sparta.

386 ....Artaxerxes dictates the King's Peace to the city-states of Greece, ending the Corinthian War.

377–350....................................Persian authority in Anatolia is shaken by numerous rebellions among satraps and vassal rulers.

374 ....Persian expedition to reconquer Egypt is defeated.

371 ....Second King's Peace fails to suppress warfare among Greeks.

358 ....Egyptians defeat second Persian effort to reconquer Egypt.

355 ....Persians foment a rebellion that destroys the Second Delian League, gutting Athens's power.

351–343....................................Artaxerxes III finally reconquers Egypt.

348 ....Carthage's second trade treaty with Rome.

338–336....................................Dynastic turmoil in Egypt following the death of Artaxerxes III.

336 ....Philip II of Macedon establishes a bridgehead in Anatolia.

334 ....Alexander the Great invades Anatolia, winning the Battle of the Granicus.

333 ....Alexander defeats Darius III at Issus and conquers Syria and the Levant.

332 ....Alexander takes Egypt.

331 ....Alexander invades Mesopotamia, defeating Darius at Arbela.

330 ....Alexander takes Susa and Persepolis; Darius murdered by Bessus; Alexander takes Persian crown.

241	Roman fleet defeats a Carthaginian squadron at Aegates Islands off Sicily; exhausted, Carthage sues for peace, and Rome wins control of Sicily; birth of the Roman Empire.
241–237	The "Truceless War" (mutiny of Carthage's mercenary troops); native Libyans of North Africa and a number of Phoenician subject communities join the revolt; Carthage savagely puts down the rebellion.
237	Capitalizing on Carthage's weakness, Rome seizes Sardinia and Corsica.
235–221	Hamilcar Barca conquers southern and southeastern Spain; he dies in an accident, and his son-in-law Hasdrubal succeeds him; foundation of Nova Carthago (Cartagena).
221	Following Hasdrubal's assassination, the army in Spain chooses Hamilcar's son Hannibal to succeed him.
220–219	Hannibal and Rome dispute control of Saguntum in eastern Spain; the town falls to Hannibal.
218	Second Punic War begins; Hannibal leads Carthaginian army overland from Spain to invade Italy, while Roman army marches overland from Italy to invade Spain; Hannibal defeats Scipio, who had aborted his invasion of Spain, at the Ticinus in northern Italy; Hannibal inflicts a crushing defeat on Roman forces at the Trebia.

217	Hannibal destroys Roman consular army at Lake Trasimene.
216	Hannibal destroys combined armies of both Roman consuls at Cannae.
215	At Ibera in Spain, Romans destroy a Carthaginian army; Rome recovers Saguntum.
215–214	Carthage fails in a bid to regain Sardinia.
213–210	Carthaginian invasion of Sicily is defeated.
211	Carthaginians destroy Roman army in Spain at the Battle of the Tader Valley; Hannibal marches on Rome but fails to take the city.
210	P. Cornelius Scipio (later Africanus) receives command over the Roman forces in Spain.
209	Scipio captures Nova Carthago by a ruse.
208	Scipio defeats the Carthaginians at Baecula.
207	A Carthaginian army marching from Spain to reinforce Hannibal in Italy is destroyed on the Metaurus.
206	Scipio defeats Carthaginians at Ilipa. Remaining Carthaginian troops abandon Spain and march to Italy.
204	Scipio invades North Africa.
203	Carthaginian troops sent to reinforce Hannibal from Spain are defeated in northern Italy; confronted by Scipio, Carthage makes peace.

Glossary

All dates are before the common era (B.C.).

Achaemenids: The royal dynasty of Persia that began with Darius I (522–486) and continued until the fall of the empire to Alexander of Macedon (Alexander the Great).

Ahhiyava: The name used in Hittite texts for the Mycenaean Greek realms in the Aegean. It is a Hittite transliteration of "Akhaia."

Akhaia/Akhaians: The name used by Homer for Greece and the Greeks during the Mycenaean period.

Amarna letters: A large cache of tablets discovered at Tel el-Amarna, the former Akhetaten, in Egypt. The letters illuminate diplomatic relations among the great powers of the Near East during the 14th century.

Anitta text: A Hittite document recounting the exploits of Anitta, ancestor of the Hittite kings, during the early 2nd millennium.

Annals of Thutmose III: Texts inscribed on the walls of the Temple at Karnak detailing Thutmose III's numerous military campaigns.

'apiru: A generic term meaning "outcast," applied in the ancient Near East to nomadic groups living on the fringes of settled agricultural areas.

Apology of Hattusilis: A text issued by the Hittite king Hattusilis III (1264–1239) justifying his violation of the Edict of Telepinus by usurping the throne of his brother, Mursilis III.

Aqaiwasha: An element within the marauders known to the Egyptians as the Sea Peoples. It is an Egyptian transliteration of "Akhaia."

aten: Egyptian officer in command of a company.

baivarabam: In the Persian army, a division of 10,000 men.

bala: A word meaning "exchange" that refers to the food and goods depositories of the highly centralized resource-extraction system of Third-Dynasty Ur (Ur III).

Behistun inscription: A lengthy autobiographical inscription erected by Darius I of Persia.

brother: The term used by rulers of the 2nd millennium to signify another ruler's equality of status.

corvus: A grapple and boarding ramp, used by the Romans in the First Punic War to negate Carthage's superior seamanship but eventually abandoned because it made ships dangerously top-heavy.

Council of 104: Also called the Council of Judges, the most important governing body at Carthage, charged with overseeing the generals and the suffetes.

cuneiform: Literally "wedge-shaped," a form of script employed for incising letters on clay tablets; the standard script used for record keeping in the Near East outside Egypt.

deportation: A widespread practice among Near Eastern empires, employed both to reduce the likelihood of revolt in trouble-prone areas and to populate regions in the interest of improving agricultural productivity.

Djahy: The Egyptian name for the coastal region better known as Phoenicia.

Edict of Telepinus: A decree issued by the Hittite king Telepinus (r. c. 1525–c. 1500), regulating the rules for accession to the throne of Hatti.

enkhos: The thrusting spear wielded by Mycenaean warriors.

ensi: A term that originally meant "king," it was used by the Akkadian empire to designate royal governors and kept that meaning thereafter.

Etemenanki: Meaning "house of the frontier between heaven and earth," this was the name of the great ziggurat, or temple platform, built in Babylon by Nebuchadrezzar, possibly the inspiration for the story of the Tower of Babel.

Gasga: A tribal people dwelling in the mountains of northern Anatolia who plagued the Hittites throughout their history, often sacking the capital of Hatussas.

gibborim: A term meaning "mighty men," referring to the Israelite contingent in David's royal guard.

Grave Circles A and B: The burial grounds of the ruling dynasties of Mycenae in the mid-2nd millennium.

Great Ones: The high aristocracy of Hatti.

gur: An Akkadian unit of dry volume equivalent to about 300 modern liters.

gurush: Literally "lads," these were male conscript workers in the centralized labor system of Ur III.

Hanigalbat: An alternative name for the kingdom of Mitanni.

Hatti: The name by which the Hittites called their kingdom.

haut: Egyptian officer in command of a division.

hazannu: The title of mayors in the Assyrian empire.

hazarabam: The basic unit of the Persian army, a battalion of 1,000 men.

hoplite: A heavily armed and armored Greek infantryman. His main weapon was a long thrusting spear, or pike.

Hurrians: The people who created the kingdom of Mitanni.

inu: The Egyptian term for levies in kind, typically horses and chariots, applied to the city-states of Canaan.

karum: A large Assyrian merchant colony in Anatolia during the early 2nd millennium.

King's Peace, the: The treaty imposed by Artaxerxes III on the warring poleis in 386, ending the Corinthian War.

King's Son of Kush and Overseer of the Southern Lands, the: The title of the viceroy of the provinces of the Egyptian empire beyond the first cataract of the Nile.

King's Sons, the: The extended family of the Hittite king.

kudurru: The Kassite Babylonian term for royal deeds conferring land ownership.

Kush: A kingdom located in Nubia, with its heartland between the third and fourth cataracts of the Nile.

Land of Ashur: The portion of the Assyrian empire under direct Assyrian rule, comprising the Assyrian homeland and the provinces of the empire.

Levant: The geographical term for the eastern coastal region of the Mediterranean Sea—currently Syria, Lebanon, and Israel.

Libyphoenicians: The inhabitants of the colonies Carthage established on the coast of northwest Africa.

limmus: The corps of high court officials of the Assyrian empire during the middle and early Neo-Assyrian periods.

Linear A: The undeciphered syllabary script used for record keeping in the palaces of Minoan Crete.

Linear B: A syllabary script derived from Linear A, shown by Michael Ventris in 1953 to represent an archaic form of Greek, used for record keeping in Mycenaean palaces and citadels.

Lower Sea, the: The name by which the Persian Gulf was known in the ancient Near East.

loyalty oaths: Solemn oaths, sworn on the gods of those involved, by which Assyrian subjects promised their fealty to Assyria.

mariyannu: The elite chariot corps of the Mitannian army.

mātum: The Assyrian term meaning "the country," referring to the Assyrian heartland, the environs of the city of Ashur.

Medize: The Greek term meaning "to submit to Persia."

menh: Egyptian officer in command of a platoon.

mer: Egyptian officer in command of a battalion.

New Kingdom: The period of Egyptian history between about 1550 and 1069, including Dynasties 18, 19, and 20, during which Egypt conquered, ruled, and then lost an empire in Nubia and the Levant.

ngeme: A "slave girl"; female conscript workers in the centralized labor system of Ur III.

nomes: Units of local administration in Egypt.

Nubia: The region beyond the first cataract of the Nile.

pakhana: A Mycenaean warrior's sword, which originally had a long, narrow blade but later became shorter and broader.

Palatial period: The term modern scholars use to designate the heyday of Minoan civilization on Crete, between about 2000 and about 1450.

panku: The Hittite assembly of notables, probably consisting of high military commanders and court officials.

penteconter: A light warship propelled in combat by 50 oars.

phalanx: The dense formation in which hoplites fought, typically 8 ranks deep and 100 or more men wide.

polearm: An Egyptian infantry weapon, a combination mace and ax.

polis (pl. poleis): Usually translated as "city-state," the polis was a self-governing community of citizens. The Greek world comprised hundreds of independent poleis.

Qart-Hadasht: "New Town," the actual name of Carthage.

quinquireme: A heavy warship propelled in battle by five banks of oars. Used in the Punic Wars.

ras sha muhhi: The majordomo, or chamberlain, of the Assyrian empire.

Rctjcnu: The Egyptian name for Canaan, the region between the Mediterranean coast and the Jordan River and Dead Sea.

royal ideology: The galaxy of attributes associated with kingship in a particular society.

Royal Road, the: The carefully guarded and supplied road that ran from Sardis to the Persian capital of Susa.

Sacred Band, the: A body of Carthaginian natives 3,000 strong who formed an elite band in the army, often used as an officer training pool.

šangû **of Ashur**: The "viceroy of Ashur," the official title of the king of Assyria, signifying his role as deputy of the god Ashur and thus emphasizing that he is not a god himself.

satrap: The governor of a Persian satrapy. Often a member of the extended royal family.

satrapy: One of the roughly two dozen large territorial units into which the Persian empire was divided; these were themselves subdivided into provinces.

Sea Peoples: The Egyptian name for several diverse waves of migrants and brigands who marauded their way through the eastern Mediterranean during the late 13th and early 12th centuries, destroying numerous towns and cities as well as the Egyptian empire in the Levant.

Sealand, the: The name by which Lower Mesopotamia was known in the mid-2nd millennium.

seal-houses: The local and regional warehouses where Hittite revenues, collected in kind, were stored.

shagina: An Akkadian term meaning "military governor."

Sharru-kin: The actual form of the name we render as Sargon, meaning "the king is legitimate." Its use implies that the person bearing the name has a questionable claim to his throne.

Shasu: The name Egyptian records give to nomadic groups living beyond the frontier of the Egyptian empire, south of the Dead Sea, who preyed on caravans. Egyptian texts locate Israel among the Shasu.

suffetes: The Latinized form of the Semitic word *špṭm*, usually rendered in English as "judges."

sukkulmah: The viceroy who presided over the frontier regions of the Ur III empire.

Sumerian king list: A document probably of the 19th century that lists rulers of Mesopotamia and Sumeria from the mythic past down to the time the list was compiled. It artificially assigns overall kingship of Mesopotamia to one city at a time.

tamkar: Ur III official charged with overseeing trade and commerce.

Ten Thousand Immortals, the: The elite royal guard of the Persian army, called the Immortals because whenever one of them died or retired, a replacement was immediately appointed.

thalassocracy: Literally, "mastery of the sea," or a sea empire. The legendary Minos of Crete was credited by later Greek authors with having created the first thalassocracy.

Thirty, the: The royal guard of David's army.

tholos (pl. *tholoi*): A large, beehive- or igloo-shaped masonry structure used as a dynastic tomb in Mycenaean Greece.

trireme: A heavy warship propelled in combat by numerous oars arranged in three banked tiers.

tuhkanti: The title of the Hittite crown prince.

turtanu: The chief army commander of Assyria.

tyrant: A ruler of a Greek polis who either seized power or was placed in power in defiance of the laws of that city.

ummanu: The chancellor of the Assyrian empire.

United Monarchy: The union of the clans of Israel and Judah under a single monarch, between the anointment of Saul (c. 1025) and the death of Solomon (c. 920).

vassal treaties: Texts defining relations between subordinate rulers and the Great King of Hatti, usually inscribed on metal plaques.

wabartum: A small Assyrian trading post in Anatolia in the early 2nd millennium.

wanax: The word meaning "king" in Mycenaean Greek.

Yoke of Ashur: The vassal states of the Assyrian empire.

Biographical Notes

All dates are before the common era (B.C.).

Adad-Nirari I (r. 1305–1274): Assyrian ruler who annexed the rump of Mitanni, extended Assyrian power into northern Syria, and pushed the Kassites out of northern Babylonia.

Adad-Nirari II (r. 912–890): Second king of the New Assyrian period, who began the practice of regular campaigning to extort tribute from peoples on Assyria's borders.

Adad-Nirari III (810–783): Neo-Assyrian king who humbled the principality of Damascus and the kingdom of Israel.

Adad-shum-usur (r. 1218–1189): Kassite ruler under whom the Kassite kingdom enjoyed a brief resurgence.

Adasi (fl. 16th century): Progenitor of the kings of Assyria.

Agum II (r. c. 1570): First Kassite ruler of Babylon, following the city's sack by the Hittites and the end of the First Dynasty.

Ahmose (r. 1550–1525): Founder of Dynasty 18, New Kingdom Egypt, and the Egyptian empire, he drove the Hyksos back into Palestine and began to establish Egyptian control over the southern Levant.

Akhenaten (a.k.a. **Amenhotep IV**; r. 1352–1336): Religious visionary and Dynasty 18 pharaoh under whom the Amarna letters (diplomatic correspondence with Egyptian vassals and with other Near Eastern monarchs) were compiled.

Alexander III of Macedon (a.k.a. **Alexander the Great**; r. 336–323): The most dazzling military genius in history. After coming to the throne of his small country at the age of 20, Alexander invaded and conquered the Persian empire in a three-year campaign.

Amenhotep I (r. 1525–1504): Son of Ahmose, this Dynasty 18 pharaoh expanded the Egyptian frontier far up the Nile Valley into Nubia.

Amenhotep II (r. 1427–1400): Dynasty 18 pharaoh who fought the Mitanni to a standstill in northern Syria.

Ammuna (r. c. 1550–1530): Son of the Hittite king Zidanta. He murdered his father and seized the throne for himself.

Anitta (r. c. 1750): Lord of Kussara in central Anatolia, claimed by Hittite kings as their predecessor.

Ariamnes (r. c. 650): Claimed by Darius I as his ancestor, he was progenitor of the Achaemenid dynasty that ruled Persia from Darius on.

Arik-den-ili (r. 1317–1306): Assyrian ruler who fended off attacks from the hill people of the eastern Taurus and took the title "mighty king, king of Assyria."

Aristagoras (r. c. 500): Tyrant of the city of Miletus, whose intrigues sparked the Ionian revolt and the great wars between Persia and the Greeks.

Artadama I (r. c. 1390): Mitannian king who concluded a treaty with Egypt, resolving their disputes over northern Syria.

Artadama II (r. c. 1350): Hittite-sponsored pretender to the throne of Mitanni.

Artaxerxes I (r. 464–424): Persian king who crushed Athenian efforts in 453 to aid Egyptian rebels and who concluded a *modus vivendi* with Athens in 449.

Artaxerxes II (r. 405–359): Although the longest-reigning Persian king, he lost control of Egypt and struggled to maintain control of Asia Minor and the Levant, but he held the Greeks at bay through skillful diplomacy.

Artaxerxes III (r. 358–338): Persian king who, though cruel and tyrannical, managed to reconquer Egypt and briefly restore the fortunes of the Persian empire.

Ashurbanipal (r. 668–c. 630): The last great ruler of Assyria, he completed the conquest of Egypt but soon lost it. Lydia in western Anatolia submitted to him, and he destroyed the kingdom of Elam in southwestern Iran after it aided a Babylonian rebellion against Assyria.

Ashur-Dan II (r. 934–912): Creator of the New Assyrian kingdom, from which the empire developed, he secured Assyria's frontiers and reformed the army.

Ashurnasirpal II (r. 883–859): Assyrian king and active campaigner who asserted Assyria's power as far east as the Zagros, as far west as Anatolia, and as far south as the Levant.

Ashur-uballit I (r. 1363–1328): Founder of the Middle Kingdom of Assyria, he annexed the region around Nineveh and made Kassite Babylonia into an Assyrian vassal.

Ashur-uballit II (r. 611–c. 608): Fugitive Assyrian prince who took refuge in Harran after the fall of the Assyrian empire and, with Egyptian backing, held out for about two more years before being defeated and disappearing from history.

Astyages (r. c. 585–550): Son and successor of Cyaxares as king of the Medes, he lost his kingdom when his army mutinied rather than face Cyrus of Persia.

Atarissiya (r. c. 1400): Ruler of a Mycenaean Greek principality located in the islands of the Aegean and mentioned in Hittite documents as a cause of insecurity in western Anatolia.

Bagoas (d. 336): Persian royal eunuch who engineered the murder of Artaxerxes III but was himself executed by Darius III.

Bardiya (a.k.a. **Smerdis**; d. 522): Brother of Cambyses II, Herodotus narrates the story of the intrigues that surrounded his death.

Belshazzar (a.k.a. **Bel-shar-usur**; fl. c. 540): Son of the Neo-Babylonian king Nabonidus and viceroy of Babylonia during his father's 10-year absence in Arabia (553–543).

Bessus (d. 330): Persian nobleman who assassinated Darius III, the last king of Persia. Alexander had Bessus tried under Persian law by a court of Persian aristocrats, and after they condemned him, Alexander had Bessus executed.

Cambyses I (r. c. 585–559): King of Persis/Anshan and father of Cyrus II.

Cambyses II (r. 530–522): Son and successor of Cyrus II, he conquered and annexed Egypt and Cyrene to the Persian empire but died in a riding accident.

Cimon (c. 520–451): Athenian commander, son of Miltiades, who masterminded the Athenian-led counteroffensive against Persia in the eastern Mediterranean after 479.

Croesus (r. c. 560–546): The last king of Lydia, whose kingdom fell to Cyrus II.

Cyaxares (r. c. 625–585): Chieftain who united the Medes and aided Nabopolassar of Babylonia in destroying the Assyrian empire.

Cyrus I (r. c. 620–585): King of Persis/Anshan, son of Teispes, father of Cambyses I, and grandfather of Cyrus II.

Cyrus II (a.k.a. **Cyrus the Great**; r. 559–530): King of Persis/Anshan who defeated the Medes, the Lydians, and the Babylonians to create the Persian empire, the largest empire the world had known to that date.

Cyrus the Younger (d. 401): Youngest son of Darius II, he challenged his brother, Artaxerxes II, for the throne, using an army of Peloponnesian War veterans whom he had recruited thanks to his role as viceroy of Anatolia. Although he won the Battle of Cunaxa, he was killed in the fight.

Darius I (r. 522–486): Founder of the Achaemenid line of Persian kings, he completed the expansion of the Persian empire and gave the empire its distinctive administrative structure.

Darius II (r. 424–405): Persian king who capitalized on Athens's weakness after its defeat in Sicily to funnel aid to Athens's enemy, Sparta, and thus to gain diplomatic leverage for Persia in internal Greek politics.

Darius III (r. 336–331): As king of Persia, he was a capable ruler and sound strategist but had the misfortune of having to face Alexander the Great. Alexander defeated him twice in battle but gave him a royal funeral after he was assassinated by the nobleman Bessus.

David (r. c. 1000–960): Bandit chieftain from the southern clans of Judah who was anointed king of Israel after Saul's death. He extended his power east of the Jordan River and north beyond Damascus.

Elissa (a.k.a. **Dido**; r. c. 800): Legendary founder of Carthage, a princess of Tyre driven into exile by King Pygmalion, who murdered his brother, her husband.

Enheduanna (fl. c. 2300): Daughter of Sargon of Akkad, installed by her father as priestess of the moon god Nanna at Ur, inaugurating a tradition among subsequent Mesopotamian rulers. She is the first known female author in human history.

Enlil-nirari (r. 1327–1318): Assyrian ruler who defeated a Kassite counterattack on Assyria after the Kassites threw off Assyrian overlordship.

Enmebaraggesi (r. c. 2700): Ruler (*ensi*) of Kish. The first arguably historical ruler in the Sumerian king list.

Esarhaddon (r. 680–669): Like most Assyrian kings, he had to suppress multiple rebellions, but he was able to begin the conquest of Egypt toward the end of his reign.

Gaumata (a.k.a. **pseudo-Smerdis**; r. c. 522–521): In Herodotus's account of the intrigues surrounding Bardiya/Smerdis's death, a Persian priest, or *magus*, who posed as the dead prince.

Gelon (r. c. 491–477): Becoming tyrant of Gela on Sicily around 491, he seized control of Syracuse and made himself tyrant there. He defeated the Carthaginians at Himera in 480, making him the virtual ruler of Greek Sicily.

Gilgamesh (r. c. 2650): Ruler (*ensi*) of Uruk, who left behind such a powerful memory that he was reckoned semidivine and became the central figure of the Sumerian national epic.

Hamilcar Barca (d. 229): Carthaginian commander who waged a successful campaign of naval and land raids against Italy and Sicily during the latter stages of the First Punic War, then went on to mastermind the expansion of the Carthaginian empire in Spain.

Hamilcar Mago (fl. c. 480): Carthaginian commander defeated by Gelon of Syracuse at the Battle on Himera in 480.

Hammurabi (r. 1792–1750): Founder of the First Dynasty of Babylon and the short-lived Old Babylonian Empire. After the death of Shamshi-Adad, he rapidly conquered an empire that included all of Mesopotamia. Under him, Babylon became the greatest city of Mesopotamia.

Hannibal Barca (247–182): Brilliant Carthaginian commander, the son of Hamilcar Barca, he launched a daring overland invasion of Italy that came close to destroying Rome's power, but he failed and was defeated at Zama, after which he went into exile.

Hantilis (r. c. 1590–c. 1560): Brother-in-law to Mursilis I. He murdered Mursilis and usurped the throne of Hatti, inaugurating a period of chaos and decline.

Harpagus (fl. c. 585): In Herodotus's account, the servant of Astyages who was responsible for sparing the life of the infant Cyrus II and who later encouraged Cyrus to rebel against Astyages.

Hasdrubal Barca (d. 207): Younger brother of Hannibal, left in command of Carthaginian forces in Spain when Hannibal marched on Italy. Hasdrubal was successful at holding Spain against Roman attacks until the advent of Scipio Africanus, who forced Hasdrubal to evacuate Spain. Marching to Italy, he was defeated and killed at the Battle of the Metaurus.

Hattusilis I (r. c. 1650–1620): Heir to the throne of Kussara and founder of the Hittite Old Kingdom. He moved his capital to Hattusas and conquered much of Anatolia.

Hattusilis III (r. c. 1264–c. 1240): Hittite king who came to the throne after a debilitating civil war. Under him, Hittite power began to wane.

Herodotus (c. 480–c. 420): Founder of the discipline of history and historian of the Greco-Persian Wars of 499–479.

Hieron II (r. c. 271–216): Tyrant, later king, of Syracuse, leading that city through the First Punic War and into the early years of the Second Punic War.

Horemheb (r. 1323–1295): The last pharaoh of Dynasty 18, under whom defeat by the Hittites and rebellions temporarily cost Egypt much of its empire in the Levant.

Huzziya (r. c. 1530–c. 1525): Hittite king who came to the throne after a palace conspiracy murdered his predecessor, Ammuna. He and his family fell victim to another palace massacre.

Ibbi-Sin (r. 2028–2004): The fourth and last ruler of Third-Dynasty Ur (Ur III). External pressures collapsed the centralized Ur III system, and Ur fell to the Elamites.

Ishbi-Erra (r. 2017–1985): A rebel official of Ur III who founded the First Dynasty of Isin when Ur III collapsed.

Kamose (r. 1555–1550): Ruler of Upper Egypt and last pharaoh of Dynasty 17, his bold attack on the Hyksos capital at Avaris began the reconquest of lower Egypt.

Kandalanu (r. c. 647–627): Last and shadowy Assyrian ruler of Babylonia. Kandalanu is perhaps a throne name for Ashurbanipal, but he may be a separate figure.

Kashtiliashu IV (r. 1232–1225): Kassite ruler who was defeated and taken prisoner by the Assyrian Tikulti-Ninurta I, after which the Assyrians appointed puppet rulers in Babylon.

Kurigalzu I (r. c. 1400): Kassite ruler who temporarily moved the capital from Babylon to a new site, the fortress of Dur-Kurigalzu, which he had built.

Lugalzaggesi (r. c. 2350–2316): Tyrannical king of Uruk, overthrown and humbled by Sargon of Akkad.

Madduwatta (fl. c. 1410): Fractious southwest Anatolian vassal of the Hittite king Tudhaliyas II. Their relations, documented in "The Indictment of Madduwatta," cast great light on how Hittite kings managed vassal relations.

Mago (r. c. 550): Leader who was chiefly responsible for launching Carthage's ascent to imperial power and greatness. Patriarch of the Magonid clan that led Carthage well into the 5th century.

Mago Barca (d. 203): Youngest brother of Hannibal and the last Carthaginian commander in Spain. He was forced to evacuate Spain, and after failing to take the Balearic Islands, he landed in Italy, where he was defeated and mortally wounded in 203.

Malchus (r. c. 550): Carthaginian general under whom Carthage became involved in Sardinia. He returned to Carthage and briefly made himself tyrant.

Mandane (fl. c. 585): According to Herodotus, the daughter of Astyages the Mede and mother of Cyrus II.

Manishtushu (r. 2269–2255): Second son of Sargon of Akkad. Like his older brother, Rimush, he fought to preserve rather than expand his father's realm.

Mardonius (c. 530–479): Achaemenid noble who commanded a failed Persian expedition against Greece in 492 and was killed fighting at Plataea in 479.

Merneptah (r. 1213–1203): Dynasty 19 pharaoh who had to battle rebellions in Nubia and the Levant as well as increasing pressure from marauding Sea Peoples.

Miltiades (c. 560–489): Athenian commander who defeated a Persian punitive attack on Athens at Marathon in 490.

Minos (r. c. 2nd millennium): According to classical Greek legend, the ruler of Crete. His ethnicity (Greek or Minoan) is unclear. Alternatively, "minos" may be the Minoan word for "king."

Mursilis I (r. c. 1620–1590): Hittite king who sacked Babylon and destroyed the last vestiges of Hammurabi's empire.

Mursilis II (r. c. 1330–c. 1290): Hittite king who expanded Hittite power into western Anatolia, conquering Arzawa and defeating Ahhiyawa.

Mursilis III (r. c. 1271–c. 1264): *See* **Urhi-Teshub**.

Muwatallis II (r. c. 1290–c. 1271): King who expanded Hittite power into southern Syria and defeated an Egyptian offensive in the Battle of Kadesh (1274).

Nabonidus (r. 555–539): Last king of the Neo-Babylonian empire, he spent much of his reign in a mysterious self-imposed exile at the oasis of Teima in northern Arabia but returned to Mesopotamia to be defeated by Cyrus II of Persia.

Nabopolassar (r. 626–605): Founder of the Neo-Babylonian empire, he came to the throne of Babylonia under mysterious circumstances and, over the course of the following 15 years, destroyed the Assyrian empire.

Naram-Sin (r. 2255–2218): Grandson of Sargon of Akkad, he expanded the Akkadian empire down the Persian Gulf into southwestern Iran and declared himself a god.

Nebuchadrezzar II (a.k.a. **Nebuchadnezzar**; r. 604–562): Second king of the Neo-Babylonian empire, he was frustrated in his efforts to conquer Egypt but succeeded in subjugating Tyre after a long siege. He destroyed the kingdom of Judah and the Temple after multiple rebellions.

Pitkhana (r. c. 1800): Lord of Kussara in central Anatolia. Claimed by the Hittite kings as their predecessor.

pseudo-Smerdis: *See* **Gaumata**.

Pygmalion (r. c. 800): King of Tyre whose intrigues, according to legend, drove his sister-in-law Elissa (Dido) to flee Tyre and to found Carthage.

Ramesses II (r. 1279–1213): The famous Dynasty 19 pharaoh who defeated the Hittite king Muwatallis at Kadesh (1274) but lost control of central Syria in the wake of the victory. Afterward, he concluded the first formal peace treaty in history with Hatti.

Ramesses III (r. 1184–1153): Dynasty 20 pharaoh who faced and defeated two concerted assaults on Egypt by the Libyans and the Sea Peoples.

Ramesses VI (r. 1143–1136): Dynasty 20 pharaoh under whom Egypt permanently lost control over Palestine, bringing an end to its empire in the Levant.

Rim-Sin I (r. 1822–1763): Ruler of Larsa, he defeated Isin and established a regional kingdom in southern Mesopotamia that finally fell to Hammurabi.

Rimush (r. 2278–2270): Eldest son of Sargon of Akkad, he struggled to maintain his father's realm.

Sargon of Akkad (r. c. 2334–2278): Beginning his career as cupbearer to Ur-Zababa of Kish, he went on to conquer Mesopotamia and northern Syria and to create the first empire in human history.

Sargon II (r. 721–705): Assyrian king who deported 27,290 people from Israel, conquered southeastern Anatolia, and crushed rebellions in Babylonia but was killed in battle with the Cimmerians.

Saul (r. c. 1025–1000): The first king of Israel, anointed when the clans united to defend themselves against Philistine pressure.

Sausattar (r. mid-15th century B.C.): King of Mitanni who conquered Ashur and advanced Mitannian power into eastern Anatolia.

Scipio Africanus (a.k.a. **P. Cornelius Scipio Africanus**; 236–183): Given extraordinary command of the Roman forces battling Carthage in Spain, he destroyed the Carthaginian empire there and then invaded North Africa, defeating Hannibal at Zama and winning the Second Punic War.

Sennacherib (r. 704–681): Assyrian king who crushed rebellions in Babylonia and campaigned into southern Anatolia but was assassinated by his own sons.

Sety I (r. 1294–1279): Dynasty 19 pharaoh who aggressively reasserted Egyptian power in the Levant, winning back what had been lost under Horemheb.

Shalmaneser III (r. 858–824): Plagued by revolts, he spent much of his very active military career defending and consolidating the conquests of his father, Ashurnasirpal II.

Shalmaneser V (r. 727–722): Assyrian conqueror of the northern kingdom of Israel, the capital of which (Samaria) fell after a three-year siege.

Shamshi-Adad (r. c. 1808–1776): Conqueror of northern Mesopotamia and Syria, creator of the short-lived kingdom of Upper Mesopotamia.

Shattiwaza (r. c. 1340): Mitanni prince installed by the Hittites as their vassal in a rump Mitanni state in western Anatolia, marking the end of the kingdom of Mitanni.

Shulgi (r. 2094–2047): The son and successor of Ur-Nammu. He built on his father's foundation and made Ur III into a tightly centralized state.

Shur-Sin (r. 2037–2029): Ur III dynast.

Shutruk-Nahhunte (r. c. 1165): Elamite king who conquered Babylonia and destroyed the last vestiges of the Kassite kingdom.

Shuttarna II (r. c. 1370): King of Mitanni. His murder led to a period of bloody civil war.

Sin-shar-ishkun (r. 623–612): Last king of Assyria, he fought hard to contain the rising power of Nabopolassar in Babylonia but was defeated and finally saw Nabopolassar destroy Ashur, Nineveh, and the Assyrian empire.

Smerdis: *See* **Bardiya**.

Solomon (r. c. 960–920): Last king of the United Monarchy of Israel, he built the first Temple, but his harsh treatment of the northern clans alienated them and led to the dissolution of the United Monarchy immediately following his death.

Suppiluliumas I (r. c. 1370–c. 1326): The real founder of the Hittite empire. He destroyed Mitanni and subjugated northern Syria.

Suppiluliumas II (r. after 1210): The last king of Hatti. Under him, the Hittite kingdom collapsed and vanished. His fate is unknown.

Tawagalawas (r. c. 1250): Mycenaean ruler of an island principality in the Aegean who sheltered Hittite renegades and launched raids on western Anatolia.

Teispes (r. c. 650–620): Founder of the royal line of Persis/Anshan and ancestor of Cyrus II.

Telepinus (r. c. 1525–c. 1500): Ruler who restored stability to the Hittite kingdom after 75 years of chaos and regularized the rules of succession to the throne in the Edict of Telepinus.

Themistocles (c. 524–459): Athenian leader who persuaded Athens in 483 to build a large fleet. He led Athens in resisting Persia in 480/79 but took refuge at the Persian court late in life and became Persian governor of the city of Magnesia.

Thutmose I (r. 1504–1492): Dynasty 18 pharaoh who advanced the frontiers of Egypt's empire to the fourth cataract of the Nile and into southern Syria, marching his army as far as the Euphrates.

Thutmose III (r. 1479–1425): The greatest conqueror in Egyptian history, he won the Battle of Megiddo (Armageddon), waged 17 campaigns in the Levant, advanced Egypt's frontier into central Syria, and crossed the Euphrates into eastern Syria. Early in his reign, Thutmose's stepmother, Queen Hatshepsut, was his regent; he was established as sole ruler in 1458.

Thutmose IV (r. 1400–1390): Dynasty 18 pharaoh who achieved peace on Egypt's frontier in the Levant by concluding a treaty with Mitanni fixing their boundary in central Syria.

Tiglath-pileser I (r. 1114–1076): Stabilized Assyria after a period of dynastic instability, driving the Babylonians out of Assyria and then campaigning as far as Phoenicia.

Tiglath-pileser III (r. 744–727): Inaugurated the golden age of Assyrian imperial power by conquering Syria, defeating Urartu, and placing Babylonia under direct Assyrian rule.

Tikulti-Ninurta I (r. 1243–1207): Capitalized on the collapse of the Hittite empire to push into Anatolia, then crushed the remainder of the Kassite kingdom.

Tudhaliyas II (r. c. 1430–c. 1410): Founder of the Hittite New Kingdom who inaugurated an era of renewed Hittite expansion. (Tudhaliyas I may have been an obscure Old Kingdom Hittite ruler).

Tudhaliyas III (r. c. 1380–c. 1370): Hittite king under whom the kingdom nearly collapsed under simultaneous assault from all sides.

Tudhaliyas IV (r. c. 1240–c. 1210): Weakened by concessions to powerful Hittite barons, Tudhaliyas was unable to halt the disintegration of Hittite royal power.

Tushratta (r. c. 1350): King of Mitanni who overthrew his predecessor in a bloody coup.

Ulam-Buriash (r. c. 1475): Kassite ruler who defeated the King of the Sealand and established Kassite control over southern Mesopotamia, as well as points along the coast of the lower Persian Gulf.

Urhi-Teshub (a.k.a. **Mursilis III**; r. c. 1271–c. 1264): Hittite king, nephew of Muwatallis II; he ascended the throne as Mursilis III but was overthrown by his uncle (who became Hattusilis III) and fled to Egypt.

Ur-Nammu (r. 2112–2095): Founder of Ur III, he conquered an empire that stretched from Nineveh to the Persian Gulf.

Utuhegal (r. 2119–2112): Ruler of Uruk who defeated the Gutians and expelled them from Mesopotamia.

Xanthippus (r. c. 255): Spartan mercenary commander who led the Carthaginians to a crushing victory over a Roman invasion force in 255 at the Battle of Bagradas.

Xerxes (r. 486–465): Son and successor to Darius I, he led the greatest military expedition of antiquity, the Persian invasion of Greece in 480, but despite a victory at Thermopylae, he was badly defeated at Salamis.

Zidanta (r. c. 1560–c. 1550): Hittite usurper who seized the throne after murdering Hantilis's family.

Bibliography

Note: The various volumes of *The Cambridge Ancient History* (2nd ed. Cambridge: Cambridge University Press, 1982) are invaluable resources for anyone with a scholarly interest in the ancient Near East and the encounter between the Near East and the rising powers of Greece and Rome.

Textbooks

Dunstan, W. E. *The Ancient Near East*. Fort Worth, TX: Harcourt Brace College Publishers, 1998. An excellent college-level textbook, valuable for any student interested in acquiring an understanding of the Near East before delving more deeply into particular areas or subjects.

Hallo, W. W., and W. K. Simpson. *The Ancient Near East: A History*. 2nd ed. Fort Worth, TX: Harcourt Brace College Publishers, 1998. This college-level textbook adopts a chronological approach to Near Eastern history rather than a national one, though it hives Egyptian history off into its own section, but it is a good volume for beginning students.

Knapp, A. Bernard. *The History and Culture of Ancient Western Asia and Egypt*. Belmont, CA: Wadsworth Publishing, 1988. A somewhat dated but still useful college-level text with useful detail for a volume of its genre.

Stiebing, W. H., Jr. *Ancient Near Eastern History and Culture*. New York: Longman, 2003. A college-level text with excellent notes and bibliographies of suggested readings.

Van de Mieroop, M. *A History of the Ancient Near East ca. 3000–323 B.C.* 2nd ed. Oxford: Blackwell Publishing, 2006. An examination of political history with a good emphasis on imperial issues, but marred by the exclusion of Egypt and a cursory treatment of Achaemenid Persia. It also contains a well-organized appendix of further reading suggestions.

Scholarly Surveys

Diakonoff, I. M., ed. *Early Antiquity*. Chicago: University of Chicago Press, 1991. A collection of chapters by Russian Near Eastern scholars of the late Soviet era, with a Marxist slant but much useful information.

Kuhrt, A. *The Ancient Near East, c. 3000–330 B.C.* 2 vols. London: Routledge, 1995. A detailed survey of all the states of the ancient Near East, including Egypt, that offers novel interpretations of the evidence and is particularly valuable for including extensive quotations from ancient Near Eastern texts in translation.

Reference Works

Bertman, S. *Handbook to Life in Ancient Mesopotamia.* Oxford: Oxford University Press, 2003. A good resource for those new to the study of the ancient Near East, offering short, topical articles and encyclopedia-style entries on people, institutions, life, and culture. Does not cover Egypt.

Bienkowski, P., and A. Millard. *Dictionary of the Ancient Near East.* Philadelphia: University of Pennsylvania Press, 2000. A single-volume encyclopedia with good articles by reputable scholars, but narrow in the range of subjects that it covers.

Bunson, M. *Encyclopedia of Ancient Egypt.* Rev. ed. New York: Facts on File, 2002. A comprehensive single-volume reference that emphasizes text rather than illustrations.

David, R. *Handbook to Life in Ancient Egypt.* Oxford: Oxford University Press, 1998. A valuable introductory resource featuring short, topical articles and brief, encyclopedia-style entries on gods and rulers.

Redford, D. B., ed. *The Oxford Encyclopedia of Ancient Egypt.* 3 vols. Oxford: Oxford University Press, 2001. A comprehensive and authoritative encyclopedia of articles contributed by numerous scholars, most of which include bibliographies for further reading.

Sasson, J. M., ed. *Civilizations of the Ancient Near East.* 4 vols. Peabody, MA: Hendrickson, 1995. A collection of more than 100 articles contributed by important scholars, covering a wide range of topics down to the fall of Achaemenid Persia.

Shaw, I., and P. Nicholson, eds. *The Dictionary of Ancient Egypt.* New York: Abrams, 1995. A useful single-volume encyclopedia of ancient Egyptian life, history, and culture, with good illustrations and maps.

Snell, D. C., ed. *A Companion to the Ancient Near East.* New York: Blackwell, 2007. A volume of 32 articles by various scholars, unevenly covering the history and culture of the ancient Near East and Egypt.

Atlases

Baines, J., and J. Málek. *Atlas of Ancient Egypt*. New York: Facts on File, 1980. Outstanding, detailed maps accompanied by abundant illustrations and a thoughtful text.

Haywood, J. *The Penguin Historical Atlas of Ancient Civilizations*. London: Penguin, 2005. Taking in the Far East, South Asia, and the New World as well as the Near East and Mediterranean, this slim volume has fine full-color maps and good summary text.

Manley, B. *The Penguin Historical Atlas of Ancient Egypt*. London: Penguin, 1996. Excellent full-color maps with very useful accompanying text.

Roaf, M. *Cultural Atlas of Mesopotamia and the Ancient Near East*. New York: Facts on File, 1990. An extremely useful volume of highly detailed maps accompanied by abundant illustrations and thoughtful text.

Original Sources in Translation—General Collections

Chavalas, M. W., ed. *The Ancient Near East*. Oxford: Blackwell, 2006. Translated texts from early Sumeria to the Achaemenid period.

Pritchard, J. B., ed. *The Ancient Near East: An Anthology of Texts and Pictures*. 2 vols. Princeton, NJ: Princeton University Press, 1958. The single most comprehensive collection of translated ancient Near Eastern and Egyptian texts, covering the full spectrum of topics.

Mesopotamian Empires from Akkad to the Neo-Babylonians

Ahmed, S. S. *Southern Mesopotamia in the Time of Ashurbanipal*. The Hague: Mouton, 1968. An analysis of Assyrian rule in Babylonia under the last great Assyrian king and of the Great Revolt against Assyria.

Balkan, K. *Studies in Babylonian Feudalism of the Kassite Period*. Malibu, CA: Undena, 1986. A brief work on the feudal-style obligations that landholders held toward the Kassite monarch, focused on Kassite administration in the provinces of Nippur.

Barton, G. A. *The Royal Inscriptions of Sumer and Akkad*. New Haven, CT: Yale University Press, 1929. Translations of hundreds of texts from 3rd-millennium Mesopotamia, arranged by city.

Beaulieu, P.-A. *The Reign of Nabonidus, King of Babylon, 556–530 B.C.* New Haven, CT: Yale University Press, 1989. A biographical study of the enigmatic last ruler of the Neo-Babylonian empire, with careful attention to the inscriptional sources that afford most of our information.

Brinkman, J. A. *A Political History of Post-Kassite Babylonia, 1158–722 B.C.* Rome: Pontificum Institutum Biblicum, 1968. A specialist volume covering the period on a reign-by-reign basis, with technical discussion of the issues and problems involved.

————. *Prelude to Empire: Babylonian Society and Politics, 747–626 B.C.* Philadelphia, PA: Babylonian Fund, 1984. A study of how Assyrian rule in Babylonia between 747 and 626 laid the foundations for the rise of the Neo-Babylonian empire.

Dougherty, R. P. *Nabonidus and Belshazzar: A Study of the Closing Events of the Neo-Babylonian Empire.* New Haven, CT: Yale University Press, 1929. Reprint, 1980. The only single-volume treatment of Nabonidus's reign and Belshazzar's viceroyalty in Babylon during Nabonidus's 10-year sojourn in Arabia.

Frame, G., and L. Wilding. *From the Upper Sea to the Lower Sea: Studies on the History of Assyria and Babylonia in Honour of A. K. Grayson.* Leiden, The Netherlands: Nederlands Institut voor het Nabije Oosten, 2004. An edited volume of articles contributed by 30 scholars focusing on the Neo-Assyrian empire.

Frayne, D. R. *Sargonic and Gutian Periods, 2334–2113 B.C.* Toronto: University of Toronto Press, 1993. Translated texts of several dozen inscriptions from the dawn of empire.

Grayson, A. K. *Assyrian and Babylonian Chronicles.* Locust Valley, NY: J. J. Augustin, 1975. Translations of the annals from which much of our understanding of the chronology of the ancient Near East is derived, with commentary and an appendix of names that appear in the chronicles, accompanied by discussion.

————. *Assyrian Royal Inscriptions.* 2 vols. Wiesbaden, Germany: Otto Harrassowitz, 1972, 1976. Translated texts covering the years 1133–853.

————. *Babylonian Historical-Literary Texts.* Toronto: University of Toronto Press, 1975. Translation and commentary on several texts from the Akkadian, Kassite, and Neo-Babylonian periods.

Harrak, A. *Assyria and Hanigalbat: A Historical Reconstruction of Bilateral Relations from the Middle of the Fourteenth to the End of the Twelfth Centuries B.C.* New York: G. Olms Verlag, 1987. A scholarly investigation of relations between Assyria and Mitanni (Hanigalbat) from Ashur-uballit I to Tikulti-Ninurta I.

King, L. W. *The Letters and Inscriptions of Hammurabi, King of Babylon*. Vol. 3, *English Translations*. London: Luzac, 1900. A selection of translated texts, many dealing with legal or social matters.

Læscøe, J. *People of Ancient Assyria: Their Inscriptions and Correspondence*. Translated by F. S. Leigh-Browne. New York: Barnes and Noble, 1963. Far more than a study of texts, this is a history of the peoples of northern Mesopotamia from about 2000 to the collapse of the Assyrian empire. It contains a valuable discussion of the Hurrians and their kingdom of Mitanni.

Leick, G. *The Babylonians: An Introduction*. London: Routledge, 2003. An introductory overview of history, society, religion, and culture, covering the period from about 1800 to about 540.

Oates, J. *Babylon*. Rev. ed. London: Thames & Hudson, 1986. A well-illustrated introduction aimed at the general reader.

Oppenheim, A. L. *Ancient Mesopotamia: Portrait of a Dead Civilization*. Rev. ed. Chicago: University of Chicago Press, 1977. A broad-ranging cultural survey with useful information on social, economic, and governmental organization, though organized by topic rather than by kingdom or period.

Parpola, S., and K. Watanabe, eds. *Neo-Assyrian Treaties and Loyalty Oaths*. Helsinki: Helsinki University Press, 1988. Translations of Assyrian treaties and their accompanying loyalty oaths from the 9th to 7th centuries (ending with Esarhaddon), illustrating this central element in the Neo-Assyrian imperial system.

Parpola, S., and R. M. Whiting, eds. *Assyria 1995. Proceedings of the 10th Anniversary Symposium of the Neo-Assyrian Text Corpus Project*. Helsinki: Helsinki University Press, 1997. Twenty-nine articles, all but three in English, on topics ranging from religion to warfare and the reasons for Assyria's fall.

Porter, B. N., ed. *Ritual and Politics in Ancient Mesopotamia*. New Haven, CT: American Oriental Society, 2005. A scholarly volume of four articles, three in English, exploring the relationship between political power and religion, with a strong emphasis on Assyria.

Roux, G. *Ancient Iraq*. 3rd ed. London: Penguin, 1992. An excellent survey text, arranged chronologically by kingdom from Akkad to the Neo-Babylonians.

Sack, R. H. *Images of Nebuchadnezzar: The Emergence of a Legend.* 2nd rev. exp. ed. London: Associated University Presses, 2004. A discussion of the sources for Nebuchadrezzar's reign and how their perspectives mold the historical image of the great Neo-Babylonian monarch.

Saggs, H. W. F. *The Might That Was Assyria.* London: Sidgwick & Jackson, 1984. A thorough study of Assyrian history, imperial expansion, and administration, as well as culture and life.

Van de Mieroop, M. *King Hammurabi of Babylon: A Biography.* Oxford: Blackwell, 2005. The only biography of this important figure in the history of ancient Mesopotamia, by a prominent scholar on the period.

Westenholz, J. G. *Legends of the Kings of Akkade: The Texts.* Winona Lake, IN: Eisenbrauns, 1997. A translation of and commentary on 22 texts containing tales about Sargon and his heirs.

Wilhelm, Gernot. *The Hurrians.* Warminster, UK: Aris & Phillips, 1989. The sole English-language volume devoted to the Hurrians and their kingdom, Mitanni, offering a detailed treatment of their origins, culture, and history.

Wiseman, D. J. *Nebuchadrezzar and Babylon.* Oxford: Oxford University Press, 1985. Most of this text focuses on Nebuchadrezzar's construction projects in Babylon itself, but there is also useful material on foreign hostages and labor and on Nebuchadrezzar's imperial conquests.

Yamada, S. *The Construction of the Assyrian Empire: A Historical Study of the Inscriptions of Shalmaneser III Relating to His Campaigns to the West.* Leiden, The Netherlands: Brill, 2000. A scholarly study of the texts documenting Shalmaneser's military activity and detailing his administration of the Assyrian empire's subject territories.

The Hittites

Beckman, G. *Hittite Diplomatic Texts.* 2nd ed. Atlanta, GA: Society of Biblical Literature, 1999. Translations of texts recovered from the Hittite capital of Hattusas.

Bryce, Trevor. *The Kingdom of the Hittites.* New ed. Oxford: Oxford University Press, 2006. A rearrangement of the contents of the 1998 edition, this is the standard history of the Hittites, useful to general readers as well as scholars.

————. *Life and Society in the Hittite World*. Oxford: Oxford University Press, 2002. A topical cultural survey of the Hittite world, with sections on government and the military.

Gurney, O. R. *The Hittites*. 2nd ed. Baltimore, MD: Penguin Books, 1954. Reprint, 1990. A readable (though now dated) survey with useful chapters on Hittite warfare and government.

Güterbock, H. G., and T. P. J. van den Hout. *The Hittite Instruction for the Royal Bodyguard*. Chicago: The Oriental Institute of the University of Chicago, 1991. A translation of an important text illuminating procedures in royal processions and trials.

Lehmann, J. *The Hittites*. Translated by J. M. Brownjohn. New York: Viking, 1975. A chatty and informal look at Hittite sites and what we know about Hittite life.

Macqueen, J. G. *The Hittites and Their Contemporaries in Asia Minor*. Revised and enlarged edition. London: Thames & Hudson, 1986. Illustrated with numerous black-and-white photographs, this volume is intended for general readers rather than specialists.

Orlin, L. L. *Assyrian Colonies in Cappadocia*. The Hague: Mouton, 1970. A highly technical study of the early Assyrian merchant colonies that helped spark the emergence of the Hittite monarchy.

The Persian Empire

Allen, L. *The Persian Empire*. Chicago: University of Chicago Press, 2005. An introductory survey of the life and culture of Achaemenid Persia (550–330), abundantly illustrated with full-color photographs.

Briant, P. *From Cyrus to Alexander: A History of the Persian Empire*. Translated by P. T. Daniels. Winona Lake, IN: Eisenbrauns, 2002. An exhaustive, 1,000-page analysis of the Achaemenid empire, with extensive treatments of royal ideology, imperial administration, the tribute system, and the military.

Brosius, M. *The Persians: An Introduction*. London: Routledge, 2006. A very good nonspecialist survey of the Persians and their empires, which includes the Parthians and Sassanids (247 B.C.–A.D. 651) as well as the Achaemenids.

Burn, A. R. *Persia and the Greeks: The Defense of the West 546–478 B.C.* New York: Minerva/St. Martin's, 1962. A classic study of the Greco-Persian Wars down to the aftermath of Plataea, told from the Greek perspective, but with much discussion of the origins and growth of the Persian empire.

Cook, J. M. *The Persian Empire*. London: J. M. Dent & Sons, 1983. A solid but accessible survey of Achaemenid Persia, including chapters devoted to imperial administration. Not overly focused on the Greco-Persian Wars.

Green, P. *The Greco-Persian Wars*. Berkeley: University of California Press, 1996. A solidly researched and capably narrated account of the confrontation between Persia and the Greeks down to 479, by a leading Greek historian.

Olmstead, A. T. *History of the Persian Empire*. Chicago: University of Chicago Press, 1948. The classic history of Achaemenid Persia.

Wiesehöfer, J. *Ancient Persia*. London: I. B. Tauris, 1996. Grounded in Persian sources and archeological research, this scholarly text shuns Greek and Roman stereotypes of the Persians and includes the Parthian and Sassanid Persian periods (247 B.C.–A.D. 651).

The Minoans and Mycenaeans

Branigan, K. *The Foundations of Palatial Crete*. New York: Praeger, 1970. A tour through the archeological evidence from the Minoan period on Crete that teases out historical information from the material remains.

Castleden, R. *Minoans: Life in Bronze Age Crete*. London: Routledge, 2005. A strongly revisionist view of the Minoans by a prolific popular author, perhaps overemphasizing the role of religion in Minoan life.

Chadwick, J. *The Mycenaean World*. Cambridge: Cambridge University Press, 1976. A slender, scholarly study of the Mycenaean world through the lens of the Linear B tablets from Pylos, which shed much light on the internal administration of a Mycenaean palace in the last months of its existence.

Cotterell, A. *The Minoan World*. New York: Scribner, 1980. A slender beginner's volume, lavishly illustrated and written in a chatty and informal style.

Dickinson, O. *The Aegean Bronze Age*. Cambridge: Cambridge University Press, 1994. Not for the beginner, this careful, scholarly volume covering both Minoan Crete and Mycenaean Greece presumes a willingness on the reader's part to immerse oneself in the archeology of the Bronze Age.

Drews, R. *The End of the Bronze Age: Changes in Warfare and the Catastrophe ca. 1200 B.C.* Princeton, NJ: Princeton University Press,

1993. Drews suggests that it was the shift to heavy infantry that sparked the collapse of the Bronze Age empires.

Friedrich, W. *Fire in the Sea: The Santorini Volcano: Natural History and the Legend of Atlantis*. Translated by Alexander R. McBirney. Cambridge: Cambridge University Press, 2000. Strong on scientific details, this book provides a detailed examination of the geological history of the Santorini volcano, including useful material on the Minoan settlement at Akrotiri, buried by the cataclysmic eruption of c. 1640, leaving a "Bronze Age Pompeii."

Nardo, D. *The Minoans*. San Diego: Thomson/Lucent, 2005. A readable and well-illustrated introduction to Minoan life and civilization.

Vermeule, E. *Greece in the Bronze Age*. Chicago: University of Chicago Press, 1972. The classic scholarly treatment of the Aegean during the 2nd millennium, not overly dominated by technical archeological discussion.

Willetts, R. F. *The Civilization of Ancient Crete*. New York: Phoenix, 1976. A volume aimed at specialists, covering Crete from the Minoans to the period following the Dorian settlement.

Wood, M. *In Search of the Trojan War*. London: Facts on File, 1985. Companion to a television series; sometimes credulous, but a useful overview of the closing era of Mycenaean Greece for the nonspecialist in a field too dominated by highly technical volumes.

Carthage

Bagnall, N. *The Punic Wars*. New York: St. Martin's, 1990. A very good account of the Punic wars, with a useful introductory chapter on the history and government of Carthage.

Caven, B. *The Punic Wars*. New York: St. Martin's, 1980. A study aimed at the general reader and focused exclusively on the wars themselves, not on the political and social organization of Carthage or Rome.

Goldsworthy, A. *The Fall of Carthage: The Punic Wars 265–146 B.C.* New York: Phoenix, 2000. First issued under the title *The Punic Wars* (2000), a detailed but approachable investigation of the Punic Wars by one of the leading scholars of the Roman army.

Lancel, S. *Carthage: A History*. Translated by A. Nevill. Oxford: Blackwell Publishing, 1995. Very archeological in its focus, this is an often rambling effort at a narrative of Phoenician expansion and Carthaginian history.

Picard, G. *Carthage*. Translated by M. and L. Kochan. New York: Ungar, 1965. A beginner's survey of Carthaginian history, well illustrated with black-and-white photographs.

———. *Daily Life in Carthage*. Translated by A. E. Foster. New York: MacMillan, 1961. A good, though somewhat dated, topical survey of Carthaginian life and institutions, which benefits from not being diluted by discussion of Carthage's wars.

Picard, G. C., and C. Picard. *The Life and Death of Carthage*. Translated by D. Collon. New York: Taplinger, 1968. Focused on Carthage rather than on the Punic Wars, this volume is important for its attention to Carthaginian government and imperial expansion.

Warmington, B. H. *Carthage*. New York: Praeger, 1969. This volume is focused primarily on the history of Carthage rather than on a topical examination of its institutions.

The Egyptian Empire

Clayton, P. A. *Chronicle of the Pharaohs*. London: Thames & Hudson, 1994. An introductory, chronologically arranged text. Lavishly illustrated.

Grimal, N. *A History of Ancient Egypt*. Translated by I. Shaw. Oxford: Blackwell, 1992. A learned study of Egyptian history down to Alexander, with an immense bibliography.

Moran, W. L., ed. and trans. *The Amarna Letters*. Baltimore, MD: Johns Hopkins University Press, 1992. A complete collection of the cuneiform correspondence recovered from Tell el-Amarna, the capital of the pharaoh Akhenaten.

Schulman, A. R. *Military Rank, Title, and Organization in the Egyptian New Kingdom*. Berlin: Hessling, 1964. A scholarly investigation of the officer elite of imperial Egypt and the structure of the Egyptian army.

Shaw, I., ed. *The Oxford History of Ancient Egypt*. New York: Oxford, 2000. A single-volume survey of Egyptian history down to the Roman conquest, but lacking in detail because of the scope of its coverage.

Spalinger, A. J. *War in Ancient Egypt*. Oxford: Blackwell, 2005. Basically a textbook on the rise and fall of the Egyptian empire, seen through a military lens.

Steindorff, G., and K. C. Seele. *When Egypt Ruled the East*. Rev. ed. Chicago: University of Chicago Press, 1957. An old but still valuable survey that focuses on New Kingdom Egypt and its empire.

Israel

Bright, J. A. *A History of Israel.* 4th ed. Philadelphia, PA: Westminster Press, 2001. A detailed narrative from the patriarchal period to the Maccabees.

Finkelstein, I., and N. A. Silbermann. *David and Solomon: In Search of the Bible's Sacred Kings and the Roots of the Western Tradition.* New York: Free Press, 2006. A very valuable archeologically based reassessment of what we can, and cannot, know about the period of the United Monarchy in Israel.

Gottwald, N. K. *The Politics of Ancient Israel.* Louisville, KY: Westminster John Knox Press, 2001. A revisionist study of the political history of the Israelite kingdoms, characterized by a text-critical approach to Biblical sources.

Grant, M. *The History of Ancient Israel.* New York: Scribner, 1984. A solid and substantial analysis of the history of Canaan and its peoples from the early 2nd millennium to the Great Jewish Revolt in A.D. 66–70.

Ishida, T. *The Royal Dynasties of Ancient Israel: A Study on the Formation and Development of Royal-Dynastic Ideology.* Berlin: Walter DeGruyter, 1977. A specialist treatment of the ideology of kingship in Israel, focusing on the period of the United Monarchy.

Miller, J. M., and J. H. Hayes. *A History of Ancient Israel and Judah.* Philadelphia, PA: Westminster Press, 1986. A detailed and well-balanced study of the history of the Israelites from their legendary beginnings to the Persian period.

Redford, D. B. *Egypt, Canaan, and Israel in Ancient Times.* Princeton, NJ: Princeton University Press, 1992. A classic study of the history of relations between Egypt and Levant down to the fall of Judah.

The Hellenistic and Roman Near East

Bowman, A. K. *Egypt After the Pharaohs: 332 BC–AD 642.* Berkeley: University of California Press, 1986. A well-illustrated and accessible overview of how Egyptian culture adapted to Greco-Roman rule and Greco-Roman culture.

Green, P. *Alexander to Actium: The Historical Evolution of the Hellenistic Age.* Berkeley: University of California Press, 1990. A thorough scholarly treatment of Hellenistic history and civilization, from one of the greatest names in the scholarship of the period.

Millar, F. *The Roman Near East 31 BC–AD 337*. Cambridge, MA: Harvard University Press, 1993. The best single-volume study of Roman rule in the Near East down to the dawn of the Byzantine period.

Miscellaneous Topics

Cotterell, A. *Chariot: The Astounding Rise and Fall of the World's First War Machine*. New York: Pimlico, 2005. A survey of the emergence, technology, and use of chariots not only in the Near East but also in the Mediterranean, India, and China, this volume contains much useful information but suffers from a rambling and undisciplined approach that requires the reader to dig for the nuggets it contains.

Hamblin, W. J. *Warfare in the Ancient Near East to 1600 B.C.: Holy Warriors at the Dawn of History*. New York: Routledge, 2006. An extremely valuable study of military history, techniques, and organization.